MW01194153

THE RETURN OF THE PRODIGAL SON

ANNIVERSARY EDITION

THE

RETURN

OF THE

PRODIGAL

SON

· ANNIVERSARY EDITION ·

A Special Two-in-One Volume,
Including *Home Tonight*

HENRI J. M. NOUWEN

Foreword by James Martin, SJ

CONVERGENT
New York

2016 Convergent Omnibus Edition

The Return of the Prodigal Son copyright © 1992 by Henri J. M.
Nouwen
Home Tonight copyright © 2009 by Henri Nouwen Legacy Trust

Published in the United States by Convergent Books,
an imprint of the Crown Publishing Group, a division of
Penguin Random House LLC, New York.
crownpublishing.com

Convergent Books is a registered trademark and the C
colophon is a trademark of Penguin Random House LLC.

For further information about the Henri Nouwen Legacy
Trust, please go to www.henrinouwensociety.com

The Return of the Prodigal Son was originally published in the
United States in hardcover by Doubleday, a division of Penguin
Random House LLC, New York, in 1992 and subsequently
in paperback by Image Books, an imprint of the Crown
Publishing Group, a division of Penguin Random House LLC,
in 1994. *Home Tonight* was originally published in the United
States in paperback by Doubleday, a division of Penguin
Random House LLC, New York, in 2009.

LIBRARY OF CONGRESS CATALOGING-IN-PUBLICATION DATA
IS AVAILABLE UPON REQUEST.

ISBN 978-0-8041-8928-6
EBOOK ISBN 978-0-4514-9604-1

Printed in the United States of America

Book design Pei Loi Koay
Jacket design: Jessie Sayward Bright
*Jacket art and gatefold insert: Return of the Prodigal Son, c. 1668–
69 (oil on canvas), Rembrandt Harmensz, van Rijn (1606–69)/State
Hermitage Museum, St. Petersberg, Russia/Bridgeman Images*
Foreword by James Martin, SJ

1 3 5 7 9 10 8 6 4 2

To my father

Laurent Jean Marie Nouwen

for his ninetieth birthday

CONTENTS

T he book that you are about to begin has changed lives. I know dozens of people—Christians and Jews, devout and doubtful, agnostics and seekers—who consider *The Return of the Prodigal Son* their favorite work of spirituality. For many people this is also Henri Nouwen's most powerful work. Ironically, at one point in this intensely honest book, he expresses, guiltily, his longing to be remembered after his death. He couldn't have known that this would be the work that would assure his place in Christian spiritual history.

What makes a book that changes lives? Why do so many people, decades after its printing and years after the death of its author, still respond to it? What is different about this work compared with other books that have come before and after it?

These answers vary from person to person, depending on where they are in their spiritual journeys, how they relate to God and what they are looking for.

Let me, then, answer that question for myself, as one of many readers and admirers of Henri Nouwen.

For me, the book's power can be explained by three factors. First, it is brutally honest. Second, it offers advice from not only a deeply spiritual man but also a gifted psychologist. And third, it provides a masterful reflection on a single passage from the New Testament.

My first encounter with this wise book was in the midst of a weeklong retreat during my Jesuit training, a few years after the book was first published. I had heard of Henri Nouwen, knew vaguely that he was a Dutch priest and psychologist, but had never read any of his writings. I picked up his book off a dusty shelf in the retreat house library primarily because I liked the Rembrandt painting reproduced on the cover. *Return,* then, was my introduction to Nouwen.

And what an introduction! The most arresting feature of this book is, for me, the author's near total candor. I had already encountered spiritual writers who wrote candidly about their lives but Nouwen's voice seemed to be the most honest I had yet encountered. Perhaps that's because the struggles he discusses at length are those that most people are embarrassed even to admit. A writer might describe the sadness of, say, confronting the death of a loved one or a failed project. But it is a rare writer who describes his or her naked desire to be noticed, loved, or "rich, powerful, and very famous," as he says in the book. The burning desire to be liked seemed to be at the heart of many of Nouwen's difficulties—as it is with so many of us, myself included.

His transparency still has the power to shock. "A friendship that had first seemed promising and life-giving," he writes, "gradually pulled me farther and farther away from home until I found myself completely obsessed." One is almost embarrassed reading such intimacies.

Yet this is what drew me almost immediately into the book, cemented my relationship with the author and made me pay attention. Since Nouwen was so frank about his failings, I believed him when he described how he overcame his struggles. "He's honest with me about dark times," thinks the reader, "and so I'm sure that he's honest with me about the lighter ones." Moreover, his wisdom is hard-won; he does not offer easy platitudes or cheap sentimentality, but the reality of grace that comes after suffering. In short, his trust *in* the reader evokes trust *from* the reader.

The second factor that made me love this book is related: the tremendous amount of solid advice that one receives from the author. These days the word "self-help" is often used pejoratively, as in, "That's just a self-help book." But why wouldn't someone treasure a book that is a help to the self—especially one that combines the insights of a spiritual master with a psychologist? To that end, let me confess something: Often when I read a book written by a spiritual guru, I find myself wondering, "Does this make any sense psychologically?" And when I read a book by a psychologist, I wonder, "How does this take into account my relationship with God?"

With Nouwen the reader discovers an artful synthesis: a deeply spiritual man with psychological training. Consider, for example, this bit of sound advice: "Complaining is self-perpetuating and counterproductive. Whenever I express my complaints in the hope of evoking pity and receiving the satisfaction I so much desire, the result is always the opposite of what I tried to get." This is counsel from someone who understands from two vantage points why complaining is so insidious. Not only does it turn people against you, as he explains later, it also extinguishes the desire for gratitude to God. Nouwen's wisdom is a fusion of the psychological and the spiritual. And the longer I live the more I realize that both are necessary for lasting human growth.

The third factor that made this book a treasure for me is its intense study of the parable of the prodigal son. This was the first time I had ever come across a Bible story that was, as one of my spiritual directors liked to say, "fully unpacked." "Exegesis" is the theological term: an "opening up" of a Scripture passage. Most readers, even before reading Nouwen's work, will probably be familiar with Jesus's famous parable, which appears in the Gospel of Luke, and will even have some of their own interpretations. As did I. But it wasn't until I read Nouwen that I understood what it meant to immerse oneself so deeply into a single passage. To climb into it. To live it.

The result of such heartfelt immersion is a brilliant meditation on the text, which illuminates it in countless new ways for readers, and, in the process, can change lives. Of course a parable is inexhaustible in its interpretations and can never be fully "understood." That's the beauty of a story. Whereas a strictly worded definition closes down the mind, a parable opens it up. This is one of the many reasons that Jesus answered questions with stories, rather than with theological arguments.

Nonetheless, who would have thought that the familiar parable normally taken to be a simple one about forgiveness would be a springboard to talk about, among other topics: resentment, isolation, complaining, envy, maturation, loneliness, longing, and compassion? At times it seems like the whole world of Christian spirituality is contained in this one story!

One of the invaluable insights of the book comes, ironically, not from Nouwen himself, but from a friend, who invites him to realize the overarching message of the book: while we sometimes act like the selfish younger son and feel like the resentful older brother in the parable, we are called to be the merciful Father. One could spend a lifetime putting that lesson into action. As I have—and still am. And guess what? I'm not there yet!

In this new edition the book has been paired with its sequel, *Home Tonight,* a kind of retreat based on *The Return of the Prodigal Son.* In your hands, then, you have one of the great spiritual classics of our time, by one of the great spiritual masters of our time, as well as a helpful way to reflect on it more at length. So let Nouwen's wisdom speak to you. Then let your prayer speak to you.

It's hard not to think of Jesus smiling at Nouwen's take on the parable and marveling at the ways that he spun it out. Perhaps they're discussing it right now.

THE

RETURN

OF THE

PRODIGAL

SON

THE STORY OF TWO SONS
AND THEIR FATHER

T here was a man who had two sons. The younger one said to his father, "Father, let me have the share of the estate that will come to me." So the father divided the property between them. A few days later, the younger son got together everything he had and left for a distant country where he squandered his money on a life of debauchery.

When he had spent it all, that country experienced a severe famine, and now he began to feel the pinch so he hired himself out to one of the local inhabitants who put him on his farm to feed the pigs. And he would willingly have filled himself with the husks the pigs were eating but no one would let him have them. Then he came to his senses and said, "How many of my father's hired men have all the food they want and more, and here am I dying of hunger! I will leave this place and go to my father and say: Father, I have sinned against heaven and against you; I no longer deserve to be called your son; treat me as one of your hired men. . . ." So he left the place and went back to his father.

While he was still a long way off, his father saw him and was moved with pity. He ran to the boy, clasped him in his arms and kissed him. Then his son said, "Father, I have sinned against heaven and against you. I no longer deserve to be called your son." But the father said to his servants, "Quick! Bring out the best robe and put it on him; put a ring on his finger and sandals on his feet. Bring the calf we have been fattening, and kill it; we will celebrate by having a feast, because this son of mine was dead and has come back to life; he was lost and is found." And they began to celebrate.

Now the elder son was out in the fields, and on his way back, as he drew near the house, he could hear music and dancing. Calling one of the servants he asked what it was all about. The servant told him, "Your brother has come, and your father has killed the calf we had been fattening because he has got him back safe and sound." He was angry then and refused to go in, and his father came out and began to urge him to come in; but he retorted to his father, "All these years I have slaved for you and never once disobeyed any orders of yours, yet you never offered me so much as a kid for me to celebrate with my friends. But, for this son of yours, when he comes back after swallowing up your property—he and his loose women—you kill the calf we had been fattening."

The father said, "My son, you are with me always, and all I have is yours. But it was only right we should celebrate and rejoice, because your brother here was dead and has come to life; he was lost and is found."

ENCOUNTER WITH A PAINTING

THE POSTER

A seemingly insignificant encounter with a poster presenting a detail of Rembrandt's *Return of the Prodigal Son* set in motion a long spiritual adventure that brought me to a new understanding of my vocation and offered me new strength to live it. At the heart of this adventure is a seventeenth-century painting and its artist, a first-century parable and its author, and a twentieth-century person in search of life's meaning.

The story begins in the fall of 1983 in the village of Trosly, France, where I was spending a few months at L'Arche, a community that offers a home to people with mental handicaps. Founded in 1964 by a Canadian, Jean Vanier, the Trosly community is the first of more than ninety L'Arche communities spread throughout the world.

One day I went to visit my friend Simone Landrien in the community's small documentation center. As we spoke, my eyes fell on a large poster pinned on her door. I saw a man in a great red cloak tenderly touching the shoulders of a disheveled boy kneeling before him. I could not take my eyes away. I felt drawn by the intimacy between the two figures, the warm red of the man's cloak, the golden yellow of the boy's tunic, and the mysterious light engulfing them both. But, most of all, it was the hands—the old man's hands—as they touched the boy's shoulders that reached me in a place where I had never been reached before.

Realizing that I was no longer paying much attention to the conversation, I said to Simone, "Tell me about that poster." She said, "Oh, that's a reproduction of Rembrandt's *Prodigal Son*. Do you like it?" I kept staring at the poster and finally stuttered, "It's beautiful, more than beautiful . . . it makes me want to cry and laugh at the same time . . . I can't tell you what I feel as I look at it, but it touches me deeply." Simone said, "Maybe you should have your own copy. You can buy it in Paris." "Yes," I said, "I must have a copy."

When I first saw the *Prodigal Son*, I had just finished an exhausting six-week lecturing trip through the United States, calling Christian communities to do anything they possibly could to prevent violence and war in Central America. I was dead tired, so much so that I could barely walk. I was anxious, lonely, restless, and very needy. During the trip I had felt like a strong fighter for justice and peace, able to face the dark world without fear. But after it was all over I felt like a vulnerable little child who wanted to crawl onto its mother's lap and cry. As soon as the cheering or cursing crowds were gone, I experienced a devastating loneliness and could easily have surrendered myself to the seductive voices that promised emotional and physical rest.

It was in this condition that I first encountered Rembrandt's

Prodigal Son on the door of Simone's office. My heart leapt when I saw it. After my long self-exposing journey, the tender embrace of father and son expressed everything I desired at that moment. I was, indeed, the son exhausted from long travels; I wanted to be embraced; I was looking for a home where I could feel safe. The son-come-home was all I was and all that I wanted to be. For so long I had been going from place to place: confronting, beseeching, admonishing, and consoling. Now I desired only to rest safely in a place where I could feel a sense of belonging, a place where I could feel at home.

Much happened in the months and years that followed. Even though the extreme fatigue left me and I returned to a life of teaching and traveling, Rembrandt's embrace remained imprinted on my soul far more profoundly than any temporary expression of emotional support. It had brought me into touch with something within me that lies far beyond the ups and downs of a busy life, something that represents the ongoing yearning of the human spirit, the yearning for a final return, an unambiguous sense of safety, a lasting home. While I was busy with many people, involved in many issues, and quite visible in many places, the homecoming of the prodigal son stayed with me and continued to take on even greater significance in my spiritual life. The yearning for a lasting home, brought to consciousness by Rembrandt's painting, grew deeper and stronger, somehow making the painter himself into a faithful companion and guide.

Two years after first seeing the Rembrandt poster, I resigned from my teaching position at Harvard University and returned to L'Arche in Trosly, there to spend a full year. The purpose of this move was to determine whether or not I was called to live a life with mentally handicapped people in one of the L'Arche communities. During that year of transition, I felt especially close to Rembrandt and his *Prodigal Son*. After all, I was looking for a new home. It seemed as though my fellow Dutchman had been given to me as a special companion. Before the year was over, I had made the decision to make L'Arche my new home and to join Daybreak, the L'Arche community in Toronto.

THE PAINTING

Just before leaving Trosly, I was invited by my friends Bobby Massie and his wife, Dana Robert, to join them on a trip to the Soviet Union. My immediate reaction was: "Now I can see the real painting." Ever since becoming interested in this great work, I had known that the original had been acquired in 1766 by Catherine the Great for the Hermitage in Saint Petersburg (which after the revolution was given the name of Leningrad, and which has recently reclaimed its original name of Saint Petersburg) and was still there. I never dreamt that I would have a chance to see it so soon. Although I was very eager to get first-hand knowledge of a country that had so strongly influenced my thoughts, emotions, and feelings during most of my life, this became almost trivial when compared with the opportunity to sit before the painting that had revealed to me the deepest yearnings of my heart.

From the moment of my departure, I knew that my decision to join L'Arche on a permanent basis and my visit to the Soviet Union were closely linked. The link—I was sure—was Rembrandt's *Prodigal Son*. Somehow, I sensed that seeing this painting would allow me to enter into the mystery of homecoming in a way I never had before.

Returning from an exhausting lecture tour to a safe place had been a homecoming; leaving the world of teachers and students to live in a community for mentally handicapped men and women felt like returning home; meeting the people of a country which had separated itself from the rest of the world by walls and heavily guarded borders, that, too, was, in its own way, a manner of going home. But, beneath or beyond all that, "coming home" meant, for me, walking step by step toward the One who awaits me with open arms and wants to hold me in an eternal embrace. I knew that Rembrandt deeply understood this spiritual homecoming. I knew that, when Rembrandt painted his *Prodigal Son*, he had lived a life that had left him with no doubt about his true and final home. I felt that, if I could meet Rembrandt right where he had painted father and son, God and humanity, compassion and misery, in one circle of love, I would come to know as much as I ever would about death and life. I also sensed the hope that through Rembrandt's masterpiece I would one day be able to express what I most wanted to say about love.

Being in Saint Petersburg is one thing. Having the opportunity to quietly reflect upon the *Prodigal Son* in the Hermitage is quite something else. When I saw the mile-long line of people waiting to enter the museum, I wondered anxiously how and for how long I would be able to see what I most wanted to see.

My anxiety, however, was relieved. In Saint Petersburg our official tour ended, and most members of the group returned home. But Bobby's mother, Suzanne Massie, who was in the Soviet Union during our trip, invited us to stay a few days with her. Suzanne is an expert in Russian culture and art, and her book *The Land of the Firebird* had greatly helped me to get ready for our trip. I asked Suzanne, "How do I ever get close to the

Prodigal Son?" She said, "Now, Henri, don't worry. I'll see to it that you have all the time you want and need with your favorite painting."

During our second day in Saint Petersburg, Suzanne gave me a telephone number and said, "This is the office number of Alexei Briantsev. He is a good friend of mine. Call him, and he will help you to get to your *Prodigal Son*." I dialed the number immediately and was surprised to hear Alexei, in his gently accented English, promise to meet me at a side door, away from the tourist entrance.

On Saturday, July 26, 1986, at 2:30 P.M., I went to the Hermitage, walked along the Neva River past the main entrance, and found the door Alexei had directed me to. I entered, and someone behind a large desk let me use the house phone to call Alexei. After a few minutes, he appeared and welcomed me with great kindness. He led me along splendid corridors and elegant staircases to an out-of-the-way place not on the tourists' itinerary. It was a long room with high ceilings and looked like an old artist's studio. Paintings were stacked everywhere. In the middle there were large tables and chairs covered with papers and objects of all sorts. As we sat down for a moment, it soon became clear to me that Alexei was the head of the Hermitage's restoration department. With great gentleness and obvious interest in my desire to spend time with Rembrandt's painting, he offered me all the help I wanted. Then he took me straight to the *Prodigal Son*, told the guard not to bother me, and left me there.

And so there I was; facing the painting that had been on my mind and in my heart for nearly three years. I was stunned by its majestic beauty. Its size, larger than life; its abundant reds, browns, and yellows; its shadowy recesses and bright fore-

ground, but most of all the light-enveloped embrace of father
and son surrounded by four mysterious bystanders, all of this
gripped me with an intensity far beyond my anticipation. There
had been moments in which I had wondered whether the real
painting might disappoint me. The opposite was true. Its gran-
deur and splendor made everything recede into the background
and held me completely captivated. Coming here was indeed a
homecoming.

While many tourist groups with their guides came and left
in rapid succession, I sat on one of the red velvet chairs in front
of the painting and just looked. Now I was seeing the real thing!
Not only the father embracing his child-come-home, but also
the elder son and the three other figures. It is a huge work in oil
on canvas, eight feet high by six feet wide. It took me a while to
simply *be* there, simply absorbing that I was truly in the presence of what I had so long hoped to see, simply enjoying the
fact that I was all by myself sitting in the Hermitage in Saint
Petersburg looking at the *Prodigal Son* for as long as I wanted.

The painting was exposed in the most favorable way, on a
wall that received plenty of natural light through a large nearby
window at an eighty-degree angle. Sitting there, I realized that
the light became fuller and more intense as the afternoon pro-
gressed. At four o'clock the sun covered the painting with a new
brightness, and the background figures—which had remained
quite vague in the early hours—seemed to step out of their dark
corners. As the evening drew near, the sunlight grew more crisp
and tingling. The embrace of the father and son became stronger and deeper, and the bystanders participated more directly in
this mysterious event of reconciliation, forgiveness, and inner
healing. Gradually I realized that there were as many paintings
of the *Prodigal Son* as there were changes in the light, and, for

a long time, I was held spellbound by this gracious dance of nature and art.

Without my realizing it, more than two hours had gone by when Alexei reappeared. With a compassionate smile and a supportive gesture, he suggested that I needed a break and invited me for coffee. He led me through the majestic halls of the museum—the larger part of which was the old winter palace of the tsars—back to the work space where we had been before. Alexei and his colleague had set out a large spread of breads, cheeses, and sweets, and encouraged me to enjoy it all. Having afternoon coffee with the art restorers of the Hermitage was certainly not what I had dreamt about when I was hoping to spend some quiet time with the *Prodigal Son*. Both Alexei and his colleague shared with me all they knew about Rembrandt's painting and were very eager to know why I was so taken by it. They seemed surprised and even a bit perplexed by my spiritual observations and reflections. They listened attentively and urged me to tell more.

After coffee, I returned to the painting for another hour until the guard and the cleaning lady let me know, in no uncertain terms, that the museum was closing and that I had been there long enough.

Four days later, I returned for another visit to the painting. During that session, something amusing happened, something that I should not leave untold. Because of the angle from which the morning sun hit the painting, the varnish gave off a distracting glare. So I took one of the red velvet chairs and moved it to a place from which the glare was cut and I could once again see clearly the figures in the painting. As soon as the guard—a serious young man with cap and military-type uniform—saw what I was doing, he became very upset at my audacity in picking up my chair and putting it somewhere else. Walking up to me, he ordered me, with an outpouring of Russian words and universal gestures, to put the chair back in its place. In response, I pointed to the sun and the canvas, trying to explain to him why I had moved the chair. My efforts had absolutely no success. So I returned the chair to its place and sat on the floor instead. But that only disturbed the guard even more. After some further animated attempts to win the sympathy of the guard for my problem, he told me to sit on the radiator below the window, from where I could have a good view. However, the first Intourist guide passing by with a large group marched up to me and told me sternly to get off the radiator and sit on one of the velvet chairs. At that, the guard became very angry at the guide and told her with a profusion of words and gestures that it was he who had let me sit on the radiator. The guide did not seem satisfied but decided to return her attention to the tourists, who were looking at the Rembrandt and wondering about the size of the figures. A few minutes later, Alexei came to see how I was doing. Immediately, the guard walked up to him and both of them entered into a long conversation. The guard was obviously trying to explain what had happened, but the discussion lasted so long that I wondered somewhat anxiously where it all would lead. Then, quite suddenly, Alexei left. For a moment, I felt quite guilty at having caused such a stir and thought that I had made Alexei angry with me. Ten minutes later, however, Alexei returned carrying a large comfortable armchair with red velvet upholstery and gold-painted legs. All for me! With a big grin, he put the chair in front of the painting and bade me sit in it. Alexei, the guard, and I all smiled. I had my own chair, and nobody objected any longer. Suddenly it all seemed very comical. Three empty chairs that could not be touched and a luxurious armchair brought in from some other room in the winter palace, offered to me to be freely moved around. Elegant bureaucracy! I wondered if any of the figures in the painting, who had been witnesses to the whole scene, were smiling along with us. I will never know.

Altogether, I spent more than four hours with the *Prodigal Son*, making notes about what I heard the guides and the tourists say, about what I saw as the sun grew stronger and faded away, and about what I experienced in my innermost being as I became more and more part of the story that Jesus once told and Rembrandt once painted. I wondered whether and how these precious hours in the Hermitage would ever bear fruit.

When I left the painting, I walked up to the young guard and tried to express my gratitude for his putting up with me for so long. As I looked into his eyes under the large Russian cap, I saw a man like myself: afraid, but with a great desire to be forgiven. From his beardless young face came a very gentle smile. I smiled too, and the two of us felt safe.

THE EVENT

A few weeks after visiting the Hermitage in Saint Petersburg, I arrived at L'Arche Daybreak in Toronto to live and work as the pastor of the community. Although I had taken a full year to sort out my vocation and to discern whether God was calling me to a life with mentally handicapped people, I still felt very apprehensive and anxious about my ability to live it well. I had never before given much attention to people with a mental handicap. Much to the contrary, I had focused increasingly on university students and their problems. I learned how to give lectures and write books, how to explain things systematically, how to make titles and subtitles, how to argue and how to analyze. So I had little idea as to how to communicate with men and women who hardly speak and, if they do speak, are not interested in logical arguments or well-reasoned opinions. I knew even less about announcing the Gospel of Jesus to people who listened more with their hearts than with their minds and who were far more sensitive to what I lived than to what I said.

I came to Daybreak in August 1986, with the conviction that I had made the right choice, but with a heart still full of trepidation about what lay ahead of me. Despite this I was convinced that, after more than twenty years in the classroom, the time had come to trust that God loves the poor in spirit in a very special way and that—even though I may have had little to offer them—they had a lot to offer me.

One of the first things I did after my arrival was to look for a good place to hang my poster of the *Prodigal Son*. The work space that was given to me proved ideal. Whenever I sat down to read, write, or talk to someone, I could see that mysterious embrace of father and son that had become such an intimate part of my spiritual journey.

Since my visit to the Hermitage, I had become more aware of the four figures, two women and two men, who stood around the luminous space where the father welcomed his returning son. Their way of looking leaves you wondering how they think or feel about what they are watching. These bystanders, or observers, allow for all sorts of interpretations. As I reflect on my own journey, I become more and more aware of how long I have played the role of observer. For years I had instructed students on the different aspects of the spiritual life, trying to help them see the importance of living it. But had I, myself, really ever dared to step into the center, kneel down, and let myself be held by a forgiving God?

The simple fact of being able to express an opinion, to set up an argument, to defend a position, and to clarify a vision has given me, and gives me still, a sense of control. And, generally, I feel much safer in experiencing a sense of control over an undefinable situation than in taking the risk of letting that situation control me.

Certainly there were many hours of prayer, many days and months of retreat, and countless conversations with spiritual directors, but I had never fully given up the role of bystander. Even though there has been in me a lifelong desire to be an insider looking out, I nevertheless kept choosing over and over again the position of the outsider looking in. Sometimes this looking-in was a curious looking-in, sometimes a jealous looking-in, sometimes an anxious looking-in, and, once in a while, even a loving looking-in. But giving up the somewhat safe position of the critical observer seemed like a great leap into totally unknown territory. I so much wanted to keep some control over my spiritual journey, to remain able to predict at least a part of the outcome, that relinquishing the security of the observer for the vulnerability of the returning son seemed close to impossible. Teaching students, passing on the many explanations given over the centuries to the words and actions of Jesus, and showing them the many spiritual journeys that people have chosen in the past seemed very much like taking the position of one of the four figures surrounding the divine embrace. The two women standing behind the father at different distances, the seated man staring into space and looking at no one in particular, and the tall man standing erect and looking critically at the event on the platform in front of him—they all represent different ways of not getting involved. There is in-difference, curiosity, daydreaming, and attentive observation; there is staring, gazing, watching, and looking; there is stand-ing in the background, leaning against an arch, sitting with arms crossed, and standing with hands gripping each other. Every one of these inner and outer postures is all too familiar to me. Some are more comfortable than others, but all of them are ways of not getting directly involved.

Moving from teaching university students to living with mentally handicapped people was, for me at least, a step toward the platform where the father embraces his kneeling son. It is the place of light, the place of truth, the place of love. It is the place where I so much want to be, but am so fearful of being. It is the place where I will receive all I desire, all that I ever hoped for, all that I will ever need, but it is also the place where I have to let go of all I most want to hold on to. It is the place that con-fronts me with the fact that truly accepting love, forgiveness, and healing is often much harder than giving it. It is the place beyond earning, deserving, and rewarding. It is the place of sur-render and complete trust.

Soon after I came to Daybreak, Linda, a beautiful young woman with Down's syndrome, put her arms around me and said: "Welcome." She does that to every newcomer, and every time she does it, she does it with unreserved conviction and love. But how to receive such an embrace? Linda had never met me. She had no understanding at all of what I had lived before coming to Daybreak. She had never had the chance to encoun-ter my dark side, nor to discover my corners of light. She had never read any of my books, heard me speak, or even had a de-cent conversation with me.

So, should I just smile, call her cute, and walk on as if nothing had happened? Or was Linda standing somewhere on the plat-form and saying with her gesture, "Come on up, don't be so bashful, your Father wants to hold you too!" It seems that every time—be it Linda's welcome, Bill's handshake, Gregory's smile, Adam's silence, or Raymond's words—I have to make a choice between "explaining" these gestures or simply accepting them as invitations to come higher up and closer by.

These years at Daybreak have not been easy. There has been much inner struggle, and there has been mental, emotional, and spiritual pain. Nothing, absolutely nothing, had about it the quality of having arrived. However, the move from Harvard to L'Arche proved to be but one little step from bystander to participant, from judge to repentant sinner, from teacher about love to being loved as the beloved. I really did not have an in-kling of how difficult the journey would be. I did not realize how deeply rooted my resistance was and how agonizing it would be to "come to my senses," fall on my knees, and let my tears flow freely. I did not realize how hard it would be to become truly part of the great event that Rembrandt's painting portrays.

Each little step toward the center seemed like an impossible demand, a demand requiring me to let go one more time from wanting to be in control, to give up one more time the desire to predict life, to die one more time to the fear of not know-ing where it all will lead, and to surrender one more time to a love that knows no limits. And still, I knew that I would never be able to live the great commandment to love without allow-ing myself to be loved without conditions or prerequisites. The journey from teaching about love to allowing myself to be loved proved much longer than I realized.

THE VISION

Much of what has happened since my arrival at Daybreak is written down in diaries and notebooks, but, as it stands, little of it is fit to share with others. The words are too raw, too noisy, too "bloody," and too naked. But now a time has come when it is possible to look back on those years of turmoil and to describe, with more objectivity than was possible before, the place to which all of that struggle has brought me. I am still not free enough to let myself be held completely in the safe embrace of the Father. In many ways I am still moving toward the center. I am still like the prodigal: traveling, preparing speeches, anticipating how it will be when I finally reach my Father's house. But I am, indeed, on my way home. I have left the distant country and come to feel the nearness of love. And so, I am ready now to share my story. There is some hope, some light, some consolation to be found in it. Much of what I have lived in the past few years will be part of this story, not as an expression of confusion or despair, but as moments in my journey toward the light.

Rembrandt's painting has remained very close to me throughout this time. I have moved it around many times: from my office to the chapel, from the chapel to the living room of the Dayspring (the house of prayer at Daybreak), and from the living room of the Dayspring back to the chapel. I have spoken about it many times inside and outside of the Daybreak community: to handicapped people and their assistants, to ministers and priests, and to men and women from diverse walks of life. The more I spoke of the *Prodigal Son*, the more I came to see it as, somehow, my personal painting, the painting that contained not only the heart of the story that God wants to tell me, but also the heart of the story that I want to tell to God and

God's people. All of the Gospel is there. All of my life is there. All of the lives of my friends is there. The painting has become a mysterious window through which I can step into the Kingdom of God. It is like a huge gate that allows me to move to the other side of existence and look from there back into the odd assortment of people and events that make up my daily life.

For many years I tried to get a glimpse of God by looking carefully at the varieties of human experience: loneliness and love, sorrow and joy, resentment and gratitude, war and peace. I sought to understand the ups and downs of the human soul, to discern there a hunger and thirst that only a God whose name is Love could satisfy. I tried to discover the lasting beyond the passing, the eternal beyond the temporal, the perfect love beyond all paralyzing fears, and the divine consolation beyond the desolation of human anguish and agony. I tried constantly to point beyond the mortal quality of our existence to a presence larger, deeper, wider, and more beautiful than we can imagine, and to speak about that presence as a presence that can already now be seen, heard, and touched by those who are willing to believe.

However, during my time here at Daybreak, I have been led to an inner place where I had not been before. It is the place within me where God has chosen to dwell. It is the place where I am held safe in the embrace of an all-loving Father who calls me by name and says, "You are my beloved son, on you my favor rests." It is the place where I can taste the joy and the peace that are not of this world.

This place had always been there. I had always been aware of it as the source of grace. But I had not been able to enter it and truly live there. Jesus says, "Anyone who loves me will keep my word and my Father will love him, and we shall come to him and make our home in him." These words have always impressed me deeply. I am God's home!

But it had always been very hard to experience the truth of these words. Yes, God dwells in my innermost being, but how could I accept Jesus' call: "Make your home in me as I make mine in you"? The invitation is clear and unambiguous. To make my home where God had made his, this is the great spiritual challenge. It seemed an impossible task.

With my thoughts, feelings, emotions, and passions, I was constantly away from the place where God had chosen to make home. Coming home and staying there where God dwells, listening to the voice of truth and love, that was, indeed, the journey I most feared because I knew that God was a jealous lover who wanted every part of me all the time. When would I be ready to accept that kind of love?

God himself showed me the way. The emotional and physical crises that interrupted my busy life at Daybreak compelled me—with violent force—to return home and to look for God where God can be found—in my own inner sanctuary. I am unable to say that I have arrived; I never will in this life, because the way to God reaches far beyond the boundary of death. While it is a long and very demanding journey, it is also one full of wonderful surprises, often offering us a taste of the ultimate goal.

When I first saw Rembrandt's painting, I was not as familiar with the home of God within me as I am now. Nevertheless, my intense response to the father's embrace of his son told me that I was desperately searching for that inner place where I too could be held as safely as the young man in the painting. At the time, I did not foresee what it would take to come a few steps closer to that place. I am grateful for not having known in advance what God was planning for me. But I am grateful as well for the new place that has been opened in me through all the inner pain. I have a new vocation now. It is the vocation to speak and write from that place back into the many places of my own and other people's restless lives. I have to kneel before the Father, put my ear against his chest and listen, without interruption, to the heartbeat of God. Then, and only then, can I say carefully and very gently what I hear. I know now that I have to speak from eternity into time, from the lasting joy into the passing realities of our short existence in this world, from the house of love into the houses of fear, from God's abode into the dwellings of human beings. I am well aware of the enormity of this vocation. Still, I am confident that it is the only way for me. One could call it the "prophetic" vision: looking at people and this world through the eyes of God.

Is this a realistic possibility for a human being? More important: Is it a true option for me? This is not an intellectual question. It is a question of vocation. I am called to enter into the inner sanctuary of my own being where God has chosen to dwell. The only way to that place is prayer, unceasing prayer. Many struggles and much pain can clear the way, but I am certain that only unceasing prayer can let me enter it.

THE YOUNGER SON,
THE ELDER SON,
AND THE FATHER

During the year after I first saw the *Prodigal Son*, my spiritual journey was marked by three phases which helped me to find the structure of my story.

The first phase was my experience of being the younger son. The long years of university teaching and the intense involvement in South and Central American affairs had left me feeling quite lost. I had wandered far and wide, met people with all sorts of life-styles and convictions, and become part of many movements. But at the end of it all, I felt homeless and very tired. When I saw the tender way in which the father touched the shoulders of his young son and held him close to his heart, I felt very deeply that I was that lost son and wanted to return, as he did, to be embraced as he was. For a long time I thought of myself as the prodigal son on his way home, anticipating the moment of being welcomed by my Father.

Then, quite unexpectedly, something in my perspective shifted. After my year in France and my visit to the Hermitage in Saint Petersburg, the feelings of desperation that had made me identify so strongly with the younger son moved to the background of my consciousness. I had made up my mind to go to Daybreak in Toronto and, as a result, felt more self-confident than before.

The second phase in my spiritual journey was initiated one evening while talking about Rembrandt's painting to Bart Gavigan, a friend from England who had come to know me quite intimately during the past year. While I explained to Bart how strongly I had been able to identify with the younger son, he looked at me quite intently and said, "I wonder if you are not more like the elder son." With these words he opened a new space within me.

Frankly, I had never thought of myself as the elder son, but once Bart confronted me with that possibility, countless ideas started running through my head. Beginning with the simple fact that I am, indeed, the eldest child in my own family, I came to see how I had lived a quite dutiful life. When I was six years old, I already wanted to become a priest and never changed my mind. I was born, baptized, confirmed, and ordained in the same church and had always been obedient to my parents, my teachers, my bishops, and my God. I had never run away from home, never wasted my time and money on sensual pursuits, and had never gotten lost in "debauchery and drunkenness." For my entire life I had been quite responsible, traditional, and homebound. But, with all of that, I may, in fact, have been just as lost as the younger son. I suddenly saw myself in a completely new way. I saw my jealousy, my anger, my touchiness, doggedness and sullenness, and, most of all, my subtle self-righteousness. I saw how much of a complainer I was and how much of my thinking and feeling was ridden with resentment. For a time it became impossible to see how I could ever have thought of myself as the younger son. I was the elder son for sure, but just as lost as his younger brother, even though I had stayed "home" all my life.

I had been working very hard on my father's farm, but had never fully tasted the joy of being at home. Instead of being grateful for all the privileges I had received, I had become a very resentful person: jealous of my younger brothers and sisters who had taken so many risks and were so warmly welcomed back. During my first year and a half at Daybreak, Bart's insightful remark continued to guide my inner life.

There was more to come. In the months following the celebration of the thirtieth anniversary of my ordination to the priesthood, I gradually entered into very dark interior places and began to experience immense inner anguish. I came to a point where I could no longer feel safe in my own community and had to leave to seek help in my struggle and to work directly on my inner healing. The few books I could take with me were all about Rembrandt and the parable of the prodigal son. While living in a rather isolated place, far away from my friends and community, I found great consolation in reading the tormented life of the great Dutch painter and learning more about the agonizing journey that ultimately had enabled him to paint this magnificent work.

For hours I looked at the splendid drawings and paintings he created in the midst of all his setbacks, disillusionment, and grief, and I came to understand how from his brush there emerged the figure of a nearly blind old man holding his son in a gesture of all-forgiving compassion. One must have died many deaths and cried many tears to have painted a portrait of God in such humility.

It was during this period of immense inner pain that another friend spoke the word that I most needed to hear and opened up the third phase of my spiritual journey. Sue Mosteller, who had been with the Daybreak community from the early seventies and had played an important role in bringing me there, had given me indispensable support when things had become difficult, and had encouraged me to struggle through whatever needed to be suffered to reach true inner freedom. When she visited me in my "hermitage" and spoke with me about the *Prodigal Son*, she said, "Whether you are the younger son or the elder son, you have to realize that you are called to become the father."

Her words struck me like a thunderbolt because, after all my years of living with the painting and looking at the old man holding his son, it had never occurred to me that the father was the one who expressed most fully my vocation in life.

Sue did not give me much chance to protest: "You have been looking for friends all your life; you have been craving for affection as long as I've known you; you have been interested in thousands of things; you have been begging for attention, appreciation, and affirmation left and right. The time has come to claim your true vocation—to be a father who can welcome his children home without asking them any questions and without wanting anything from them in return. Look at the father in your painting and you will know who you are called to be. We, at Daybreak, and most people around you don't need you to be a good friend or even a kind brother. We need you to be a father who can claim for himself the authority of true compassion."

Looking at the bearded old man with his full red cloak, I felt deep resistance to thinking about myself in that way. I felt quite ready to identify myself with the spendthrift younger son or the resentful elder son, but the idea of being like the old man who had nothing to lose because he had lost all, and only to give, overwhelmed me with fear. Nevertheless, Rembrandt died when he was sixty-three years old and I am a lot closer to that age than to the age of either of the two sons. Rembrandt was willing to put himself in the father's place; why not I?

The year and a half since Sue Mosteller's challenge has been a time to begin claiming my spiritual fatherhood. It has been a slow and arduous struggle, and sometimes I still feel the desire to remain the son and never to grow old. But I also have tasted the immense joy of children coming home and of laying hands on them in a gesture of forgiveness and blessing. I have come to know in a small way what it means to be a father who asks no questions, wanting only to welcome his children home.

All that I have lived since my first encounter with the Rembrandt poster has not only given me the inspiration to write this book, but also suggested its structure. I will first reflect upon the younger son, then upon the elder son, and ultimately upon the father. For, indeed, I am the younger son; I am the elder son; and I am on my way to becoming the father. And for you who will make this spiritual journey with me, I hope and pray that you too will discover within yourselves not only the lost children of God, but also the compassionate mother and father that is God.

PART I

THE YOUNGER SON

T he younger son said to his father, "Father, let me have the share of the estate that will come to me." So the father divided the property between them. A few days later, the younger son got together everything he had and left for a distant country where he squandered his money on a life of debauchery.

When he had spent it all, that country experienced a severe famine, and now he began to feel the pinch so he hired himself out to one of the local inhabitants who put him on his farm to feed the pigs. And he would willingly have filled himself with the husks the pigs were eating but no one would let him have them. Then he came to his senses and said, "How many of my father's hired men have all the food they want and more, and here am I dying of hunger! I will leave this place and go to my father and say: Father, I have sinned against heaven and against you; I no longer deserve to be called your son; treat me as one of your hired men." So he left the place and went back to his father.

CHAPTER I

REMBRANDT AND THE
YOUNGER SON

Rembrandt was close to his death when he painted his *Prodigal Son.* Most likely it was one of Rembrandt's last works. The more I read about it and look at it, the more I see it as a final statement of a tumultuous and tormented life. Together with his unfinished painting *Simeon and the Child Jesus,* the *Prodigal Son* shows the painter's perception of his aged self—a perception in which physical blindness and a deep inner seeing are intimately connected. The way in which the old Simeon holds the vulnerable child and the way in which the old father embraces his exhausted son reveal an inner vision that reminds one of Jesus' words to his disciples: "Blessed are the eyes that see what you see." Both Simeon and the father of the returning son carry *within* themselves that mysterious light by which they see. It is an inner light, deeply hidden, but radiating an all-pervasive tender beauty.

This inner light, however, had remained hidden for a long time. For many years it remained unreachable for Rembrandt. Only gradually and through much anguish did he come to know that light within himself and, through himself, in those he painted. Before being like the father, Rembrandt was for a long time like the proud young man who "got together everything he had and left for a distant country where he squandered his money."

When I look at the profoundly interiorized self-portraits which Rembrandt produced during his last years and which explain much of his ability to paint the luminous old father and the old Simeon, I must not forget that, as a young man, Rembrandt had all the characteristics of the prodigal son: brash, self-confident, spendthrift, sensual, and very arrogant. At the age of thirty, he painted himself with his wife, Saskia, as the lost son in a brothel. No interiority is visible there. Drunk, with his half-open mouth and sexually greedy eyes, he glares scornfully at those who look at his portrait as if to say: "Isn't this a lot of fun!" With his right hand he lifts up a half-empty glass, while with his left he touches the lower back of his girl whose eyes are no less lustful than his own. Rembrandt's long, curly hair, his velvet cap with the huge white feather, and the leather-sheathed sword with golden hilt touching the backs of the two merrymakers leave little doubt about their intentions. The drawn curtain in the upper right corner even makes one think of the brothels in Amsterdam's infamous red-light district. Gazing intently at this sensuous self-portrait of the young Rembrandt as the prodigal son, I can scarcely believe that this is the same man who, thirty years later, painted himself with eyes that penetrate so deeply into the hidden mysteries of life.

Still, all the Rembrandt biographers describe him as a proud young man, strongly convinced of his own genius and eager to explore everything the world has to offer; an extrovert who loves luxury and is quite insensitive toward those about him. There is no doubt that one of Rembrandt's main concerns was money. He made a lot, he spent a lot, and he lost a lot. A large part of his energy was wasted in long, drawn-out court cases about financial settlements and bankruptcy proceedings. The self-portraits painted during his late twenties and early thirties reveal Rembrandt as a man hungry for fame and adulation, fond of extravagant costumes, preferring golden chains to the traditional starched white collars, and sporting outlandish hats, berets, helmets, and turbans. Although much of this elaborate dressing-up can be explained as a normal way to practice and show off painting techniques, it also demonstrates an arrogant character who wasn't simply out to please his sponsors.

However, this short period of success, popularity, and wealth is followed by much grief, misfortune, and disaster. Trying to summarize the many misfortunes of Rembrandt's life can be overwhelming. They are not unlike those of the prodigal son. After having lost his son Rumbartus in 1635, his first daughter Cornelia in 1638, and his second daughter Cornelia in 1640, Rembrandt's wife Saskia, whom he deeply loved and admired, dies in 1642. Rembrandt is left behind with his nine-month-old son, Titus. After Saskia's death, Rembrandt's life continues to be marked with countless pains and problems. A very unhappy relationship with Titus' nurse, Geertje Dircx, ending in lawsuits and the confinement of Geertje in an asylum, is followed by a more stable union with Hendrickje Stoffels. She bears him a son who dies in 1652 and a daughter, Cornelia, the only child who will survive him.

During these years, Rembrandt's popularity as a painter plummeted, even though some collectors and critics continued to recognize him as one of the greatest painters of the time. His financial problems became so severe that in 1656 Rembrandt

Gemaeldegalerie Alte Meister, Dresden, Germany © Staatliche Kunstsammlungen Dresden/
Bridgeman Images

is declared insolvent and asks for the right to sign over all his property and effects for the benefit of his creditors to avoid bankruptcy. All of Rembrandt's possessions, his own and other painters' works, his large collection of artifacts, his house in Amsterdam and his furniture, are sold in three auctions during 1657 and 1658.

Although Rembrandt would never become completely free of debt and debtors, in his early fifties he is able to find a modicum of peace. The increasing warmth and interiority of his paintings during this period show that the many disillusionments did not embitter him. On the contrary, they had a purifying effect on his way of seeing. Jakob Rosenberg writes: "He began to regard man and nature with an even more penetrating eye, no longer distracted by outward splendor or theatrical display." In 1663, Hendrickje dies, and five years later, Rembrandt witnesses not only the marriage but also the death of his beloved son, Titus. When Rembrandt himself dies in 1669, he has become a poor and lonely man. Only his daughter Cornelia, his daughter-in-law Magdalene van Loo, and his granddaughter Titia survived him.

As I look at the prodigal son kneeling before his father and pressing his face against his chest, I cannot but see there the once so self-confident and venerated artist who has come to the painful realization that all the glory he had gathered for himself proved to be vain glory. Instead of the rich garments with which the youthful Rembrandt painted himself in the brothel, he now wears only a torn undertunic covering his emaciated body, and the sandals, in which he had walked so far, have become worn out and useless.

Moving my eyes from the repentant son to the compassionate father, I see that the glittering light reflecting from golden chains, harnesses, helmets, candles, and hidden lamps has died out and been replaced by the inner light of old age. It is the movement from the glory that seduces one into an ever greater search for wealth and popularity to the glory that is hidden in the human soul and surpasses death.

CHAPTER 2

THE YOUNGER SON LEAVES

The younger one said to his father, "Father, let me have the share of the estate that will come to me." So the father divided the property between them. A few days later, the younger son got together everything he had and left for a distant country.

A RADICAL REJECTION

The full title of Rembrandt's painting is, as has been said, *Return of the Prodigal Son.* Implicit in the "return" is a leaving. Returning is a homecoming after a home-leaving, a coming back after having gone away. The father who welcomes his son home is so glad because this son "was dead and has come back to life; he was lost and is found." The immense joy in welcoming back the lost son hides the immense sorrow that has gone before. The finding has the losing in the background, the returning has the leaving under its cloak. Looking at the tender and joy-filled return, I have to dare to taste the sorrowful events that preceded it. Only when I have the courage to explore in depth what it means to leave home, can I come to a true understanding of the return. The soft yellow-brown of the son's underclothes looks beautiful when seen in rich harmony with the red of the father's cloak, but the truth of the matter is that the son is dressed in rags that betray the great misery that lies behind him. In the context of a compassionate embrace, our brokenness may appear beautiful, but our brokenness has no other beauty but the beauty that comes from the compassion that surrounds it.

To understand deeply the mystery of compassion, I have to look honestly at the reality that evokes it. The fact is that, long before turning and returning, the son left. He said to his father, "Let me have the share of the estate that will come to me," then he got together everything he had received and left. The evangelist Luke tells it all so simply and so matter-of-factly that it is difficult to realize fully that what is happening here is an unheard-of event: hurtful, offensive, and in radical contradiction to the most venerated tradition of the time. Kenneth Bailey, in his penetrating explanation of Luke's story, shows that the son's manner of leaving is tantamount to wishing his father dead. Bailey writes:

> For over fifteen years I have been asking people of all walks of life from Morocco to India and from Turkey to the Sudan about the implications of a son's request for his inheritance while the father is still living. The answer has always been emphatically the same . . . the conversation runs as follows:
>
> Has anyone ever made such a request in your village? Never!

Could anyone ever make such a request?
Impossible!
If anyone ever did, what would happen?
His father would beat him, of course!
Why?
The request means—he wants his father to die.

Bailey explains that the son asks not only for the division of the inheritance, but also for the right to dispose of his part. "After signing over his possessions to his son, the father still has the right to live off the proceeds . . . as long as he is alive. Here the younger son gets, and thus is assumed to have demanded, disposition to which, even more explicitly, he has no right until the death of his father. The implication of 'Father, I cannot wait for you to die' underlies both requests."

The son's "leaving" is, therefore, a much more offensive act than it seems at first reading. It is a heartless rejection of the home in which the son was born and nurtured and a break with the most precious tradition carefully upheld by the larger community of which he was a part. When Luke writes, "and left for a distant country," he indicates much more than the desire of a young man to see more of the world. He speaks about a drastic cutting loose from the way of living, thinking, and acting that has been handed down to him from generation to generation as a sacred legacy. More than disrespect, it is a betrayal of the treasured values of family and community. The "distant country" is the world in which everything considered holy at home is disregarded.

This explanation is significant to me, not only because it provides me with an accurate understanding of the parable in its historical context, but also—and most of all—because it summons me to recognize the younger son in myself. At first it seemed hard to discover in my own life's journey such a defiant rebellion. Rejecting the values of my own heritage is not part of the way I think of myself. But when I look carefully at the many more or less subtle ways I have preferred the distant country to the home close by, the younger son quickly emerges. I am speaking here about a spiritual "leaving home"—as quite distinct from the mere physical fact that I have spent most of my years outside my beloved Holland.

More than any other story in the Gospel, the parable of the prodigal son expresses the boundlessness of God's compassionate love. And when I place myself in that story under the light of that divine love, it becomes painfully clear that leaving home is much closer to my spiritual experience than I might have thought.

Rembrandt's painting of the father welcoming his son displays scarcely any external movement. In contrast to his 1636 etching of the prodigal son—full of action, the father running to the son and the son throwing himself at his father's feet— the Hermitage painting, made about thirty years later, is one of utter stillness. The father's touching the son is an everlasting blessing; the son resting against his father's breast is an eternal peace. Christian Tümpel writes: "The moment of receiving and forgiving in the stillness of its composition lasts without end. The movement of the father and the son speaks of something that passes not, but lasts forever." Jakob Rosenberg summarizes this vision beautifully when he writes: "The group of father and son is outwardly almost motionless, but inwardly all the more moved . . . the story deals not with the human love of an earthly father . . . what is meant and represented here is the divine love and mercy in its power to transform death into life."

DEAF TO THE VOICE OF LOVE

Leaving home is, then, much more than an historical event bound to time and place. It is a denial of the spiritual reality that I belong to God with every part of my being, that God holds me safe in an eternal embrace, that I am indeed carved in the palms of God's hands and hidden in their shadows. Leaving home means ignoring the truth that God has "fashioned me in secret, moulded me in the depths of the earth and knitted me together in my mother's womb." Leaving home is living as though I do not yet have a home and must look far and wide to find one.

Home is the center of my being where I can hear the voice that says: "You are my Beloved, on you my favor rests"—the same voice that gave life to the first Adam and spoke to Jesus, the second Adam; the same voice that speaks to all the children of God and sets them free to live in the midst of a dark world while remaining in the light. I have heard that voice. It has spoken to me in the past and continues to speak to me now. It is the never-interrupted voice of love speaking from eternity and giving life and love whenever it is heard. When I hear that voice, I know that I am home with God and have nothing to fear. As the Beloved of my heavenly Father, "I can walk in the valley of darkness: no evil would I fear." As the Beloved, I can "cure the sick, raise the dead, cleanse the lepers, cast out devils." Having "received without charge," I can "give without charge." As the Beloved, I can confront, console, admonish, and encourage without fear of rejection or need for affirmation. As the Beloved, I can suffer persecution without desire for revenge and receive praise without using it as a proof of my goodness. As the Beloved, I can be tortured and killed without ever having to doubt that the love that is given to me is stronger than death.

Private Collection/Bridgeman Images

As the Beloved, I am free to live and give life, free also to die while giving life.

Jesus has made it clear to me that the same voice that he heard at the River Jordan and on Mount Tabor can also be heard by me. He has made it clear to me that just as he has his home with the Father, so do I. Praying to his Father for his disciples, he says: "They do not belong to the world, any more than I belong to the world. Consecrate them [set them aside] in the truth. As you sent me into the world, I have sent them into the world, and for their sake I consecrate myself so that they too may be consecrated in truth." These words reveal my true dwelling place, my true abode, my true home. Faith is the radical trust that home has always been there and always will be there. The somewhat stiff hands of the father rest on the prodigal's shoulders with the everlasting divine blessing: "You are my Beloved, on you my favor rests."

Yet over and over again I have left home. I have fled the hands of blessing and run off to faraway places searching for love! This is the great tragedy of my life and of the lives of so many I meet on my journey. Somehow I have become deaf to the voice that calls me the Beloved, have left the only place where I can hear that voice, and have gone off desperately hoping that I would find somewhere else what I could no longer find at home.

At first this sounds simply unbelievable. Why should I leave the place where all I need to hear can be heard? The more I think about this question, the more I realize that the true voice of love is a very soft and gentle voice speaking to me in the most hidden places of my being. It is not a boisterous voice, forcing itself on me and demanding attention. It is the voice of a nearly blind father who has cried much and died many deaths. It is a voice that can only be heard by those who allow themselves to be touched.

Sensing the touch of God's blessing hands and hearing the voice calling me the Beloved are one and the same. This became clear to the prophet Elijah. Elijah was standing on the mountain to meet God. First there came a hurricane, but God was not in the hurricane. Then there came an earthquake, but God was not in the earthquake. Then followed a fire, but God was not there either. Finally there came something very tender, called by some a soft breeze and by others a small voice. When Elijah sensed this, he covered his face because he knew that God was present. In the tenderness of God, voice was touch and touch was voice.

But there are many other voices, voices that are loud, full of promises and very seductive. These voices say, "Go out and prove that you are worth something." Soon after Jesus had heard the voice calling him the Beloved, he was led to the desert to hear those other voices. They told him to prove that he was worth love in being successful, popular, and powerful. Those same voices are not unfamiliar to me. They are always there and, always, they reach into those inner places where I question my own goodness and doubt my self-worth. They suggest that I am not going to be loved without my having earned it through determined efforts and hard work. They want me to prove to myself and others that I am worth being loved, and they keep pushing me to do everything possible to gain acceptance. They deny loudly that love is a totally free gift. I leave home every time I lose faith in the voice that calls me the Beloved and follow the voices that offer a great variety of ways to win the love I so much desire.

Almost from the moment I had ears to hear, I heard those voices, and they have stayed with me ever since. They have come to me through my parents, my friends, my teachers, and my colleagues, but, most of all, they have come and still come through the mass media that surround me. And they say: "Show me that you are a good boy. You had better be better than your friend! How are your grades? Be sure you can make it through school! I sure hope you are going to make it on your own! What are your connections? Are you sure you want to be friends with those people? These trophies certainly show how good a player you were! Don't show your weakness, you'll be used! Have you made all the arrangements for your old age? When you stop being productive, people lose interest in you! When you are dead, you are dead!"

As long as I remain in touch with the voice that calls me the Beloved, these questions and counsels are quite harmless. Parents, friends, and teachers, even those who speak to me through the media, are mostly very sincere in their concerns. Their warnings and advice are well intended. In fact, they can be limited human expressions of an unlimited divine love. But when I forget that voice of the first unconditional love, then these innocent suggestions can easily start dominating my life and pull me into the "distant country." It is not very hard for me to know when this is happening. Anger, resentment, jealousy, desire for revenge, lust, greed, antagonisms, and rivalries are the obvious signs that I have left home. And that happens quite easily. When I pay careful attention to what goes on in my mind from moment to moment, I come to the disconcerting discovery that there are very few moments during my day when I am really free from these dark emotions, passions, and feelings.

Constantly falling back into an old trap, before I am even fully aware of it, I find myself wondering why someone hurt me, rejected me, or didn't pay attention to me. Without realizing it, I find myself brooding about someone else's success, my own loneliness, and the way the world abuses me. Despite my conscious intentions, I often catch myself daydreaming about becoming rich, powerful, and very famous. All of these mental games reveal to me the fragility of my faith that I am the Beloved One on whom God's favor rests. I am so afraid of being disliked, blamed, put aside, passed over, ignored, persecuted, and killed, that I am constantly developing strategies to defend myself and thereby assure myself of the love I think I need and deserve. And in so doing I move far away from my father's home and choose to dwell in a "distant country."

SEARCHING WHERE IT CANNOT BE FOUND

At issue here is the question: "To whom do I belong? To God or to the world?" Many of my daily preoccupations suggest that I belong more to the world than to God. A little criticism makes me angry, and a little rejection makes me depressed. A little praise raises my spirits, and a little success excites me. It takes very little to raise me up or thrust me down. Often I am like a small boat on the ocean, completely at the mercy of its waves. All the time and energy I spend in keeping some kind of balance and preventing myself from being tipped over and drowning shows that my life is mostly a struggle for survival: not a holy struggle, but an anxious struggle resulting from the mistaken idea that it is the world that defines me.

As long as I keep running about asking: "Do you love me? Do you really love me?" I give all power to the voices of the world and put myself in bondage because the world is filled with "ifs." The world says: "Yes, I love you *if* you are good-looking, intelligent, and wealthy. I love you *if* you have a good education, a good job, and good connections. I love you *if* you produce much, sell much, and buy much." There are endless "ifs" hidden in the world's love. These "ifs" enslave me, since it is impossible to respond adequately to all of them. The world's love is and always will be conditional. As long as I keep looking for my true self in the world of conditional love, I will remain "hooked" to the world—trying, failing, and trying again. It is a world that fosters addictions because what it offers cannot satisfy the deepest craving of my heart.

"Addiction" might be the best word to explain the lostness that so deeply permeates contemporary society. Our addictions make us cling to what the world proclaims as the keys to self-fulfillment: accumulation of wealth and power; attainment of status and admiration; lavish consumption of food and drink, and sexual gratification without distinguishing between lust and love. These addictions create expectations that cannot but fail to satisfy our deepest needs. As long as we live within the world's delusions, our addictions condemn us to futile quests in "the distant country," leaving us to face an endless series of disillusionments while our sense of self remains unfulfilled. In these days of increasing addictions, we have wandered far away from our Father's home. The addicted life can aptly be designated a life lived in "a distant country." It is from there that our cry for deliverance rises up.

I am the prodigal son every time I search for unconditional love where it cannot be found. Why do I keep ignoring the place of true love and persist in looking for it elsewhere? Why do I keep leaving home where I am called a child of God, the Beloved of my Father? I am constantly surprised at how I keep taking the gifts God has given me—my health, my intellectual and emotional gifts—and keep using them to impress people, receive affirmation and praise, and compete for rewards, instead of developing them for the glory of God. Yes, I often carry them off to a "distant country" and put them in the service of an exploiting world that does not know their true value. It's almost as if I want to prove to myself and to my world that I do not need God's love, that I can make a life on my own, that I want to be fully independent. Beneath it all is the great rebellion, the radical "No" to the Father's love, the unspoken curse: "I wish you were dead." The prodigal son's "No" reflects Adam's original rebellion: his rejection of the God in whose love we are created and by whose love we are sustained. It is the rebellion that places me outside the garden, out of reach of the tree of life. It is the rebellion that makes me dissipate myself in a "distant country."

Looking again at Rembrandt's portrayal of the return of the younger son, I now see how much more is taking place than a mere compassionate gesture toward a wayward child. The great event I see is the end of the great rebellion. The rebellion of Adam and all his descendants is forgiven, and the original blessing by which Adam received everlasting life is restored. It seems to me now that these hands have always been stretched out— even when there were no shoulders upon which to rest them. God has never pulled back his arms, never withheld his blessing, never stopped considering his son the Beloved One. But the Father couldn't compel his son to stay home. He couldn't force his love on the Beloved. He had to let him go in freedom, even though he knew the pain it would cause both his son and himself. It was love itself that prevented him from keeping his son home at all cost. It was love itself that allowed him to let his son find his own life, even with the risk of losing it.

Here the mystery of my life is unveiled. I am loved so much

that I am left free to leave home. The blessing is there from the beginning. I have left it and keep on leaving it. But the Father is always looking for me with outstretched arms to receive me back and whisper again in my ear: "You are my Beloved, on you my favor rests."

CHAPTER 3

THE YOUNGER SON'S RETURN

He squandered his money on a life of debauchery. When he had spent it all, that country experienced a severe famine, and now he began to feel the pinch; so he hired himself out to one of the local inhabitants who put him on his farm to feed the pigs. And he would willingly have filled himself with the husks the pigs were eating, but no one would let him have them. Then he came to his senses and said, "How many of my father's hired men have all the food they want and more, and here am I dying of hunger! I will leave this place and go to my father and say: Father, I have sinned against heaven and against you; I no longer deserve to be called your son; treat me as one of your hired men." So he left the place and went back to his father.

BEING LOST

The young man held and blessed by the father is a poor, a very poor, man. He left home with much pride and money, determined to live his own life far away from his father and his community. He returns with nothing: his money, his health, his honor, his self-respect, his reputation ... everything has been squandered.

Rembrandt leaves little doubt about his condition. His head is shaven. No longer the long curly hair with which Rembrandt had painted himself as the proud, defiant prodigal son in the brothel. The head is that of a prisoner whose name has been replaced by a number. When a man's hair is shaved off, whether in prison or in the army, in a hazing ritual or in a concentration camp, he is robbed of one of the marks of his individuality. The clothes Rembrandt gives him are underclothes, barely covering his emaciated body. The father and the tall man observing the scene wear wide red cloaks, giving them status and dignity. The kneeling son has no cloak. The yellow-brown, torn undergarment just covers his exhausted, worn-out body from which all strength is gone. The soles of his feet tell the story of a long and humiliating journey. The left foot, slipped out of its worn sandal, is scarred. The right foot, only partially covered by a broken sandal, also speaks of suffering and misery. This is a man dispossessed of everything ... except for one thing, his sword. The only remaining sign of dignity is the short sword hanging from his hips—the badge of his nobility. Even in the midst of his debasement, he had clung to the truth that he still was the son of his father. Otherwise, he would have sold his so valuable sword, the symbol of his sonship. The sword is there to show me that, although he came back speaking as a beggar and an outcast, he had not forgotten that he still was the son of his father. It was this remembered and valued sonship that finally persuaded him to turn back.

I see before me a man who went deep into a foreign land and

lost everything he took with him. I see emptiness, humiliation, and defeat. He who was so much like his father now looks worse than his father's servants. He has become like a slave.

What happened to the son in the distant country? Aside from all the material and physical consequences, what were the inner consequences of the son's leaving home? The sequence of events is quite predictable. The farther I run away from the place where God dwells, the less I am able to hear the voice that calls me the Beloved, and the less I hear that voice, the more entangled I become in the manipulations and power games of the world.

It goes somewhat like this: I am not so sure anymore that I have a safe home, and I observe other people who seem to be better off than I. I wonder how I can get to where they are. I try hard to please, to achieve success, to be recognized. When I fail, I feel jealous or resentful of these others. When I succeed, I worry that others will be jealous or resentful of me. I become suspicious or defensive and increasingly afraid that I won't get what I so much desire or will lose what I already have. Caught in this tangle of needs and wants, I no longer know my own motivations. I feel victimized by my surroundings and distrustful of what others are doing or saying. Always on my guard, I lose my inner freedom and start dividing the world into those who are for me and those who are against me. I wonder if anyone really cares. I start looking for validations of my distrust. And wherever I go, I see them, and I say: "No one can be trusted." And then I wonder whether *anyone* ever really loved me. The world around me becomes dark. My heart grows heavy. My body is filled with sorrows. My life loses meaning. I have become a lost soul.

The younger son became fully aware of how lost he was when no one in his surroundings showed the slightest interest in him.

They noticed him only as long as he could be used for their purposes. But when he had no money left to spend and no gifts left to give, he stopped existing for them. It is hard for me to imagine what it means to be a complete foreigner, a person to whom no one shows any sign of recognition. Real loneliness comes when we have lost all sense of having things in common. When no one wanted to give him the food he was giving to the pigs, the younger son realized that he wasn't even considered a fellow human being. I am only partially aware of how much I rely on some degree of acceptance. Common background, history, vision, religion, and education; common relationships, life-styles, and customs; common age and profession; all of these can serve as bases for acceptance. Whenever I meet a new person, I always look for something we have in common. That seems a normal, spontaneous reaction. When I say, "I am from Holland," the response is often: "Oh, I have been there," or "I have a friend there," or "Oh, windmills, tulips, and wooden shoes!"

Whatever the reaction, there is always a mutual search for a common link. The less we have in common, the harder it is to be together and the more estranged we feel. When I know neither the language nor the customs of others, when I do not understand their life-style or religion, their rituals or their art, when I do not know their food and manner of eating . . . then I feel even more foreign and lost.

When the younger son was no longer considered a human being by the people around him, he felt the profundity of his isolation, the deepest loneliness one can experience. He was truly lost, and it was this complete lostness that brought him to his senses. He was shocked into the awareness of his utter alienation and suddenly understood that he had embarked on the road to death. He had become so disconnected from what gives life—family, friends, community, acquaintances, and even food—that he realized that death would be the natural next step. All at once he saw clearly the path he had chosen and where it would lead him; he understood his own death choice; and he knew that one more step in the direction he was going would take him to self-destruction.

In that critical moment, what was it that allowed him to opt for life? It was the rediscovery of his deepest self.

CLAIMING CHILDHOOD

Whatever he had lost, be it his money, his friends, his reputation, his self-respect, his inner joy and peace—one or all—he still remained his father's child. And so he says to himself: "How many of my father's hired men have all the food they want and more, and here am I dying of hunger! I will leave this place and go to my father and say: Father, I have sinned against heaven and against you; I no longer deserve to be called your son; treat me as one of your hired men." With these words in his heart, he was able to turn, to leave the foreign country, and go home.

The meaning of the younger son's return is succinctly expressed in the words: "Father, . . . I no longer deserve to be called your son." On the one hand the younger son realizes that he has lost the dignity of his sonship, but at the same time that sense of lost dignity makes him also aware that he is indeed the *son* who had dignity to lose.

The younger son's return takes place in the very moment that he reclaims his sonship, even though he has lost all the dignity that belongs to it. In fact, it was the loss of everything that brought him to the bottom line of his identity. He hit the bedrock of his sonship. In retrospect, it seems that the prodigal had to lose everything to come into touch with the ground of his being. When he found himself desiring to be treated as one of the pigs, he realized that he was not a pig but a human being, a son of his father. This realization became the basis for his choice to live instead of to die. Once he had come again in touch with the truth of his sonship, he could hear—although faintly—the voice calling him the Beloved and feel—although distantly—the touch of blessing. This awareness of and confidence in his father's love, misty as it may have been, gave him the strength to claim for himself his sonship, even though that claim could not be based on any merit.

A few years ago, I, myself, was very concretely confronted with the choice: to return or not to return. A friendship that at first seemed promising and life-giving gradually pulled me farther and farther away from home until I finally found myself completely obsessed by it. In a spiritual sense, I found myself squandering all I had been given by my father to keep the friendship alive. I couldn't pray any longer. I had lost interest in my work and found it increasingly hard to pay attention to other people's concerns. As much as I realized how self-destructive my thoughts and actions were, I kept being drawn by my love-hungry heart to deceptive ways of gaining a sense of self-worth.

Then, when finally the friendship broke down completely, I had to choose between destroying myself or trusting that the love I was looking for did, in fact, exist . . . back home! A voice, weak as it seemed, whispered that no human being would ever be able to give me the love I craved, that no friendship, no intimate relationship, no community would ever be able to satisfy the deepest needs of my wayward heart. That soft but persistent voice spoke to me about my vocation, my early commitments, the many gifts I had received in my father's house. That voice called me "son."

The anguish of abandonment was so biting that it was hard, almost impossible, to believe that voice. But friends, seeing my despair, kept urging me to step over my anguish and to trust that there was someone waiting for me at home. Finally, I chose for containment instead of more dissipation and went to a place where I could be alone. There, in my solitude, I started to walk home slowly and hesitantly, hearing ever more clearly the voice that says: "You are my Beloved, on you my favor rests."

This painful, yet hopeful, experience brought me to the core of the spiritual struggle for the right choice. God says: "I am offering you life or death, blessing or curse. Choose life, then, so that you ... may live in the love of Yahweh your God, obeying his voice, holding fast to him." Indeed, it is a question of life or death. Do we accept the rejection of the world that imprisons us, or do we claim the freedom of the children of God? We must choose.

Judas betrayed Jesus. Peter denied him. Both were lost children. Judas, no longer able to hold on to the truth that he remained God's child, hung himself. In terms of the prodigal son, he sold the sword of his sonship. Peter, in the midst of his despair, claimed it and returned with many tears. Judas chose death. Peter chose life. I realize that this choice is always before me. Constantly I am tempted to wallow in my own lostness and lose touch with my original goodness, my God-given humanity, my basic blessedness, and thus allow the powers of death to take charge. This happens over and over again whenever I say to myself: "I am no good. I am useless. I am worthless. I am unlovable. I am a nobody." There are always countless events and situations that I can single out to convince myself and others that my life is just not worth living, that I am only a burden, a problem, a source of conflict, or an exploiter of other people's time and energy. Many people live with this dark, inner sense of themselves. In contrast to the prodigal, they let the darkness absorb them so completely that there is no light left to turn toward and return to. They might not kill themselves physically, but spiritually they are no longer alive. They have given up faith in their original goodness and, thus, also in their Father who has given them their humanity.

But when God created man and woman in his own image, he saw that "it was very good," and, despite the dark voices, no man or woman can ever change that.

The choice for my own sonship, however, is not an easy one. The dark voices of my surrounding world try to persuade me that I am no good and that I can only become good by earning my goodness through "making it" up the ladder of success. These voices lead me quickly to forget the voice that calls me "my son, the Beloved," reminding me of my being loved independently of any acclaim or accomplishment. These dark voices drown out that gentle, soft, light-giving voice that keeps calling me "my favorite one"; they drag me to the periphery of my existence and make me doubt that there is a loving God waiting for me at the very center of my being.

But leaving the foreign country is only the beginning. The way home is long and arduous. What to do on the way back to the Father? It is very clear what the prodigal son does. He prepares a scenario. As he turned, remembering his sonship, he said to himself: "I will leave this place and go to my father and say: Father, I have sinned against heaven and against you; I no longer deserve to be called your son; treat me as one of your hired men." As I read these words, I am keenly aware of how full my inner life is with this kind of talk. In fact, I am seldom without some imaginary encounter in my head in which I explain myself, boast or apologize, proclaim or defend, evoke praise or pity. It seems that I am perpetually involved in long dialogues with absent partners, anticipating their questions and preparing my responses. I am amazed by the emotional energy that goes into these inner ruminations and murmurings. Yes, I *am* leaving the foreign country. Yes, I *am* going home ... but why all this preparation of speeches which will never be delivered?

The reason is clear. Although claiming my true identity as a child of God, I still live as though the God to whom I am returning demands an explanation. I still think about his love as conditional and about home as a place I am not yet fully sure of. While walking home, I keep entertaining doubts about whether I will be truly welcome when I get there. As I look at my spiritual journey, my long and fatiguing trip home, I see how full it is of guilt about the past and worries about the future. I realize my failures and know that I have lost the dignity of my sonship, but I am not yet able to fully believe that where my failings are great, "grace is always greater." Still clinging to my sense of worthlessness, I project for myself a place far below that which belongs to the son. Belief in total, absolute forgiveness does not come readily. My human experience tells me that forgiveness boils down to the willingness of the other to forgo revenge and to show me some measure of charity.

THE LONG WAY HOME

The prodigal's return is full of ambiguities. He is traveling in the right direction, but what confusion! He admits that he was unable to make it on his own and confesses that he would get better treatment as a slave in his father's home than as an outcast in a foreign land, but he is still far from trusting his father's love. He knows that he is still the son, but tells himself that he has lost the dignity to be called "son," and he prepares himself to accept the status of a "hired man" so that he will at least survive. There is repentance, but not a repentance in the light of the immense love of a forgiving God. It is a self-serving repentance that offers the possibility of survival. I know this state of mind and heart quite well. It is like saying: "Well, I couldn't make it on my own, I have to acknowledge that God is the only resource left to me. I will go to God and ask for forgiveness in the hope that I will receive a minimal punishment and be allowed to survive on the condition of hard labor." God remains a harsh, judgmental God. It is this God who makes me feel guilty and worried and calls up in me all these self-serving apologies. Submission to this God does not create true inner freedom, but breeds only bitterness and resentment.

One of the greatest challenges of the spiritual life is to receive God's forgiveness. There is something in us humans that keeps us clinging to our sins and prevents us from letting God erase our past and offer us a completely new beginning. Sometimes it even seems as though I want to prove to God that my darkness is too great to overcome. While God wants to restore me to the full dignity of sonship, I keep insisting that I will settle for being a hired servant. But do I truly want to be restored to the full responsibility of the son? Do I truly want to be so totally forgiven that a completely new way of living becomes possible? Do I trust myself and such a radical reclamation? Do I want to break away from my deep-rooted rebellion against God and surrender myself so absolutely to God's love that a new person can emerge? Receiving forgiveness requires a total willingness to let God be God and do all the healing, restoring, and renewing. As long as I want to do even a part of that myself, I end up with partial solutions, such as becoming a hired servant. As a hired servant, I can still keep my distance, still revolt, reject, strike, run away, or complain about my pay. As the beloved son, I have to claim my full dignity and begin preparing myself to become the father.

It is clear that the distance between the turning around and the arrival at home needs to be traveled wisely and with discipline. The discipline is that of becoming a child of God. Jesus makes it clear that the way to God is the same as the way to a new childhood. "Unless you turn and become like little children you will never enter the Kingdom of Heaven." Jesus does not ask me to remain a child but to become one. Becoming a child is living toward a second innocence: not the innocence of the newborn infant, but the innocence that is reached through conscious choices.

How can those who have come to this second childhood, this second innocence, be described? Jesus does this very clearly in the Beatitudes. Shortly after hearing the voice calling him the Beloved, and soon after rejecting Satan's voice daring him to prove to the world that he is worth being loved, he begins his public ministry. One of his first steps is to call disciples to follow him and share in his ministry. Then Jesus goes up onto the mountain, gathers his disciples around him, and says: "How blessed are the poor, the gentle, those who mourn, those who hunger and thirst for uprightness, the merciful, the pure of heart, the peacemakers, and those who are persecuted in the cause of uprightness."

These words present a portrait of the child of God. It is a

self-portrait of Jesus, the Beloved Son. It is also a portrait of me as I must be. The Beatitudes offer me the simplest route for the journey home, back into the house of my Father. And along this route I will discover the joys of the second childhood: comfort, mercy, and an ever clearer vision of God. And as I reach home and feel the embrace of my Father, I will realize that not only heaven will be mine to claim, but that the earth as well will become my inheritance, a place where I can live in freedom without obsessions and compulsions.

Becoming a child is living the Beatitudes and so finding the narrow gate into the Kingdom. Did Rembrandt know about this? I don't know whether the parable leads me to see new aspects of his painting, or whether his painting leads me to discover new aspects of the parable. But looking at the head of the boy-come-home, I can see the second childhood portrayed.

I vividly remember showing the Rembrandt painting to friends and asking them what they saw. One of them, a young woman, stood up, walked to the large print of the *Prodigal Son*, and put her hand on the head of the younger son. Then she said, "This is the head of a baby who just came out of his mother's womb. Look, it is still wet, and the face is still fetus-like." All of us who were present saw suddenly what she saw. Was Rembrandt portraying not simply the return to the Father, but also the return to the womb of God who is Mother as well as Father?

Until then I had thought of the shaved head of the boy as the head of someone who had been a prisoner, or lived in a concentration camp. I had thought of his face as the emaciated face of an ill-treated hostage. And that may still be all that Rembrandt wanted to show. But since that meeting with my friends, it is no longer possible for me to look at his painting without seeing there a little baby reentering the mother's womb. This helps me to understand more clearly the road I am to walk on my way home.

Isn't the little child poor, gentle, and pure of heart? Isn't the little child weeping in response to every little pain? Isn't the little child the peacemaker hungry and thirsty for uprightness and the final victim of persecution? And what of Jesus himself, the Word of God who became flesh, dwelt for nine months in Mary's womb, and came into this world as a little child worshipped by shepherds from close by and by wise men from far away? The eternal Son became a child so that I might become a child again and so re-enter with him into the Kingdom of the Father. "In all truth I tell you," Jesus said to Nicodemus, "no one can see the Kingdom of God without being born from above."

THE TRUE PRODIGAL

I am touching here the mystery that Jesus himself became the prodigal son for our sake. He left the house of his heavenly Father, came to a foreign country, gave away all that he had, and returned through his cross to his Father's home. All of this he did, not as a rebellious son, but as the obedient son, sent out to bring home all the lost children of God. Jesus, who told the story to those who criticized him for associating with sinners, himself lived the long and painful journey that he describes.

When I began to reflect on the parable and Rembrandt's portrayal of it, I never thought of the exhausted young man with the face of a newborn baby as Jesus. But now, after so many hours of intimate contemplation, I feel blessed by this vision. Isn't the broken young man kneeling before his father the "lamb of God that takes away the sin of the world"? Isn't he the innocent one who became sin for us? Isn't he the one who didn't "cling to his equality with God," but "became as human beings are"? Isn't he the sinless Son of God who cried out on the cross: "My God, my God, why have you forsaken me?" Jesus is the prodigal son of the prodigal Father who gave away everything the Father had entrusted to him so that I could become like him and return with him to his Father's home.

Seeing Jesus himself as the prodigal son goes far beyond the traditional interpretation of the parable. Nonetheless, this vision holds a great secret. I am gradually discovering what it means to say that my sonship and the sonship of Jesus are one, that my return and the return of Jesus are one, that my home and the home of Jesus are one. There is no journey to God outside of the journey that Jesus made. The one who told the story of the prodigal son is the Word of God, "through whom all things came into being." He "became flesh, lived among us," and made us part of his fullness.

Once I look at the story of the prodigal son with the eyes of faith, the "return" of the prodigal becomes the return of the Son of God who has drawn all people into himself and brings them home to his heavenly Father. As Paul says: "God wanted all fullness to be found in him and through him to reconcile all things to him, everything in heaven and everything on earth."

Frère Pierre Marie, the founder of the Fraternity of Jerusalem, a community of monks living in the city, reflects on Jesus as the prodigal son in a very poetic and biblical way. He writes:

> He, who is born not from human stock, or human desire
> or human will, but from God himself, one day took to
> himself everything that was under his footstool and he
> left with his inheritance, his title of Son, and the whole

ransom price. He left for a far country . . . the faraway
land . . . where he became as human beings are and emptied himself. His own people did not accept him and his
first bed was a bed of straw! Like a root in arid ground,
he grew up before us, he was despised, the lowest of men,
before whom one covers his face. Very soon, he came to
know exile, hostility, loneliness . . . After having given
away everything in a life of bounty, his worth, his peace,
his light, his truth, his life . . . all the treasures of knowledge and wisdom and the hidden mystery kept secret for
endless ages; after having lost himself among the lost
children of the house of Israel, spending his time with the
sick (and not with the well-to-do), with the sinners (and
not with the just), and even with the prostitutes to whom
he promised entrance into the Kingdom of his Father;
after having been treated as a glutton and a drunkard, as
a friend of tax collectors and sinners, as a Samaritan, a
possessed, a blasphemer; after having offered everything,
even his body and his blood; after having felt deeply in
himself sadness, anguish, and a troubled soul; after having gone to the bottom of despair, with which he volun-
tarily dressed himself as being abandoned by his Father
far away from the source of living water, he cried out from
the cross on which he was nailed: "I am thirsty." He was
laid to rest in the dust and the shadow of death. And
there, on the third day, he rose up from the depths of hell
to where he had descended, burdened with the crimes of
us all, he bore our sins, our sorrows he carried. Standing
straight, he cried out: "Yes, I am ascending to my Father,
and your Father, to my God, and your God." And he reas-
cended to heaven. Then in the silence, looking at his Son

and all his children, since his Son had become all in all, the Father said to his servants, "Quick! Bring out the best robe and put it on him; put a ring on his finger and sandals on his feet; let us eat and celebrate! Because my children who, as you know, were dead have returned to life; they were lost and have been found again! My prodigal Son has brought them all back." They all began to have a feast dressed in their long robes, washed white in the blood of the Lamb.

Looking again at Rembrandt's *Prodigal Son*, I see him now in a new way. I see him as Jesus returning to his Father and my Father, his God and my God.

It is unlikely that Rembrandt himself ever thought of the prodigal son in this way. This understanding was not a customary part of the preaching and writing of his time. Nevertheless, to see in this tired, broken young man the person of Jesus himself brings much comfort and consolation. The young man being embraced by the Father is no longer just one repentant sinner, but the whole of humanity returning to God. The broken body of the prodigal becomes the broken body of humanity, and the baby-like face of the returning child becomes the face of all suffering people longing to reenter the lost paradise. Thus Rembrandt's painting becomes more than the mere portrayal of a moving parable. It becomes the summary of the history of our salvation. The light surrounding both Father and Son now speaks of the glory that awaits the children of God. It calls to mind the majestic words of John: ". . . we are already God's children, but what we shall be in the future has not yet been revealed. We are well aware that when he appears we shall be like him, because we shall see him as he really is."

But neither Rembrandt's painting nor the parable it depicts leaves us in a state of ecstasy. When I saw the central scene of the father embracing his returning son on the poster in Simone's office, I was not yet aware of the four bystanders watching the scene. But now I know the faces of those surrounding the "return." They are enigmatic to say the least, especially that of the tall man standing at the right side of the painting. Yes, there is beauty, glory, salvation . . . but there are also the critical eyes of uncommitted onlookers. They add a restraining note to the painting and prevent any notions of a quick, romantic solution to the question of spiritual reconciliation. The journey of the younger son cannot be separated from that of his elder brother. And so it is to him that I now—with some temerity—turn my attention.

PART II

THE ELDER SON

N ow the elder son was out in the fields, and on his way back, as he drew near the house, he could hear music and dancing. Calling one of the servants he asked what it was all about. The servant told him, "Your brother has come, and your father has killed the calf we had been fattening because he has got him back safe and sound." He was angry then and refused to go in, and his father came out and began to urge him to come in; but he retorted to his father, "All these years I have slaved for you and never once disobeyed any orders of yours, yet you never offered me so much as a kid for me to celebrate with my friends. But, for this son of yours, when he comes back after swallowing up your property—he and his loose women—you kill the calf we had been fattening."

The father said, "My son, you are with me always, and all I have is yours. But it was only right we should celebrate and rejoice, because your brother here was dead and has come to life; he was lost and is found."

CHAPTER 4

REMBRANDT AND THE ELDER SON

D uring my hours in the Hermitage, quietly looking at the *Prodigal Son*, I never for a moment questioned that the man standing at the right of the platform on which the father embraces his returned son was the elder son. The way he stands there looking at the great gesture of welcome leaves no room for doubt as to whom Rembrandt wanted to portray. I made many notes describing this stern-looking, distant observer and saw there everything Jesus tells us about the elder son.

Still, the parable makes it clear that the elder son is not yet home when the father embraces his lost son and shows him his mercy. To the contrary, the story shows that, when the elder son finally returns from his work, the welcome-home party for his brother is already in full swing.

I am surprised at how easily I missed the discrepancy between Rembrandt's painting and the parable, and simply took it for granted that Rembrandt wanted to paint both brothers in his portrayal of the prodigal son.

When I returned home and began to read all the historical studies of the painting, I quickly realized that many critics were much less sure than I as to the identity of the man standing at the right. Some described him as an old man, and some even questioned whether Rembrandt himself had painted him.

But then one day, more than a year after my visit to the Hermitage, a friend, Ivan Dyer, with whom I had often discussed my interest in the *Prodigal* painting, sent me a copy of Barbara Joan Haeger's "The Religious Significance of Rembrandt's Return of the Prodigal Son." This brilliant study, which puts the painting into the context of the visual and iconographic tradition of Rembrandt's time, brought the elder son back into the picture.

Haeger shows that, in the biblical commentaries and paintings of Rembrandt's time, the parable of the Pharisee and the tax collector and the parable of the prodigal son were closely linked. Rembrandt follows that tradition. The seated man beating his breast and looking at the returning son is a steward representing the sinners and tax collectors, while the standing man looking at the father in a somewhat enigmatic way is the elder son, representing the Pharisees and scribes. By putting the elder son in the painting as the most prominent witness, however, Rembrandt goes not only beyond the literal text of the parable, but also beyond the painting tradition of his time. Thus Rembrandt holds on, as Haeger says, "not to the letter but to the spirit of the biblical text."

Barbara Haeger's findings are much more than a happy affirmation of my earliest intuition. They help me to see *Return of the Prodigal Son* as a work that summarizes the great spiritual battle and the great choices this battle demands. By painting not only the younger son in the arms of his father, but also the elder son who can still choose for or against the love that is offered to him, Rembrandt presents me with the "inner drama of the soul"—his as well as my own. Just as the parable of the prodigal son encapsulates the core message of the Gospel and calls the listeners to make their own choices in the face of it, so, too, does Rembrandt's painting sum up his own spiritual struggle and invite his viewers to make a personal decision about their lives.

Thus Rembrandt's bystanders make his painting a work that engages the viewer in a very personal way. In the fall of 1983, when I first saw the poster showing the central part of the painting, I immediately felt that I was personally called to something. Now that I am better acquainted with the whole painting and especially with the meaning of the prominent witness on the right, I am more than ever convinced of what an enormous spiritual challenge this painting represents.

Looking at the younger son and reflecting on Rembrandt's life, it became quite apparent to me that Rembrandt must have understood him in a personal way. When he painted *Return of the Prodigal Son*, he had lived a life marked by great self-confidence, success, and fame, followed by many painful losses, disappointments, and failures. Through it all he had moved from the exterior light to the interior light, from the portrayal of external events to the portrayal of the inner meanings, from a life full of things and people to a life more marked by solitude and silence. With age, he grew more interior and still. It was a spiritual homecoming.

But the elder son is also part of Rembrandt's life experience, and many modern biographers are, in fact, critical of the romantic vision of his life. They stress that Rembrandt was much more subject to the demands of his sponsors and his need for money than is generally believed, that his subjects are often more the result of the prevailing fashions of his time than of his spiritual vision, and that his failures have as much to do with his self-righteous and obnoxious character as with the lack of appreciation on the part of his milieu.

Different new biographies see in Rembrandt more a selfish, calculating manipulator than a searcher for spiritual truth. They contend that many of his paintings, brilliant as they are, are much less spiritual than they seem. My initial reaction to these demythologizing studies of Rembrandt was one of shock. In particular, the biography by Gary Schwartz—which leaves little room for romanticizing Rembrandt—made me wonder if anything like a "conversion" had ever taken place. It is quite clear from the many recent studies of Rembrandt's relation-ships with his patrons, those who ordered and bought his work, as well as with family and friends, that he was a very difficult person to get along with. Schwartz describes him as a "bitter, revengeful person who used all permissible and impermissible weapons to attack those who came in his way."

Indeed, Rembrandt was known to act often selfishly, arro-gantly, and even vengefully. This is most vividly shown in the way he treated Geertje Dircx, with whom he had been living for six years. He used Geertje's brother, who had been given the power of attorney by Geertje herself, to "collect testimony from neighbors against her, so that she could be sent away to an insane asylum." The outcome was Geertje's confinement in a mental institution. When the possibility later arose that she could be released, "Rembrandt hired an agent to collect evi-dence against her, to make certain that she stay locked up."

During the year 1649, when these tragic events began to hap-pen, Rembrandt was so consumed by them that he produced no work. At this point another Rembrandt emerges, a man lost in bitterness and desire for revenge, and capable of betrayal.

This Rembrandt is hard to face. It is not so difficult to sympathize with a lustful character who indulges in the hedonistic pleasures of the world, then repents, returns home, and becomes a very spiritual person. But appreciating a man with deep resentments, wasting much of his precious time in rather petty court cases and constantly alienating people by his arrogant behavior, is much harder to do. Yet, to the best of my knowledge, that, too, was a part of his life, a part I cannot ignore.

Rembrandt is as much the elder son of the parable as he is the younger. When, during the last years of his life, he painted both sons in his *Return of the Prodigal Son*, he had lived a life in which neither the lostness of the younger son nor the lostness of the elder son was alien to him. Both needed healing and forgiveness. Both needed to come home. Both needed the embrace of a forgiving father. But from the story itself, as well as from Rembrandt's painting, it is clear that the hardest conversion to go through is the conversion of the one who stayed home.

CHAPTER 5

THE ELDER SON LEAVES

Now the elder son was out in the fields, and on his way back, as he drew near the house, he could hear music and dancing. Calling one of the servants, he asked what it was all about. The servant told him, "Your brother has come, and your father has killed the calf we had been fattening because he has got him back safe and sound." He was angry then and refused to go in, and his father came out and began to urge him to come in; but he retorted to his father, "All these years I have slaved for you and never once disobeyed any orders of yours, yet you never offered me so much as a kid for me to celebrate with my friends. But, for this son of yours, when he comes back after swallowing up your property—he and his loose women—you kill the calf we had been fattening."

STANDING WITH CLASPED HANDS

During the hours I spent in the Hermitage looking at Rembrandt's painting, I became increasingly fascinated by the figure of the elder son. I recall gazing at him for long periods and wondering what was going on in this man's mind and heart. He is, without any doubt, the main observer of the younger son's homecoming. At the time when I was familiar only with the detail of the painting in which the father embraces his returning son, it was rather easy to perceive it as inviting, moving, and reassuring. But when I saw the whole painting, I quickly realized the complexity of the reunion. The main observer, watching the father embracing his returning son, appears very withdrawn. He looks at the father, but not with joy. He does not reach out, nor does he smile or express welcome. He simply stands there—at the side of the platform—apparently not eager to come higher up.

It is true that the "return" is the central event of the painting; however, it is not situated at the physical center of the canvas. It takes place at the left side of the painting, while the tall, stern elder son dominates the right side. There is a large open space separating the father and his elder son, a space that creates a tension asking for resolution.

With the elder son in the painting, it is no longer possible for me to sentimentalize the "return." The main observer is keeping his distance, seemingly unwilling to participate in the father's welcome. What is going on inside this man? What will he do? Will he come closer and embrace his brother as his father did, or will he walk away in anger and disgust?

Ever since my friend Bart remarked that I may be much more like the elder brother than the younger, I have observed this "man at the right" with more attentiveness and have seen many new and hard things. The way in which the elder son has been painted by Rembrandt shows him to be very much like his father. Both are bearded and wear large red cloaks over their shoulders. These externals suggest that he and his father have much in common, and this commonality is underlined by the light on the elder son which connects his face in a very direct way with the luminous face of his father.

But what a painful difference between the two! The father bends over his returning son. The elder son stands stiffly erect, a posture accentuated by the long staff reaching from his hand to the floor. The father's mantle is wide and welcoming; the son's hangs flat over his body. The father's hands are spread out and touch the homecomer in a gesture of blessing; the son's are clasped together and held close to his chest. There is light on both faces, but the light from the father's face flows through his whole body—especially his hands—and engulfs the younger son in a great halo of luminous warmth; whereas the light on the face of the elder son is cold and constricted. His figure remains in the dark, and his clasped hands remain in the shadows.

The parable that Rembrandt painted might well be called "The Parable of the Lost Sons." Not only did the younger son, who left home to look for freedom and happiness in a distant country, get lost, but the one who stayed home also became a lost man. Exteriorly he did all the things a good son is supposed to do, but, interiorly, he wandered away from his father. He did his duty, worked hard every day, and fulfilled all his obligations but became increasingly unhappy and unfree.

LOST IN RESENTMENT

It is hard for me to concede that this bitter, resentful, angry man might be closer to me in a spiritual way than the lustful younger brother. Yet the more I think about the elder son, the more I recognize myself in him. As the eldest son in my own family, I know well what it feels like to have to be a model son.

I often wonder if it is not especially the elder sons who want to live up to the expectations of their parents and be considered obedient and dutiful. They often want to please. They often fear being a disappointment to their parents. But they often also experience, quite early in life, a certain envy toward their younger brothers and sisters, who seem to be less concerned about pleasing and much freer in "doing their own thing." For me, this was certainly the case. And all my life I have harbored a strange curiosity for the disobedient life that I myself didn't dare to live, but which I saw being lived by many around me. I did all the proper things, mostly complying with the agendas set by the many parental figures in my life—teachers, spiritual directors, bishops, and popes—but at the same time I often wondered why I didn't have the courage to "run away" as the younger son did.

It is strange to say this, but, deep in my heart, I have known the feeling of envy toward the wayward son. It is the emotion that arises when I see my friends having a good time doing all sorts of things that I condemn. I called their behavior reprehensible or even immoral, but at the same time I often wondered why I didn't have the nerve to do some of it or all of it myself.

The obedient and dutiful life of which I am proud or for which I am praised feels, sometimes, like a burden that was laid on my shoulders and continues to oppress me, even when I have accepted it to such a degree that I cannot throw it off. I have no difficulty identifying with the elder son of the parable who complained: "All these years I have slaved for you and never once disobeyed any orders of yours, yet you never offered me so much as a kid for me to celebrate with my friends." In this complaint, obedience and duty have become a burden, and service has become slavery.

All of this became very real for me when a friend who had

recently become a Christian criticized me for not being very prayerful. His criticism made me very angry. I said to myself, "How dare he teach me a lesson about prayer! For years he has lived a carefree and undisciplined life, while I since childhood have scrupulously lived the life of faith. Now he is converted and starts telling me how to behave!" This inner resentment reveals to me my own "lostness." I had stayed home and didn't wander off, but I had not yet lived a free life in my father's house. My anger and envy showed me my own bondage.

This is not something unique to me. There are many elder sons and elder daughters who are lost while still at home. And it is this lostness—characterized by judgment and condemnation, anger and resentment, bitterness and jealousy—that is so pernicious and so damaging to the human heart. Often we think about lostness in terms of actions that are quite visible, even spectacular. The younger son sinned in a way we can easily identify. His lostness is quite obvious. He misused his money, his time, his friends, his own body. What he did was wrong; not only his family and friends knew it, but he himself as well. He rebelled against morality and allowed himself to be swept away by his own lust and greed. There is something very clear-cut about his misbehavior. Then, having seen that all his wayward behavior led to nothing but misery, the younger son came to his senses, turned around, and asked for forgiveness. We have here a classical human failure, with a straightforward resolution. Quite easy to understand and sympathize with.

The lostness of the elder son, however, is much harder to identify. After all, he did all the right things. He was obedient, dutiful, law-abiding, and hardworking. People respected him, admired him, praised him, and likely considered him a model son. Outwardly, the elder son was faultless. But when confronted by his father's joy at the return of his younger brother, a dark power erupts in him and boils to the surface. Suddenly, there becomes glaringly visible a resentful, proud, unkind, selfish person, one that had remained deeply hidden, even though it had been growing stronger and more powerful over the years.

Looking deeply into myself and then around me at the lives of other people, I wonder which does more damage, lust or resentment? There is so much resentment among the "just" and the "righteous." There is so much judgment, condemnation, and prejudice among the "saints." There is so much frozen anger among the people who are so concerned about avoiding "sin."

The lostness of the resentful "saint" is so hard to reach precisely because it is so closely wedded to the desire to be good and virtuous. I know, from my own life, how diligently I have tried to be good, acceptable, likable, and a worthy example for others. There was always the conscious effort to avoid the pitfalls of sin and the constant fear of giving in to temptation. But with all of that there came a seriousness, a moralistic intensity—and even a touch of fanaticism—that made it increasingly difficult to feel at home in my Father's house. I became less free, less spontaneous, less playful, and others came to see me more and more as a somewhat "heavy" person.

WITHOUT JOY

When I listen carefully to the words with which the elder son attacks his father—self-righteous, self-pitying, jealous words—I hear a deeper complaint. It is the complaint that comes from a heart that feels it never received what it was due. It is the complaint expressed in countless subtle and not-so-subtle ways, forming a bedrock of human resentment. It is the complaint that cries out: "I tried so hard, worked so long, did so much, and still I have not received what others get so easily. Why do people not thank me, not invite me, not play with me, not honor me, while they pay so much attention to those who take life so easily and so casually?"

It is in this spoken or unspoken complaint that I recognize the elder son in me. Often I catch myself complaining about little rejections, little impolitenesses, little negligences. Time and again I discover within me that murmuring, whining, grumbling, lamenting, and griping that go on and on even against my will. The more I dwell on the matters in question, the worse my state becomes. The more I analyze it, the more reason I see for complaint. And the more deeply I enter it, the more complicated it gets. There is an enormous, dark drawing power to this inner complaint. Condemnation of others and self-condemnation, self-righteousness and self-rejection keep reinforcing each other in an ever more vicious way. Every time I allow myself to be seduced by it, it spins me down in an endless spiral of self-rejection. As I let myself be drawn into the vast interior labyrinth of my complaints, I become more and more lost until, in the end, I feel myself to be the most misunderstood, rejected, neglected, and despised person in the world.

Of one thing I am sure. Complaining is self-perpetuating and counterproductive. Whenever I express my complaints in the hope of evoking pity and receiving the satisfaction I so much desire, the result is always the opposite of what I tried to get. A complainer is hard to live with, and very few people know how to respond to the complaints made by a self-rejecting person. The tragedy is that, often, the complaint, once expressed, leads to that which is most feared: further rejection.

From this perspective, the elder son's inability to share in the joy of his father becomes quite understandable. When he came home from the fields, he heard music and dancing. He knew there was joy in the household. Immediately, he became suspicious. Once the self-rejecting complaint has formed in us, we lose our spontaneity to the extent that even joy can no longer evoke joy in us.

The story says: "Calling one of the servants, he asked what it was all about." There is the fear that I am excluded again, that someone didn't tell me what was going on, that I was kept out of things. The complaint resurges immediately: "Why was I not informed, what is this all about?" The unsuspecting servant, full of excitement and eager to share the good news, explains: "Your brother has come, and your father has killed the calf we had been fattening because he has got him back safe and sound." But this shout of joy cannot be received. Instead of relief and gratitude, the servant's joy summons up the opposite: "He was angry then and refused to go in." Joy and resentment cannot coexist. The music and dancing, instead of inviting to joy, become a cause for even greater withdrawal.

I have very vivid memories of a similar situation. Once, when I felt quite lonely, I asked a friend to go out with me. Although he replied that he didn't have time, I found him just a little later at a mutual friend's house where a party was going on. Seeing me, he said, "Welcome, join us, good to see you." But my anger was so great at not being told about the party that I couldn't stay. All of my inner complaints about not being accepted, liked, and loved surged up in me, and I left the room, slamming the door behind me. I was completely incapacitated—unable to receive and participate in the joy that was there. In an instant, the joy in that room had become a source of resentment.

This experience of not being able to enter into joy is the

THE RETURN OF THE PRODIGAL SON

experience of a resentful heart. The elder son couldn't enter into the house and share in his father's joy. His inner complaint paralyzed him and let the darkness engulf him.

Rembrandt sensed the deepest meaning of this when he painted the elder son at the side of the platform where the younger son is received in the father's joy. He didn't depict the celebration, with its musicians and dancers; they were merely the external signs of the father's joy. The only sign of a party is the relief of a seated flute player carved into the wall against which one of the women (the prodigal's mother?) leans. In place of the party, Rembrandt painted light, the radiant light that envelops both father and son. The joy that Rembrandt portrays is the still joy that belongs to God's house.

In the story one can imagine the elder son standing outside in the dark, not wanting to enter the lighted house filled with happy noises. But Rembrandt paints neither the house nor the fields. He portrays it all with darkness and light. The father's embrace, full of light, is God's house. All the music and dancing are there. The elder son stands outside the circle of this love, refusing to enter. The light on his face makes it clear that he, too, is called to the light, but he cannot be forced.

Sometimes, people wonder: Whatever happened to the elder son? Did he let himself be persuaded by his father? Did he finally enter into the house and participate in the celebration? Did he embrace his brother and welcome him home as his father had done? Did he sit down with the father and his brother at the same table and enjoy with them the festive meal?

Neither Rembrandt's painting nor the parable it portrays tells us about the elder son's final willingness to let himself be found. Is the elder son willing to confess that he, too, is a sinner in need of forgiveness? Is he willing to acknowledge that he is not better than his brother?

I am left alone with these questions. Just as I do not know how the younger son accepted the celebration or how he lived with his father after his return, I also do not know whether the elder son ever reconciled himself with his brother, his father, or himself. What I do know with unwavering certainty is the heart of the father. It is a heart of limitless mercy.

AN OPEN-ENDED QUESTION

Unlike a fairy tale, the parable provides no happy ending. Instead, it leaves us face to face with one of life's hardest spiritual choices: to trust or not to trust in God's all-forgiving love. I myself am the only one who can make that choice. In response to their complaint, "This man welcomes sinners and eats with them," Jesus confronted the Pharisees and scribes not only with the return of the prodigal son, but also with the resentful elder son. It must have come as a shock to these dutiful religious people. They finally had to face their own complaint and choose how they would respond to God's love for the sinners. Would they be willing to join them at the table as Jesus did? It was and still is a real challenge: for them, for me, for every human being who is caught in resentment and tempted to settle on a complaintive way of life.

The more I reflect on the elder son in me, the more I realize how deeply rooted this form of lostness really is and how hard it is to return home from there. Returning home from a lustful escapade seems so much easier than returning home from a cold anger that has rooted itself in the deepest corners of my being. My resentment is not something that can be easily distinguished and dealt with rationally.

It is far more pernicious: something that has attached itself

to the underside of my virtue. Isn't it good to be obedient, dutiful, law-abiding, hardworking, and self-sacrificing? And still
it seems that my resentments and complaints are mysteriously
tied to such praiseworthy attitudes. This connection often
makes me despair. At the very moment I want to speak or act
out of my most generous self, I get caught in anger or resentment. And it seems that just as I want to be most selfless, I find
myself obsessed about being loved. Just when I do my utmost to
accomplish a task well, I find myself questioning why others do
not give themselves as I do. Just when I think I am capable of
overcoming my temptations, I feel envy toward those who gave
in to theirs. It seems that wherever my virtuous self is, there also
is the resentful complainer.

Here, I am faced with my own true poverty. I am totally unable to root out my resentments. They are so deeply anchored
in the soil of my inner self that pulling them out seems like
self-destruction. How to weed out these resentments without
uprooting the virtues as well?

Can the elder son in me come home? Can I be found as the
younger son was found? How can I return when I am lost in resentment, when I am caught in jealousy, when I am imprisoned
in obedience and duty lived out as slavery? It is clear that alone,
by myself, I cannot find myself. More daunting than healing
myself as the younger son is healing myself as the elder son.
Confronted here with the impossibility of self-redemption, I
now understand Jesus' words to Nicodemus: "Do not be surprised when I say: 'You must be born from above.'" Indeed,
something has to happen that I myself cannot cause to happen.
I cannot be reborn from below; that is, with my own strength,
with my own mind, with my own psychological insights. There
is no doubt in my mind about this because I have tried so hard

in the past to heal myself from my complaints and failed . . . and failed . . . and failed, until I came to the edge of complete emotional collapse and even physical exhaustion. I can only be healed from above, from where God reaches down. What is impossible for me is possible for God. "With God, everything is possible."

CHAPTER 6

THE ELDER SON'S RETURN

*The elder son . . . was angry then and refused to go in, and his father
came out and began to urge him to come in . . .*

*The father said, "My son, you are with me always, and all I have
is yours. But it was only right we should celebrate and rejoice, because your brother here was dead and has come to life; he was lost
and is found."*

A POSSIBLE CONVERSION

The father wants not only his younger son back, but his elder
son as well. The elder son, too, needs to be found and led back
into the house of joy. Will he respond to his father's plea or remain stuck in his bitterness? Rembrandt, too, leaves the elder
brother's final decision open to question. Barbara Joan Haeger
writes: "Rembrandt does not reveal whether he sees the light.
As he does not clearly condemn the elder brother, Rembrandt
holds out the hope that he too will perceive he is a sinner . . .

the interpretation of the elder brother's reaction is left up to the viewer."

The open-endedness of the story itself and Rembrandt's depiction of it leave me with much spiritual work to do. As I look at the lighted face of the elder son, and then at his darkened hands, I sense not only his captivity, but also the possibility of liberation. This is not a story that separates the two brothers into the good and the evil one. The father only is good. He loves both sons. He runs out to meet both. He wants both to sit at his table and participate in his joy. The younger brother allows himself to be held in a forgiving embrace. The elder brother stands back, looks at the father's merciful gesture, and cannot yet step over his anger and let his father heal him as well.

The Father's love does not force itself on the beloved. Although he wants to heal us of all our inner darkness, we are still free to make our own choice to stay in the darkness or to step into the light of God's love. God is there. God's light is there. God's forgiveness is there. God's boundless love is there. What is so clear is that God is always there, always ready to give and forgive, absolutely independent of our response. God's love does not depend on our repentance or our inner or outer changes.

Whether I am the younger son or the elder son, God's only desire is to bring me home. Arthur Freeman writes:

The father loves each son and gives each the freedom to be what he can, but he cannot give them freedom they will not take nor adequately understand. The father seems to realize, beyond the customs of his society, the need of his sons to be themselves. But he also knows their need for his love and a "home." How their stories will be completed is up to them. The fact that the parable is not completed makes it certain that the father's love is not dependent upon an appropriate completion of the story. The father's love is only dependent on himself and remains part of his character. As Shakespeare says in one of his sonnets: "Love is not love which alters when it alteration finds."

For me, personally, the possible conversion of the elder son is of crucial importance. There is much in me of that group of which Jesus is most critical: the Pharisees and the scribes. I have studied the books, learned about the laws, and often presented myself as an authority in religious matters. People have shown me a great deal of respect and even called me "reverend." I have been rewarded with compliments and praise, with money and prizes, and with much acclaim. I have been critical of many types of behavior and often passed judgment on others.

So when Jesus tells the parable of the prodigal son, I have to listen with the awareness that I am closest to those who elicited the story from him with the remark: "This man welcomes sinners and eats with them." Is there any chance for me to return to the Father and feel welcome in his home? Or am I so ensnared in my own self-righteous complaints that I am doomed, against my own desire, to remain outside of the house, wallowing in my anger and resentment?

Jesus says: "How blessed are you when you are poor . . . blessed are you who are hungry . . . blessed are you who are weeping . . . ," but I am not poor, hungry, or weeping. Jesus prays: "I bless you Father, Lord of heaven and of earth, for hiding these things [of the kingdom] from the learned and the clever." It is to these, the learned and the clever, that I clearly belong. Jesus shows a distinct preference for those who are marginal in society—the poor, the sick, and the sinners—but I am certainly not marginal. The painful question that arises for me out of the Gospel is: "Have I already had my reward?" Jesus is very critical of those who "say their prayers standing up in their synagogues and at street corners for people to see them." Of them, he says: "In truth I tell you, they have had their reward." With all my writing and speaking about prayer and with all the publicity that I enjoy, I cannot help but wonder if these words are not meant for me.

Indeed they are. But the story of the elder son puts all of these agonizing questions in a new light, making it very plain that God does not love the younger son more than the elder. In the story the father goes out to the elder son just as he did to the younger, urges him to come in, and says, "My son, you are with me always, and all I have is yours."

These are the words I must pay attention to and allow to penetrate to the center of my self. God calls me "my son." The Greek word for son that Luke uses here is *teknon*, "an affection-ate form of address," as Joseph A. Fitzmyer says. Literally trans-lated, what the father says is "child."

This affectionate approach becomes even clearer in the words that follow. The harsh and bitter reproaches of the son are not met with words of judgment. There is no recrimination or ac-cusation. The father does not defend himself or even comment on the elder son's behavior. The father moves directly beyond all evaluations to stress his intimate relationship with his son when he says: "You are with me always." The father's declaration of unqualified love eliminates any possibility that the younger son is more loved than the elder. The elder son has never left the house. The father has shared everything with him. He has made him part of his daily life, keeping nothing from him. "All I have is yours," he says. There could be no clearer statement of the father's unlimited love for his elder son. Thus the father's unreserved, unlimited love is offered wholly and equally to both his sons.

LETTING GO OF RIVALRY

The joy at the dramatic return of the younger son in no way means that the elder son was less loved, less appreciated, less favored. The father does not compare the two sons. He loves them both with a complete love and expresses that love according to their individual journeys. He knows them both intimately. He understands their highly unique gifts and shortcomings. He sees with love the passion of his younger son, even when it is not regulated by obedience. With the same love, he sees the obedience of the elder son, even when it is not vitalized by passion. With the younger son there are no thoughts of better or worse, more or less, just as there are no measuring sticks with the elder son. The father responds to both according to their uniqueness. The return of the younger son makes him call for a joyful celebration. The return of the elder son makes him extend an invitation to full participation in that joy.

"In the house of my father there are many places to live," Jesus says. Each child of God has there his or her unique place, all of them places of God. I have to let go of all comparison, all rivalry and competition, and surrender to the Father's love. This requires a leap of faith because I have little experience of non-comparing love and do not know the healing power of such a love. As long as I stay outside in the darkness, I can only remain in the resentful complaint that results from my comparisons. Outside of the light, my younger brother seems to be more loved by the Father than I; in fact, outside of the light, I cannot even see him as my own brother.

God is urging me to come home, to enter into his light, and to discover there that, in God, all people are uniquely and completely loved. In the light of God I can finally see my neighbor as my brother, as the one who belongs as much to God as I do. But outside of God's house, brothers and sisters, husbands and wives, lovers and friends become rivals and even enemies; each perpetually plagued by jealousies, suspicions, and resentments.

It is not surprising that, in his anger, the elder son complains to the father: ". . . you never offered me so much as a kid for me to celebrate with my friends. But, for this son of yours, when he comes back after swallowing up your property—he and his loose women—you kill the calf we had been fattening." These words reveal how deeply hurt this man must feel. His self-esteem is painfully wounded by his father's joy, and his own anger prevents him from accepting this returning scoundrel as his brother. With the words "this son of yours" he distances himself from his brother as well as from his father.

He looks at the two of them as aliens who have lost all sense of reality and engage in a relationship that is completely inappropriate, considering the true facts of the prodigal's life. The elder son no longer has a brother. Nor, any longer, a father. Both have become strangers to him. His brother, a sinner, he looks down on with disdain; his father, a slave owner, he looks up at with fear.

Here I see how lost the elder son is. He has become a foreigner in his own house. True communion is gone. Every relationship is pervaded by the darkness. To be afraid or to show disdain, to suffer submission or to enforce control, to be an oppressor or to be a victim: these have become the choices for one outside of the light. Sins cannot be confessed, forgiveness cannot be received, the mutuality of love cannot exist. True communion has become impossible.

I know the pain of this predicament. In it, everything loses its spontaneity. Everything becomes suspect, self-conscious, calculated, and full of second-guessing. There is no longer any trust. Each little move calls for a countermove; each little remark begs for analysis; the smallest gesture has to be evaluated. This is the pathology of the darkness.

Is there a way out? I don't think there is—at least not on my side. It often seems that the more I try to disentangle myself from the darkness, the darker it becomes. I need light, but that light has to conquer my darkness, and that I cannot bring about myself. I cannot forgive myself. I cannot make myself feel loved. By myself I cannot leave the land of my anger. I cannot bring myself home nor can I create communion on my own. I can desire it, hope for it, wait for it, yes, pray for it. But my true freedom I cannot fabricate for myself. That must be given to me. I am lost. I must be found and brought home by the shepherd who goes out to me.

The story of the prodigal son is the story of a God who goes searching for me and who doesn't rest until he has found me. He urges and he pleads. He begs me to stop clinging to the powers of death and to let myself be embraced by arms that will carry me to the place where I will find the life I most desire.

Recently I lived, very concretely in my own flesh, the return of the elder son. While hitchhiking, I was hit by a car and soon found myself in a hospital close to death. There I suddenly had the illuminating insight that I would not be free to die as long as I was still holding on to the complaint of not having been loved enough by the one whose son I am. I realized that I had not yet grown up completely. I felt strongly the call to lay to rest my adolescent complaints and to give up the lie that I am less loved than my younger brothers. It was frightening, but very liberating. When my dad, far advanced in years, flew over from Holland to visit me, I knew that this was the moment to claim my own God-given sonship. For the first time in my life, I told my father explicitly that I loved him and was grateful for his love for me. I said many things that I had never said before and was surprised at how long it had taken me to say them. My father was somewhat surprised and even puzzled by it all, but received my words with understanding and a smile. As I look back on this spiritual event, I see it as a true return, the return from a false dependence on a human father who cannot give me all I need to a true dependence on the divine Father who says: "You are with me always, and all I have is yours"; the return also from my complaining, comparing, resentful self to my true self that is free to give and receive love. And even though there have been, and undoubtedly will continue to be, many setbacks, it brought me to the beginning of the freedom to live my own life and die my own death. The return to the "Father from whom all fatherhood takes its name" allows me to let my dad be no less than the good, loving, but limited human being he is, and to let my heavenly Father be the God whose unlimited, unconditional love melts away all resentments and anger and makes me free to love beyond the need to please or find approval.

THROUGH TRUST AND GRATITUDE

This personal experience of the return of the elder son in me may offer some hope to people caught in the resentment that is the bitter fruit of their need to please. I guess that all of us will someday have to deal with the elder son or the elder daughter in us. The question before us is simply: What can we do to make the return possible? Although God himself runs out to us to find us and bring us home, we must not only recognize that we are lost, but also be prepared to be found and brought home. How? Obviously not by just waiting and being passive. Although we are incapable of liberating ourselves from our frozen anger, we can allow ourselves to be found by God and healed by his love through the concrete and daily practice of trust and gratitude. Trust and gratitude are the disciplines for the conversion of the elder son. And I have come to know them through my own experience.

Without trust, I cannot let myself be found. Trust is that deep inner conviction that the Father wants me home. As long as I doubt that I am worth finding and put myself down as less loved than my younger brothers and sisters, I cannot be found. I have to keep saying to myself, "God is looking for you. He will go anywhere to find you. He loves you, he wants you home, he cannot rest unless he has you with him."

There is a very strong, dark voice in me that says the opposite: "God isn't really interested in me, he prefers the repentant sinner who comes home after his wild escapades. He doesn't pay attention to me who has never left the house. He takes me for granted. I am not his favorite son. I don't expect him to give me what I really want."

At times this dark voice is so strong that I need enormous spiritual energy to trust that the Father wants me home as much as he does the younger son. It requires a real discipline to step over my chronic complaint and to think, speak, and act with the conviction that I am being sought and will be found. Without such discipline, I become prey to self-perpetuating hopelessness.

By telling myself that I am not important enough to be found, I amplify my self-complaint until I have become totally deaf to the voice calling for me. At some point, I must totally disown my self-rejecting voice and claim the truth that God does indeed want to embrace me as much as he does my wayward brothers and sisters. To prevail, this trust has to be even deeper than the sense of lostness. Jesus expresses its radicalness when he says: "Everything you ask and pray for, trust that you have it already, and it will be yours." Living in this radical trust will open the way for God to realize my deepest desire.

Along with trust there must be gratitude—the opposite of resentment. Resentment and gratitude cannot coexist, since resentment blocks the perception and experience of life as a gift. My resentment tells me that I don't receive what I deserve. It always manifests itself in envy.

Gratitude, however, goes beyond the "mine" and "thine" and claims the truth that all of life is a pure gift. In the past I always thought of gratitude as a spontaneous response to the awareness of gifts received, but now I realize that gratitude can also be lived as a discipline. The discipline of gratitude is the explicit effort to acknowledge that all I am and have is given to me as a gift of love, a gift to be celebrated with joy.

Gratitude as a discipline involves a conscious choice. I can choose to be grateful even when my emotions and feelings are still steeped in hurt and resentment. It is amazing how many occasions present themselves in which I can choose gratitude instead of a complaint. I can choose to be grateful when I am criticized, even when my heart still responds in bitterness. I can choose to speak about goodness and beauty, even when my inner eye still looks for someone to accuse or something to call ugly. I can choose to listen to the voices that forgive and to look at the faces that smile, even while I still hear words of revenge and see grimaces of hatred.

There is always the choice between resentment and gratitude because God has appeared in my darkness, urged me to come home, and declared in a voice filled with affection: "You are with me always, and all I have is yours." Indeed, I can choose to dwell in the darkness in which I stand, point to those who are seemingly better off than I, lament about the many misfortunes that have plagued me in the past, and thereby wrap myself up in my resentment. But I don't have to do this. There is the option to look into the eyes of the One who came out to search for me and see therein that all I am and all I have is pure gift calling for gratitude.

The choice for gratitude rarely comes without some real effort. But each time I make it, the next choice is a little easier, a little freer, a little less self-conscious. Because every gift I acknowledge reveals another and another until, finally, even the most normal, obvious, and seemingly mundane event or encounter proves to be filled with grace. There is an Estonian proverb that says: "Who does not thank for little will not thank for much." Acts of gratitude make one grateful because, step by step, they reveal that all is grace.

Both trust and gratitude require the courage to take risks because distrust and resentment, in their need to keep their claim on me, keep warning me how dangerous it is to let go of my careful calculations and guarded predictions. At many points I have to make a leap of faith to let trust and gratitude have a chance: to write a gentle letter to someone who will not forgive me, make a call to someone who has rejected me, speak a word of healing to someone who cannot do the same.

The leap of faith always means loving without expecting to be loved in return, giving without wanting to receive, inviting without hoping to be invited, holding without asking to be held. And every time I make a little leap, I catch a glimpse of the One who runs out to me and invites me into his joy, the joy in which I can find not only myself, but also my brothers and sisters. Thus the disciplines of trust and gratitude reveal the God who searches for me, burning with desire to take away all my resentments and complaints and to let me sit at his side at the heavenly banquet.

THE TRUE ELDER SON

The return of the elder son is becoming as important to me *as—* if not more important *than—*the return of the younger son. How will the elder son look when he is free from his complaints, free from his anger, resentments, and jealousies? Because the parable tells us nothing about the response of the elder son, we are left with the choice of listening to the Father or of remaining imprisoned in our self-rejection.

But even as I reflect on that choice and realize that the whole parable was told by Jesus and painted by Rembrandt for my conversion, it becomes clear to me that Jesus, who told the story, is himself not only the younger son, but the elder son as well. He has come to show the Father's love and to free me from the bondage of my resentments. All that Jesus says about himself reveals him as the Beloved Son, the one who lives in complete communion with the Father. There is no distance, fear, or suspicion between Jesus and the Father.

The words of the father in the parable: "My son, you are with me always, and all I have is yours" express the true relationship of God the Father with Jesus his Son. Jesus constantly affirms that all the glory that belongs to the Father belongs to the Son

too. All the Father does, the Son does too. There is no separation between Father and Son: "The Father and I are one"; no
division of work: "The Father loves the Son and has entrusted
everything to him"; no competition: "I have made known to you
everything I have learned from my Father"; no envy: "The Son
can do nothing by himself, he can do only what he sees the
Father doing." There is perfect unity between Father and Son.
This unity belongs at the center of Jesus' message: "You must
believe me when I say that I am in the Father and the Father is
in me." To believe in Jesus means to believe that he is the one
sent by the Father, the one in and through whom the fullness of
the Father's love is revealed.

This is expressed dramatically by Jesus himself in the parable of the wicked tenants. The owner of the vineyard, after
having sent in vain several stewards to collect his share of the
harvest, decides to send "his beloved son." The tenants recognize that he is the heir and kill him to obtain the inheritance
for themselves. This is the picture of the true son who obeys his
father, not as a slave, but as the Beloved, and fulfills the will of
the Father in full unity with him.

Thus Jesus is the elder Son of the Father. He is sent by the Father to reveal God's unremitting love for all his resentful children and to offer himself as the way home. Jesus is God's way of
making the impossible possible—of allowing light to conquer
darkness. Resentments and complaints, deep as they may seem,
can vanish in the face of him in whom the full light of Sonship is visible. As I look again at Rembrandt's elder son, I realize
that the cold light on his face can become deep and warm—
transforming him totally—and make him who he truly is: "The
Beloved Son on whom God's favor rests."

PART III

THE FATHER

While he was still a long way off, his father saw him and was moved with pity. He ran to the boy, clasped him in his arms and kissed him . . . the father said to his servants, "Quick! Bring out the best robe and put it on him; put a ring on his finger and sandals on his feet. Bring the calf we have been fattening, and kill it; we will celebrate by having a feast, because this son of mine was dead and has come back to life; he was lost and is found." And they began to celebrate.

. . . his father came out and began to urge him to come in . . . The father said, "My son, you are with me always, and all I have is yours. But it was only right we should celebrate and rejoice, because your brother here was dead and has come to life; he was lost and is found."

CHAPTER 7

REMBRANDT AND THE FATHER

While I was sitting in front of the painting in the Hermitage trying to absorb what I saw, many groups of tourists passed by. Even though they spent less than a minute with the painting, almost all of the guides described it as a painting of the compassionate father, and most of them mentioned that it was one of Rembrandt's last paintings, one to which he came only after a life of suffering. Indeed, this is what this painting is all about. It is the human expression of divine compassion.

Instead of its being called *Return of the Prodigal Son*, it could easily have been called "The Welcome by the Compassionate Father." The emphasis is less on the son than on the father. The parable is in truth a "Parable of the Father's Love." Looking at the way in which Rembrandt portrays the father, there came to me a whole new interior understanding of tenderness, mercy, and forgiveness. Seldom, if ever, has God's immense, compassionate love been expressed in such a poignant way. Every detail of the father's figure—his facial expression, his posture, the colors of his dress, and, most of all, the still gesture of his hands—speaks of the divine love for humanity that existed from the beginning and ever will be.

Everything comes together here: Rembrandt's story, humanity's story, and God's story. Time and eternity intersect; approaching death and everlasting life touch each other. Sin and forgiveness embrace; the human and the divine become one.

What gives Rembrandt's portrayal of the father such an irresistible power is that the most divine is captured in the most human. I see a half-blind old man with a mustache and a parted beard, dressed in a gold-embroidered garment and a deep red cloak, laying his large, stiffened hands on the shoulders of his returning son. This is very specific, concrete, and describable.

I also see, however, infinite compassion, unconditional love, everlasting forgiveness—divine realities—emanating from a Father who is the creator of the universe. Here, both the human and the divine, the fragile and the powerful, the old and the eternally young are fully expressed. This is Rembrandt's genius. The spiritual truth is completely enfleshed. As Paul Baudiquet writes: "The spiritual in Rembrandt ... pulls its strongest and most splendid accents from the flesh."

It is of special significance that Rembrandt chose a nearly blind old man to communicate God's love. Surely the parable Jesus told and the way the parable has been interpreted throughout the centuries offer the main basis for the portrayal of God's merciful love. But I should not forget that it was Rembrandt's own story that enabled him to give it its unique expression.

Paul Baudiquet says: "Since his youth, Rembrandt has had but one vocation: to grow old." And it is true that Rembrandt always displayed a great interest in older people. He had drawn them, etched them, and painted them ever since he was a young man and became increasingly fascinated by their inner beauty. Some of Rembrandt's most stunning portraits are of old people, and his most gripping self-portraits are made during his last years.

After his many trials at home and at work, he shows a special fascination with blind people. As the light in his work interiorizes, he begins to paint blind people as the real see-ers. He is attracted to Tobit and the near-blind Simeon, and he paints them several times.

As Rembrandt's own life moves toward the shadows of old age, as his success wanes, and the exterior splendor of his life diminishes, he comes more in touch with the immense beauty of the interior life. There he discovers the light that comes from an inner fire that never dies: the fire of love. His art no longer tries to "grasp, conquer, and regulate the visible," but to "transform the visible in the fire of love that comes from the unique heart of the artist."

The unique heart of Rembrandt becomes the unique heart of the father. The inner, light-giving fire of love that has grown strong through the artist's many years of suffering burns in the heart of the father who welcomes his returning son.

I understand now why Rembrandt didn't follow the literal text of the parable. There Saint Luke writes: "While the younger son was still a long way off, his father saw him and was moved with pity. He ran to the boy, clasped him in his arms and kissed him." Earlier in his life, Rembrandt had etched and drawn this event with all the dramatic movement it contains. But as he approached death, Rembrandt chose to portray a very still father who recognizes his son, not with the eyes of the body, but with the inner eye of his heart.

It seems that the hands that touch the back of the returning son are the instruments of the father's inner eye. The near-blind father sees far and wide. His seeing is an eternal seeing, a seeing that reaches out to all of humanity. It is a seeing that understands the lostness of women and men of all times and places, that knows with immense compassion the suffering of those who have chosen to leave home, that cried oceans of tears as they got caught in anguish and agony. The heart of the father burns with an immense desire to bring his children home.

Oh, how much would he have liked to talk to them, to warn them against the many dangers they were facing, and to convince them that at home can be found everything that they search for elsewhere. How much would he have liked to pull them back with his fatherly authority and hold them close to himself so that they would not get hurt.

But his love is too great to do any of that. It cannot force, constrain, push, or pull. It offers the freedom to reject that love or to love in return. It is precisely the immensity of the divine love that is the source of the divine suffering. God, creator of heaven and earth, has chosen to be, first and foremost, a Father.

As Father, he wants his children to be free, free to love. That freedom includes the possibility of their leaving home, going to a "distant country," and losing everything. The Father's heart knows all the pain that will come from that choice, but his love makes him powerless to prevent it. As Father, he desires that those who stay at home enjoy his presence and experience his affection. But here again, he wants only to offer a love that can be freely received. He suffers beyond telling when his children honor him only with lip service, while their hearts are far from him. He knows their "deceitful tongues" and "disloyal hearts," but he cannot make them love him without losing his true fatherhood.

As Father, the only authority he claims for himself is the authority of compassion. That authority comes from letting the sins of his children pierce his heart. There is no lust, greed, anger, resentment, jealousy, or vengeance in his lost children that has not caused immense grief to his heart. The grief is so deep because the heart is so pure. From the deep inner place where love embraces all human grief, the Father reaches out to his children. The touch of his hands, radiating inner light, seeks only to heal.

Here is the God I want to believe in: a Father who, from the beginning of creation, has stretched out his arms in merciful blessing, never forcing himself on anyone, but always waiting; never letting his arms drop down in despair, but always hoping that his children will return so that he can speak words of love to them and let his tired arms rest on their shoulders. His only desire is to bless.

In Latin, to bless is *benedicere*, which means literally: saying good things. The Father wants to say, more with his touch than with his voice, good things of his children. He has no desire to punish them. They have already been punished excessively by their own inner or outer waywardness. The Father wants simply to let them know that the love they have searched for in such distorted ways has been, is, and always will be there for them. The Father wants to say, more with his hands than with his mouth: "You are my Beloved, on you my favor rests." He is the shepherd, "feeding his flock, gathering lambs in his arms, holding them against his breast."

The true center of Rembrandt's painting is the hands of the father. On them all the light is concentrated; on them the eyes of the bystanders are focused; in them mercy becomes flesh; upon them forgiveness, reconciliation, and healing come together, and, through them, not only the tired son, but also the worn-out father find their rest. From the moment I first saw the poster on Simone's office door, I felt drawn to those hands. I did not fully understand why. But gradually over the years I have come to know those hands. They have held me from the hour of my conception, they welcomed me at my birth, held me close to my mother's breast, fed me, and kept me warm. They have protected me in times of danger and consoled me in times of grief. They have waved me good-bye and always welcomed me back. Those hands are God's hands. They are also the hands of my parents, teachers, friends, healers, and all those whom God has given me to remind me how safely I am held.

Not long after Rembrandt painted the father and his blessing hands, he died.

Rembrandt's hands had painted countless human faces and human hands. In this, one of his last paintings, he painted the face and the hands of God. Who had posed for this life-size portrait of God? Rembrandt himself?

The father of the prodigal son *is* a self-portrait, but not in the traditional sense. Rembrandt's own face appears in several of his paintings. It appears as the prodigal son in the brothel, as a frightened disciple on the lake, as one of the men taking the dead body of Jesus from the cross.

Yet here it is not Rembrandt's face that is reflected, but his soul, the soul of a father who had suffered so many a death. During his sixty-three years, Rembrandt saw not only his dear wife Saskia die, but also three sons, two daughters, and the two women with whom he lived. The grief for his beloved son Titus, who died at the age of twenty-six shortly after his marriage, has never been described, but in the father of the *Prodigal Son* we can see how many tears it must have cost him. Created in

REMBRANDT AND THE FATHER

the image of God, Rembrandt had come to discover through his long, painful struggle the true nature of that image. It is the image of a near-blind old man crying tenderly, blessing his deeply wounded son. Rembrandt was the son, he became the father, and thus was made ready to enter eternal life.

CHAPTER 8

THE FATHER WELCOMES HOME

While he was still a long way off, his father saw him [his younger son] and was moved with pity. He ran to the boy, clasped him in his arms and kissed him.

. . . his father came out and began to urge him [his elder son] to come in.

FATHER AND MOTHER

Often I have asked friends to give me their first impression of Rembrandt's *Prodigal Son*. Inevitably, they point to the wise old man who forgives his son: the benevolent patriarch.

The longer I looked at "the patriarch," the clearer it became to me that Rembrandt had done something quite different from letting God pose as the wise old head of a family. It all began with the hands. The two are quite different. The father's left hand touching the son's shoulder is strong and muscular. The fingers are spread out and cover a large part of the prodigal son's shoulder and back. I can see a certain pressure, especially in the thumb. That hand seems not only to touch, but, with its strength, also to hold. Even though there is a gentleness in the way the father's left hand touches his son, it is not without a firm grip.

How different is the father's right hand! This hand does not hold or grasp. It is refined, soft, and very tender. The fingers are close to each other and they have an elegant quality. It lies gently upon the son's shoulder. It wants to caress, to stroke, and to offer consolation and comfort. It is a mother's hand.

Some commentators have suggested that the masculine left hand is Rembrandt's own hand, while the feminine right hand is similar to the right hand of *The Jewish Bride* painted in the same period. I like to believe that this is true.

As soon as I recognized the difference between the two hands of the father, a new world of meaning opened up for me. The Father is not simply a great patriarch. He is mother as well as father. He touches the son with a masculine hand and a feminine hand. He holds, and she caresses. He confirms and she consoles. He is, indeed, God, in whom both manhood and womanhood, fatherhood and motherhood, are fully present. That gentle caressing right hand echoes for me the words of the prophet Isaiah: "Can a woman forget her baby at the breast, feel no pity for the child she has borne? Even if these were to forget, I shall not forget you. Look, I have engraved you on the palms of my hands."

My friend Richard White pointed out to me that the caressing feminine hand of the father parallels the bare, wounded foot of the son, while the strong masculine hand parallels the foot dressed in a sandal. Is it too much to think that the one hand protects the vulnerable side of the son, while the other hand reinforces the son's strength and desire to get on with his life?

Then there is the great red cloak. With its warm color and its arch-like shape, it offers a welcome place where it is good to be. At first, the cloak covering the bent-over body of the father looked to me like a tent inviting the tired traveler to find some rest. But as I went on gazing at the red cloak, another image, stronger than that of a tent, came to me: the sheltering wings of the mother bird. They reminded me of Jesus' words about God's maternal love: "Jerusalem, Jerusalem . . . How often have I longed to gather your children, as a hen gathers her chicks under her wings, and you refused!"

Day and night God holds me safe, as a hen holds her chicks secure under her wings. Even more than that of a tent, the image of a vigilant mother bird's wings expresses the safety that God offers her children. They express care, protection, a place to rest and feel safe.

Every time I look at the tent-like and wings-like cloak in Rembrandt's painting, I sense the motherly quality of God's love and my heart begins to sing in words inspired by the Psalmist:

> *You who dwell in the shelter of the Most High*
> *and abide in the shade of the Almighty—*
> *say to your God: "My refuge, my stronghold,*
> *my God in whom I trust!*
> *. . . You conceal me with your pinions*
> *and under your wings I shall find refuge."*

And so, under the aspect of an old Jewish patriarch, there emerges also a motherly God receiving her son home.

As I now look again at Rembrandt's old man bending over

his returning son and touching his shoulders with his hands, I begin to see not only a father who "clasps his son in his arms," but also a mother who caresses her child, surrounds him with the warmth of her body, and holds him against the womb from which he sprang. Thus the "return of the prodigal son" becomes the return to God's womb, the return to the very origins of being and again echoes Jesus' exhortation to Nicodemus, to be reborn from above.

Now I understand better also the enormous stillness of this portrait of God. There is no sentimentality here, no romanticism, no simplistic tale with a happy ending. What I see here is God as mother, receiving back into her womb the one whom she made in her own image. The near-blind eyes, the hands, the cloak, the bent-over body, they all call forth the divine maternal love, marked by grief, desire, hope, and endless waiting.

The mystery, indeed, is that God in her infinite compassion has linked herself for eternity with the life of her children. She has freely chosen to become dependent on her creatures, whom she has gifted with freedom. This choice causes her grief when they leave; this choice brings her gladness when they return. But her joy will not be complete until all who have received life from her have returned home and gather together around the table prepared for them.

And this includes the elder son. Rembrandt places him at a distance, out from under the billowing cloak, at the edge of the circle of light. The elder son's dilemma is to accept or reject that his father's love is beyond comparisons; to dare to be loved as his father longs to love him or to insist on being loved as *he* feels he ought to be loved. The father knows that the choice must be the son's, even while he waits with outstretched hands. Will the elder son be willing to kneel and be touched by the same

hands that touch his younger brother? Will he be willing to be forgiven and to experience the healing presence of the father who loves him beyond compare? Luke's story makes it very clear that the father goes out to both of his children. Not only does he run out to welcome the younger wayward son, but he comes out also to meet the elder, dutiful son as he returns from the fields wondering what the music and dancing are all about and urges him to come in.

NO MORE OR LESS

It is very important for me to understand the full meaning of what is happening here. While the father is truly filled with joy at his younger son's return, he has not forgotten the elder. He doesn't take his elder son for granted. His joy was so intense that he couldn't wait to start celebrating, but as soon as he became aware of his elder son's arrival, he left the party, went out to him, and pleaded with him to join them.

In his jealousy and bitterness, the elder son can only see that his irresponsible brother is receiving more attention than he himself, and concludes that he is the less loved of the two. His father's heart, however, is not divided into more or less. The father's free and spontaneous response to his younger son's return does not involve any comparisons with his elder son. To the contrary, he ardently desires to make his elder son part of his joy.

This is not easy for me to grasp. In a world that constantly compares people, ranking them as more or less intelligent, more or less attractive, more or less successful, it is not easy to really believe in a love that does not do the same. When I hear someone praised, it is hard not to think of myself as less praise-worthy; when I read about the goodness and kindness of other people, it is hard not to wonder whether I myself am as good and kind as they; and when I see trophies, rewards, and prizes being handed out to special people, I cannot avoid asking my-self why that didn't happen to me.

The world in which I have grown up is a world so full of grades, scores, and statistics that, consciously or unconsciously, I always try to take my measure against all the others. Much sadness and gladness in my life flows directly from my compar-ing, and most, if not all, of this comparing is useless and a ter-rible waste of time and energy.

Our God, who is both Father and Mother to us, does not compare. Never. Even though I know in my head that this is true, it is still very hard to fully accept it with my whole being. When I hear someone called a favorite son or daughter, my im-mediate response is that the other children must be less appre-ciated, or less loved. I cannot fathom how all of God's children can be favorites. And still, they are. When I look from my place in the world into God's Kingdom, I quickly come to think of God as the keeper of some great celestial scoreboard, and I will always be afraid of not making the grade. But as soon as I look from God's welcoming home into the world, I discover that God loves with a divine love, a love that cedes to all women and men their uniqueness without ever comparing.

The elder brother compares himself with the younger one and becomes jealous. But the father loves them both so much that it didn't even occur to him to delay the party in order to prevent the elder son from feeling rejected. I am convinced that many of my emotional problems would melt as snow in the sun if I could let the truth of God's motherly non-comparing love permeate my heart.

How hard that is becomes clear when I reflect on the parable of the laborers in the vineyard. Each time I read that parable in which the landowner gives as much to the workers who worked only one hour as to those who did "a heavy day's work in all the heat," a feeling of irritation still wells up inside of me. Why didn't the landowner pay those who worked many long hours first and then surprise the latecomers with his generosity? Why, instead, does he pay the workers of the eleventh hour first, raising false expectations in the others and creating unnecessary bitterness and jealousy? These questions, I now realize, come from a perspective that is all too willing to impose the economy of the temporal on the unique order of the divine.

It hadn't previously occurred to me that the landowner might have wanted the workers of the early hours to rejoice in his generosity to the latecomers. It never crossed my mind that he might have acted on the supposition that those who had worked in the vineyard the whole day would be deeply grateful to have had the opportunity to do work for their boss, and even more grateful to see what a generous man he is. It requires an interior about-face to accept such a non-comparing way of thinking. But that is God's way of thinking. God looks at his people as children of a family who are happy that those who have done only a little bit are as much loved as those who accomplish much.

God is so naive as to think that there would be great rejoicing when all those who spent time in his vineyard, whether a short time or a long time, were given the same attention. Indeed, he was so naive as to expect that they would all be so happy to be in his presence that comparing themselves with each other wouldn't even occur to them. That is why he says with the bewilderment of a misunderstood lover: "Why should you be envious because I am generous?" He could have said: "You have been with me the whole day, and I gave you all you asked for! Why are you so bitter?" It is the same bewilderment that comes from the heart of the father when he says to his jealous son: "My son, you are with me always, and all I have is yours."

Here lies hidden the great call to conversion: to look not with the eyes of my own low self-esteem, but with the eyes of God's love. As long as I keep looking at God as a landowner, as a father who wants to get the most out of me for the least cost, I cannot but become jealous, bitter, and resentful toward my fellow workers or my brothers and sisters. But if I am able to look at the world with the eyes of God's love and discover that God's vision is not that of a stereotypical landowner or patriarch but rather that of an all-giving and forgiving father who does not measure out his love to his children according to how well they behave, then I quickly see that my only true response can be deep gratitude.

THE HEART OF GOD

In Rembrandt's painting, the elder son simply observes. It is difficult to imagine what is going on in his heart. Just as with the parable, so also with the painting, I am left with the question: How will he respond to the invitation to join the celebration?

There is no doubt—in the parable or the painting—about the father's heart. His heart goes out to both of his sons; he loves them both; he hopes to see them together as brothers around the same table; he wants them to experience that, different as they are, they belong to the same household and are children of the same father.

As I let all of this sink in, I see how the story of the father and his lost sons powerfully affirms that it was not I who chose God, but God who first chose me. This is the great mystery of our faith. We do not choose God, God chooses us. From all eternity we are hidden "in the shadow of God's hand" and "engraved on his palm." Before any human being touches us, God "forms us in secret" and "textures us" in the depth of the earth, and before any human being decides about us, God "knits us together in our mother's womb." God loves us before any human person can show love to us. He loves us with a "first" love, an unlimited, unconditional love, wants us to be his beloved children, and tells us to become as loving as himself.

For most of my life I have struggled to find God, to know God, to love God. I have tried hard to follow the guidelines of the spiritual life—pray always, work for others, read the Scriptures—and to avoid the many temptations to dissipate myself. I have failed many times but always tried again, even when I was close to despair.

Now I wonder whether I have sufficiently realized that during all this time God has been trying to find me, to know me, and to love me. The question is not "How am I to find God?" but "How am I to let myself be found by him?" The question is not "How am I to know God?" but "How am I to let myself be known by God?" And, finally, the question is not "How am I to love God?" but "How am I to let myself be loved by God?" God is looking into the distance for me, trying to find me, and longing to bring me home. In all three parables which Jesus tells in response to the question of why he eats with sinners, he puts the emphasis on God's initiative. God is the shepherd who goes looking for his lost sheep. God is the woman who lights a lamp, sweeps out the house, and searches everywhere for her lost coin until she has found it. God is the father who watches and waits for his children, runs out to meet them, embraces them, pleads with them, begs and urges them to come home.

It might sound strange, but God wants to find me as much as, if not more than, I want to find God. Yes, God needs me as much as I need God. God is not the patriarch who stays home, doesn't move, and expects his children to come to him, apologize for their aberrant behavior, beg for forgiveness, and promise to do better. To the contrary, he leaves the house, ignoring his dignity by running toward them, pays no heed to apologies and promises of change, and brings them to the table richly prepared for them.

I am beginning now to see how radically the character of my spiritual journey will change when I no longer think of God as hiding out and making it as difficult as possible for me to find him, but, instead, as the one who is looking for me while I am doing the hiding. When I look through God's eyes at my lost self and discover God's joy at my coming home, then my life may become less anguished and more trusting.

Wouldn't it be good to increase God's joy by letting God find me and carry me home and celebrate my return with the angels? Wouldn't it be wonderful to make God smile by giving God the chance to find me and love me lavishly? Questions like these raise a real issue: that of my own self-concept. Can I accept that I am worth looking for? Do I believe that there is a real desire in God to simply be with me?

Here lies the core of my spiritual struggle: the struggle against self-rejection, self-contempt, and self-loathing. It is a very fierce battle because the world and its demons conspire to make me think about myself as worthless, useless, and negligible. Many consumerist economies stay afloat by manipulating the low self-esteem of their consumers and by creating spiritual expectations through material means. As long as I am kept "small," I can easily be seduced to buy things, meet people, or go places that promise a radical change in self-concept even though they are totally incapable of bringing this about. But every time I allow myself to be thus manipulated or seduced, I will have still more reasons for putting myself down and seeing myself as the unwanted child.

A FIRST AND EVERLASTING LOVE

For a very long time I considered low self-esteem to be some kind of virtue. I had been warned so often against pride and conceit that I came to consider it a good thing to deprecate myself. But now I realize that the real sin is to deny God's first love for me, to ignore my original goodness. Because without claiming that first love and that original goodness for myself, I lose touch with my true self and embark on the destructive search among the wrong people and in the wrong places for what can only be found in the house of my Father.

I do not think I am alone in this struggle to claim God's first love and my original goodness. Beneath much human assertiveness, competitiveness, and rivalry; beneath much self-confidence and even arrogance, there is often a very insecure heart, much less sure of itself than outward behavior would lead one to believe. I have often been shocked to discover that men and women with obvious talents and with many rewards for their accomplishments have so many doubts about their own goodness. Instead of experiencing their outward successes as a sign of their inner beauty, they live them as a cover-up for their sense of personal worthlessness. Not a few have said to me:

"If people only knew what goes on in my innermost self, they would stop with their applause and praise."

I vividly remember talking with a young man loved and admired by everyone who knew him. He told me how a small critical remark from one of his friends had thrown him into an abyss of depression. As he spoke, tears streamed from his eyes and his body twisted in anguish. He felt that his friend had broken through his wall of defenses and had seen him as he really was: an ugly hypocrite, a despicable man beneath his gleaming armor. As I heard his story, I realized what an unhappy life he had lived, even though the people around him had envied him for his gifts. For years he had walked around with the inner questions: "Does anyone really love me? Does anyone really care?" And every time he had climbed a little higher on the ladder of success, he had thought: "This is not who I really am; one day everything will come crashing down and then people will see that I am no good."

This encounter illustrates the way many people live their lives—never fully sure that they are loved as they are. Many have horrendous stories that offer very plausible reasons for their low self-esteem: stories about parents who were not giving them what they needed, about teachers who mistreated them, about friends who betrayed them, and about a Church which left them out in the cold during a critical moment of their life.

The parable of the prodigal son is a story that speaks about a love that existed before any rejection was possible and that will still be there after all rejections have taken place. It is the first and everlasting love of a God who is Father as well as Mother. It is the fountain of all true human love, even the most limited. Jesus' whole life and preaching had only one aim: to reveal this inexhaustible, unlimited motherly and fatherly love of his God and to show the way to let that love guide every part of our daily lives. In his painting of the father, Rembrandt offers me a glimpse of that love. It is the love that always welcomes home and always wants to celebrate.

CHAPTER 9

THE FATHER CALLS FOR
A CELEBRATION

※

The father said to his servants, "Quick! Bring out the best robe and put it on him; put a ring on his finger and sandals on his feet. Bring the calf we have been fattening, and kill it; we will celebrate by having a feast, because this son of mine was dead and has come back to life; he was lost and is found." And they began to celebrate.

GIVING THE VERY BEST

It is clear to me that the younger son is not returning to a simple farm family. Luke describes the father as a very wealthy man with extensive property and many servants. To match this description Rembrandt clothes him and the two men who are watching him richly. The two women in the background lean against an arch that looks more like a part of a palace than of a farmhouse. The splendid garb of the father and the prosperous look of his surroundings stand in sharp contrast to the long suffering so visible in his near-blind eyes, his sorrowful face, and his stooped figure.

The same God who suffers because of his immense love for his children is the God who is rich in goodness and mercy and who desires to reveal to his children the richness of his glory. The father does not even give his son a chance to apologize. He pre-empts his son's begging by spontaneous forgiveness and puts aside his pleas as completely irrelevant in the light of the joy at his return. But there is more. Not only does the father forgive without asking questions and joyfully welcome his lost son home, but he cannot wait to give him new life, life in abundance. So strongly does God desire to give life to his returning son that he seems almost impatient. Nothing is good enough. The very best must be given to him. While the son is prepared to be treated as a hired servant, the father calls for the robe reserved for a distinguished guest; and, although the son no longer feels worthy to be called son, the father gives him a ring for his finger and sandals for his feet to honor him as his beloved son and restore him as his heir.

I remember vividly the clothes I wore during the summer after my graduation from high school. My white trousers, broad belt, colorful shirt, and shining shoes all expressed how good I felt about myself. My parents were very glad to buy these new clothes for me and showed great pride in their son. And I felt grateful to be their son. I especially recall how good it felt to wear new shoes. Since those days, I have traveled a lot and seen how people go through life barefoot. Now I understand even better the symbolic significance of new shoes. Bare feet indicate poverty and often slavery. Shoes are for the wealthy and the powerful. Shoes offer protection against snakes; they give safety and strength. They turn the hunted ones into hunters. For many poor people, getting shoes is a benchmark passage. An old Afro-American spiritual expresses this beautifully: "All of God's chillun got shoes. When I get to heab'n I'm going to put on my shoes; I'm going to walk all ovah God's heab'n."

The Father dresses his son with the signs of freedom, the freedom of the children of God. He does not want any of them to be hired servants or slaves. He wants them to wear the robe of honor, the ring of inheritance, and the footwear of prestige. It is like an investiture by which God's year of favor is inaugurated. The full meaning of this investiture and inauguration is spelled out in the fourth vision of the prophet Zechariah:

> Yahweh showed me the high priest Joshua standing before the angel of Yahweh. . . . Now Joshua was dressed in dirty clothes as he stood before the angel. The latter then spoke as follows to those who were standing before him. "Take off his dirty clothes and dress him in splendid robes and put a turban on his head." So they put a turban on his head and dressed him in clean clothes, while the angel of Yahweh stood by and said, "You see, I have taken your guilt away." The angel of Yahweh then made this declaration to Joshua: "Yahweh Sabaoth says this, 'If you walk in my ways and keep my ordinances, you shall govern my house, you shall watch over my courts, and I will give you free access among those in attendance here. . . . So listen, High Priest Joshua. . . . I shall remove this country's guilt in a single day. On that day . . . invite each other to come under your vine and your fig tree.'"

As I read the story of the prodigal son with this vision of Zechariah in mind, the word "Quick," with which the father exhorts his servants to bring his son the robe, ring, and sandals, expresses much more than a human impatience. It reveals the divine eagerness to inaugurate the new Kingdom that has been prepared from the beginning of time.

There is no doubt that the father wants a lavish feast. Killing the calf that had been fattened up for a special occasion shows how much the father wanted to pull out all the stops and offer his son a party such as had never been celebrated before. His exuberant joy is obvious. After having given his order to make everything ready, he exclaims: "We will celebrate by having a feast, because this son of mine was dead and has come back to life; he was lost and is found," and immediately they begin to celebrate. There is an abundance of food, there is music and dance, and the happy party noises can be heard far beyond the house.

AN INVITATION TO JOY

I realize that I am not used to the image of God throwing a big party. It seems to contradict the solemnity and seriousness I have always attached to God. But when I think about the ways in which Jesus describes God's Kingdom, a joyful banquet is often at its center. Jesus says, "Many will come from east and west and sit down with Abraham and Isaac and Jacob at the feast in the Kingdom of Heaven." And he compares the Kingdom of Heaven with a wedding feast offered by the king to his son. The king's servants go out to invite people with the words: "Look, my banquet is all prepared, my oxen and fattened cattle have been slaughtered, everything is ready. Come to the wedding." But many were not interested. They were too busy with their own affairs.

Just as in the parable of the prodigal son, Jesus expresses here the great desire of his Father to offer his children a banquet and his eagerness to get it going even when those who are invited refuse to come. This invitation to a meal is an invitation to intimacy with God. This is especially clear at the Last Supper, shortly before Jesus' death. There he says to his disciples: "From now on, I tell you, I shall never again drink wine until the day I drink the new wine with you in the kingdom of my Father." And at the close of the New Testament, God's ultimate victory is described as a splendid wedding feast: "The reign of the Lord our God Almighty has begun; let us be glad and joyful and give glory to God, because this is the time for the marriage of the Lamb. . . . blessed are those who are invited to the wedding feast of the Lamb . . ."

Celebration belongs to God's Kingdom. God not only offers forgiveness, reconciliation, and healing, but wants to lift up these gifts as a source of joy for all who witness them. In all three of the parables which Jesus tells to explain why he eats with sinners, God rejoices and invites others to rejoice with him. "Rejoice with me," the shepherd says, "I have found my sheep that was lost." "Rejoice with me," the woman says, "I have found the drachma I lost." "Rejoice with me," the father says, "this son of mine was lost and is found."

All these voices are the voices of God. God does not want to keep his joy to himself. He wants everyone to share in it. God's joy is the joy of his angels and his saints; it is the joy of all who belong to the Kingdom.

Rembrandt paints the moment of the return of the younger son. The elder son and the three other members of the father's household keep their distance. Will they understand the father's joy? Will they let the father embrace them? Will I? Will they be able to step out of their recriminations and share in the celebration? Will I?

I can see only one moment, and I am left guessing as to what will happen next. I repeat: Will they? Will I? I know the father wants all the people around him to admire the returning son's new clothes, to join him around the table, to eat and dance with him. This is not a private affair. This is something for all in the family to celebrate in gratitude.

I repeat again: Will they? Will I? It is an important question because it touches—strange as it may sound—my resistance to living a joyful life.

God rejoices. Not because the problems of the world have been solved, not because all human pain and suffering have come to an end, nor because thousands of people have been converted and are now praising him for his goodness. No, God rejoices because *one* of his children who was lost has been found. What I am called to is to enter into that joy. It is God's joy, not the joy that the world offers. It is the joy that comes from seeing a child walk home amid all the destruction, devastation, and anguish of the world. It is a hidden joy, as inconspicuous as the flute player that Rembrandt painted in the wall above the head of the seated observer.

I am not accustomed to rejoicing in things that are small, hidden, and scarcely noticed by the people around me. I am generally ready and prepared to receive bad news, to read about wars, violence, and crimes, and to witness conflict and disarray. I always expect my visitors to talk about their problems and pain, their setbacks and disappointments, their depressions and their anguish. Somehow I have become accustomed to living with sadness, and so have lost the eyes to see the joy and the ears to hear the gladness that belongs to God and which is to be found in the hidden corners of the world.

I have a friend who is so deeply connected with God that he can see joy where I expect only sadness. He travels much and meets countless people. When he returns home, I always expect him to tell me about the difficult economic situation of the countries he visited, about the great injustices he heard about, and the pain he has seen. But even though he is very aware of the great upheaval of the world, he seldom speaks of it. When he shares his experiences, he tells about the hidden joys he has discovered. He tells about a man, a woman, or a child who brought him hope and peace. He tells about little groups of people who are faithful to each other in the midst of all the turmoil. He tells about the small wonders of God. At times I realize that I am disappointed because I want to hear "newspaper news," exciting and exhilarating stories that can be talked about among friends. But he never responds to my need for sensationalism. He keeps saying: "I saw something very small and very beautiful, something that gave me much joy."

The father of the prodigal son gives himself totally to the joy that his returning son brings him. I have to learn from that. I have to learn to "steal" all the real joy there is to steal and lift it up for others to see. Yes, I know that not everybody has been converted yet, that there is not yet peace everywhere, that all pain has not yet been taken away, but still, I see people turning and returning home; I hear voices that pray; I notice moments of forgiveness, and I witness many signs of hope. I don't have to wait until all is well, but I can celebrate every little hint of the Kingdom that is at hand.

This is a real discipline. It requires choosing for the light even when there is much darkness to frighten me, choosing for life even when the forces of death are so visible, and choosing for the truth even when I am surrounded with lies. I am tempted to be so impressed by the obvious sadness of the human condition that I no longer claim the joy manifesting itself in many small but very real ways. The reward of choosing joy is joy itself. Living among people with mental disabilities has convinced me of that. There is so much rejection, pain, and woundedness among us, but once you choose to claim the joy hidden in the midst of all suffering, life becomes celebration. Joy never denies the sadness, but transforms it to a fertile soil for more joy.

Surely I will be called naive, unrealistic, and sentimental, and I will be accused of ignoring the "real" problems, the structural evils that underlie much of human misery. But God rejoices when one repentant sinner returns. Statistically that is not very interesting. But for God, numbers never seem to matter. Who knows whether the world is kept from destruction because of one, two, or three people who have continued to pray when the rest of humanity has lost hope and dissipated itself?

From God's perspective, one hidden act of repentance, one little gesture of selfless love, one moment of true forgiveness is all that is needed to bring God from his throne to run to his returning son and to fill the heavens with sounds of divine joy.

NOT WITHOUT SORROW

If that is God's way, then I am challenged to let go of all the voices of doom and damnation that drag me into depression and allow the "small" joys to reveal the truth about the world I live in. When Jesus speaks about the world, he is very realistic. He speaks about wars and revolutions, earthquakes, plagues and famines, persecution and imprisonment, betrayal, hatred and assassinations. There is no suggestion at all that these signs of the world's darkness will ever be absent. But still, God's joy can be ours in the midst of it all. It is the joy of belonging to the household of God whose love is stronger than death and who empowers us to be in the world while already belonging to the kingdom of joy.

This is the secret of the joy of the saints. From Saint Anthony of the desert, to Saint Francis of Assisi, to Frère Roger Schultz of Taizé, to Mother Teresa of Calcutta, joy has been the mark of the people of God. That joy can be seen on the faces of the many simple, poor, and often suffering people who live today among great economic and social upheaval, but who can already hear the music and the dance in the Father's house. I, myself, see this joy every day in the faces of the mentally handicapped people of my community. All these holy men and women, whether they lived long ago or belong to our own time, can recognize the many small returns that take place every day and rejoice with the Father. They have somehow pierced the meaning of true joy.

For me it is amazing to experience daily the radical difference between cynicism and joy. Cynics seek darkness wherever they go. They point always to approaching dangers, impure motives, and hidden schemes. They call trust naive, care romantic, and forgiveness sentimental. They sneer at enthusiasm, ridicule spiritual fervor, and despise charismatic behavior. They consider themselves realists who see reality for what it truly is and who are not deceived by "escapist emotions." But in belittling God's joy, their darkness only calls forth more darkness.

People who have come to know the joy of God do not deny the darkness, but they choose not to live in it. They claim that the light that shines in the darkness can be trusted more than the darkness itself and that a little bit of light can dispel a lot of darkness. They point each other to flashes of light here and there, and remind each other that they reveal the hidden but real presence of God. They discover that there are people who heal each other's wounds, forgive each other's offenses, share their possessions, foster the spirit of community, celebrate the gifts they have received, and live in constant anticipation of the full manifestation of God's glory.

Every moment of each day I have the chance to choose between cynicism and joy. Every thought I have can be cynical or joyful. Every word I speak can be cynical or joyful. Every action can be cynical or joyful. Increasingly I am aware of all these possible choices, and increasingly I discover that every choice for joy in turn reveals more joy and offers more reason to make life a true celebration in the house of the Father.

Jesus lived this joy of the Father's house to the full. In him we can see his Father's joy. "Everything the Father has is mine," he says, including God's boundless joy. That divine joy does not obliterate the divine sorrow. In our world, joy and sorrow exclude each other. Here below, joy means the absence of sorrow and sorrow the absence of joy. But such distinctions do not exist in God. Jesus, the Son of God, is the man of sorrows, but also the man of complete joy. We catch a glimpse of this when we realize that in the midst of his greatest suffering Jesus is never separated from his Father. His union with God is never broken even when he "feels" abandoned by God. The joy of God belongs to his sonship, and this joy of Jesus and his Father is offered to me. Jesus wants me to have the same joy he enjoys: "I have loved you, just as my Father has loved me. Remain in my love. If you keep my commandments you will remain in my love just as I have kept my Father's commandments and remain in his love. I have told you this, so that my own joy may be in you and your joy be complete."

As the returned child of God, living in the Father's house, God's joy is mine to claim. There is seldom a minute in my life that I am not tempted by sadness, melancholy, cynicism, dark moods, somber thoughts, morbid speculations, and waves of depression. And often I allow them to cover up the joy of my Father's house. But when I truly believe that I have already returned and that my Father has already dressed me with a cloak, ring, and sandals, I can remove the mask of the sadness from my heart and dispel the lie it tells about my true self and claim the truth with the inner freedom of the child of God.

But there is more. A child does not remain a child. A child becomes an adult. An adult becomes father and mother. When the prodigal son returns home, he returns not to remain a child, but to claim his sonship and become a father himself. As the returned child of God who is invited to resume my place in my Father's home, the challenge now, yes the call, is to become the Father myself. I am awed by this call. For a long time I have lived with the insight that returning to my Father's home was the ultimate call. It has taken me much spiritual work to make the elder son as well as the younger son in me turn around and receive the welcoming love of the Father. The fact is that, on many levels, I am still returning. But the closer I come to home the clearer becomes the realization that there is a call beyond the call to return. It is the call to become the Father who welcomes home and calls for a celebration. Having reclaimed my sonship, I now have to claim fatherhood. When I first saw Rembrandt's *Prodigal Son*, I could never have dreamt that becoming the repentant son was only a step on the way to becoming the welcoming father. I now see that the hands that forgive, console, heal, and offer a festive meal must become my own. Becoming the Father is, therefore, for me the surprising conclusion of these reflections on Rembrandt's *Return of the Prodigal Son*.

BECOMING THE FATHER

"Be compassionate as your Father is compassionate."

A LONELY STEP

When I first saw the detail of Rembrandt's *Prodigal Son*, a spiritual journey was set in motion that led me to write this book. As I now come to its conclusion, I discover how long a journey I have made.

From the beginning I was prepared to accept that not only the younger son, but also the elder son would reveal to me an important aspect of my spiritual journey. For a long time the father remained "the other," the one who would receive me, forgive me, offer me a home, and give me peace and joy. The father was the place to return to, the goal of my journey, the final resting place. It was only gradually and often quite painfully that I came to realize that my spiritual journey would never be complete as long as the father remained an outsider.

It dawned on me that even my best theological and spiritual formation had not been able to completely free me from a Father God who remained somewhat threatening and somewhat fearsome. All I had learned about the Father's love had not fully enabled me to let go of an authority above me who had power over me and would use it according to his will. Somehow, God's love for me was limited by my fear of God's power, and it seemed wise to keep a careful distance even though the desire for closeness was immense. I know that I share this experience with countless others. I have seen how the fear of becoming subject to God's revenge and punishment has paralyzed the mental and emotional lives of many people, independently of their age, religion, or life-style. This paralyzing fear of God is one of the great human tragedies.

Rembrandt's painting and his own tragic life have offered me a context in which to discover that the final stage of the spiritual life is to so fully let go of all fear of the Father that it becomes possible to become like him. As long as the Father evokes fear, he remains an outsider and cannot dwell within me. But Rembrandt, who showed me the Father in utmost vulnerability, made me come to the awareness that my final vocation is indeed to become like the Father and to live out his divine compassion in my daily life. Though I am both the younger son and the elder son, I am not to remain them, but to become the Father. No father or mother ever became father or mother without having been son or daughter, but every son and daughter has to consciously choose to step beyond their childhood and become father and mother for others. It is a hard and lonely step to take—especially in a period of history in which parenthood is so hard to live well—but it is a step that is essential for the fulfillment of the spiritual journey.

Although Rembrandt does not place the father in the physical center of his painting, it is clear that the father is the center of the event the painting portrays. From him comes all the light, to him goes all the attention. Rembrandt, faithful to the parable, intended that our primary attention go to the father before anyone else.

I am amazed at how long it has taken me to make the father the center of my attention. It was so easy to identify with the two sons. Their outer and inner waywardness is so understandable and so profoundly human that identification happens almost spontaneously as soon as the connections are pointed out. For a long time I had identified myself so fully with the younger son that it did not even occur to me that I might be more like the elder. But as soon as a friend said, "Aren't you the elder son in the story?" it was hard to see anything else. Seemingly, we all participate to a greater or lesser degree in all the forms of human brokenness. Neither greed nor anger, neither lust nor resentment, neither frivolity nor jealousy are completely absent from any one of us. Our human brokenness can be acted out in many ways, but there is no offense, crime, or war that does not have its seeds in our own hearts.

But what of the father? Why pay so much attention to the sons when it is the father who is in the center and when it is the father with whom I am to identify? Why talk so much about being like the sons when the real question is: Are you interested in being like the father? It feels somehow good to be able to say: "These sons are like me." It gives a sense of being understood. But how does it feel to say: "The father is like me"? Do I want to be like the father? Do I want to be not just the one who is being forgiven, but also the one who forgives; not just the one who is being welcomed home, but also the one who welcomes home;

not just the one who receives compassion, but the one who offers it as well?

Isn't there a subtle pressure in both the Church and society to remain a dependent child? Hasn't the Church in the past stressed obedience in a fashion that made it hard to claim spiritual fatherhood, and hasn't our consumer society encouraged us to indulge in childish self-gratification? Who has truly challenged us to liberate ourselves from immature dependencies and to accept the burden of responsible adults? And aren't we ourselves constantly trying to escape the fearful task of fatherhood? Rembrandt certainly did. Only after much pain and suffering, when he approached death, was he able to understand and paint true spiritual paternity.

Perhaps the most radical statement Jesus ever made is: "Be compassionate as your Father is compassionate." God's compassion is described by Jesus not simply to show me how willing God is to feel for me, or to forgive me my sins and offer me new life and happiness, but to invite me to become like God and to show the same compassion to others as he is showing to me. If the only meaning of the story were that people sin but God forgives, I could easily begin to think of my sins as a fine occasion for God to show me his forgiveness. There would be no real challenge in such an interpretation. I would resign myself to my weaknesses and keep hoping that eventually God would close his eyes to them and let me come home, whatever I did. Such sentimental romanticism is not the message of the Gospels.

What I am called to make true is that whether I am the younger or the elder son, I am the son of my compassionate Father. I am an heir. No one says it more clearly than Paul when he writes: "The Spirit himself joins with our spirit to bear witness that we are children of God. And if we are children, then we are heirs, heirs of God and joint heirs with Christ, provided that we share his sufferings, so as to share his glory." Indeed, as son and heir I am to become successor. I am destined to step into my Father's place and offer to others the same compassion that he has offered me. The return to the Father is ultimately the challenge to become the Father.

This call to become the Father precludes any "soft" interpretation of the story. I know how much I long to return and be held safe, but do I really want to be son and heir with all that that implies? Being in the Father's house requires that I make the Father's life my own and become transformed in his image.

Recently, on looking into a mirror, I was struck by how much I look like my dad. Looking at my own features, I suddenly saw the man whom I had seen when I was twenty-seven years old: the man I had admired as well as criticized, loved as well as feared. Much of my energy had been invested in finding my own self in the face of this person, and many of my questions about who I was and who I was to become had been shaped by being the son of this man. As I suddenly saw this man appearing in the mirror, I was overcome with the awareness that all the differences I had been aware of during my lifetime seemed so small compared with the similarities. As with a shock, I realized that I was indeed heir, successor, the one who is admired, feared, praised, and misunderstood by others, as my dad was by me.

THE FATHERHOOD OF COMPASSION

Rembrandt's portrayal of the father of the prodigal son makes me understand that I no longer need to use my sonship to keep my distance. Having lived my sonship to its fullest, the time has come to step over all barriers and claim the truth that becoming the old man in front of me is all I really desire for myself. I cannot remain a child forever, I cannot keep pointing to my father as an excuse for my life. I have to dare to stretch out my own hands in blessing and to receive with ultimate compassion my children, regardless of how they feel or think about me. Since becoming the compassionate Father is the ultimate goal of the spiritual life, as it is expressed in the parable as well as in Rembrandt's painting, I now need to explore its full significance.

First of all, I have to keep in mind the context in which Jesus tells the story of the "man who had two sons." Luke writes: "The tax collectors and sinners . . . were all crowding around to listen to him, and the Pharisees and scribes complained saying: 'This man welcomes sinners and eats with them.'" They put his legitimacy as a teacher in question by criticizing his closeness to sinful people. In response Jesus tells his critics the parables of the lost sheep, the lost coin, and the prodigal son.

Jesus wants to make it clear that the God of whom he speaks is a God of compassion who joyously welcomes repentant sinners into his house. To associate and eat with people of ill repute, therefore, does not contradict his teaching about God, but does, in fact, live out this teaching in everyday life. If God forgives the sinners, then certainly those who have faith in God should do the same. If God welcomes sinners home, then certainly those who trust in God should do likewise. If God is compassionate, then certainly those who love God should be compassionate as well. The God whom Jesus announces and in whose name he acts is the God of compassion, the God who offers himself as example and model for all human behavior.

But there is more. Becoming like the heavenly Father is not just one important aspect of Jesus' teaching, it is the very heart of his message. The radical quality of Jesus' words and the seeming impossibility of his demands are quite obvious when heard as part of a general call to become and to be true sons and daughters of God.

As long as we belong to this world, we will remain subject to its competitive ways and expect to be rewarded for all the good we do. But when we belong to God, who loves us without conditions, we can live as he does. The great conversion called for by Jesus is to move from belonging to the world to belonging to God.

When, shortly before his death, Jesus prays to his Father for his disciples, he says: "[Father,] they do not belong to the world any more than I belong to the world. . . . May they all be one . . . just as, Father, you are in me and I am in you, so that they also may be in us, so that the world may believe it was you who sent me."

Once we are in God's house as sons and daughters of his household, we can be like him, love like him, be good like him, care like him. Jesus leaves no doubt about this when he explains that: "If you love those who love you, what credit can you expect? Even sinners love those who love them. And if you do good to those who do good to you, what credit can you expect? For even sinners do that much. And if you lend to those from whom you hope to get money back, what credit can you expect? . . . Even sinners lend to sinners to get back the same amount. Instead, love your enemies and do good to them, and lend without any hope of return. You will have a great reward, and you will be children of the Most High, for he himself is kind to the ungrateful and to the wicked. Be compassionate just as your Father is compassionate."

That is the core message of the Gospel. The way human

beings are called to love one another is God's way. We are called to love one another with the same selfless outgoing love that we see in Rembrandt's depiction of the father. The compassion with which we are to love cannot be based upon a competitive life-style. It has to be this absolute compassion in which no trace of competition can be found. It has to be this radical love of enemy. If we are not only to be received by God, but also to receive as God, we must become like the heavenly Father and see the world through his eyes.

But even more important than the context of the parable and the explicit teaching of Jesus is the person of Jesus himself. Jesus is the true Son of the Father. He is the model for our becoming the Father. In him the fullness of God dwells. All the knowledge of God resides in him; all the glory of God remains in him; all the power of God belongs to him. His unity with the Father is so intimate and so complete that to see Jesus is to see the Father. "Show us the Father," Philip says to him. Jesus responds, "Anyone who has seen me has seen the Father."

Jesus shows us what true sonship is. He is the younger son without being rebellious. He is the elder son without being resentful. In everything he is obedient to the Father, but never his slave. He hears everything the Father says, but this does not make him his servant. He does everything the Father sends him to do, but remains completely free. He gives everything, and he receives everything. He declares openly: "In all truth I tell you, by himself the Son can do nothing. He can only do what he sees the Father doing; and whatever the Father does the Son does too. For the Father loves the Son and shows him everything he himself does, and he will show him even greater things than these works that will astonish you. Thus as the Father raises the dead and gives them life, so the Son gives life to anyone he chooses; for the Father judges no one; he has entrusted all judgment to the Son, so that all may honor the Son as they honor the Father."

This is divine sonship. And it is to this sonship that I am called. The mystery of redemption is that God's Son became flesh so that all the lost children of God could become sons and daughters as Jesus is son. In this perspective, the story of the prodigal son takes on a whole new dimension. Jesus, the Beloved of the Father, leaves his Father's home to take on the sins of God's wayward children and bring them home. But, while leaving, he stays close to the Father and through total obedience offers healing to his resentful brothers and sisters. Thus, for my sake, Jesus becomes the younger son as well as the elder son in order to show me how to become the Father. Through him I can become a true son again and, as a true son, I finally can grow to become compassionate as our heavenly Father is.

As the years of my life pass, I discover how arduous and challenging, but also how fulfilling it is to grow into this spiritual fatherhood. Rembrandt's painting rules out any thought that this has anything to do with power, influence, or control. I might once have held the illusion that one day the many bosses would be gone and I could finally be the boss myself. But this is the way of the world in which power is the main concern. And it is not difficult to see that those who have tried most of their lives to get rid of their bosses are not going to be very different from their predecessors when they finally step into their places. Spiritual fatherhood has nothing to do with power or control. It is a fatherhood of compassion. And I have to keep looking at the father embracing the prodigal son to catch a glimpse of this.

Against my own best intentions, I find myself continually striving to acquire power. When I give advice, I want to know whether it is being followed; when I offer help, I want to be thanked; when I give money, I want it to be used my way; when I do something good, I want to be remembered. I might not get a statue, or even a memorial plaque, but I am constantly concerned that I not be forgotten, that somehow I will live on in the thoughts and deeds of others.

But the father of the prodigal son is not concerned about himself. His long-suffering life has emptied him of his desires to keep in control of things. His children are his only concern, to them he wants to give himself completely, and for them he wants to pour out all of himself.

Can I give without wanting anything in return, love without putting any conditions on my love? Considering my immense need for human recognition and affection, I realize that it will be a lifelong struggle. But I am also convinced that each time I step over this need and act free of my concern for return, I can trust that my life can truly bear the fruits of God's Spirit.

Is there a way to this spiritual fatherhood? Or am I doomed to remain so caught up in my own need to find a place in my world that I end up ever and again using the authority of power instead of the authority of compassion? Has competition so pervaded my entire being that I will continue to see my own children as rivals? If Jesus truly calls me to be compassionate as his heavenly Father is compassionate and if Jesus offers himself as the way to that compassionate life, then I cannot keep acting as though competition is, in fact, the last word. I must trust that I am capable of becoming the Father I am called to be.

GRIEF, FORGIVENESS, AND GENEROSITY

Looking at Rembrandt's painting of the father, I can see three ways to a truly compassionate fatherhood: grief, forgiveness, and generosity.

It might sound strange to consider grief a way to compassion. But it is. Grief asks me to allow the sins of the world—my own included—to pierce my heart and make me shed tears, many tears, for them. There is no compassion without many tears. If they can't be tears that stream from my eyes, they have to be at least tears that well up from my heart. When I consider the immense waywardness of God's children, our lust, our greed, our violence, our anger, our resentment, and when I look at them through the eyes of God's heart, I cannot but weep and cry out in grief:

> Look, my soul, at the way one human being tries to inflict
> as much pain on another as possible; look at these people
> plotting to bring harm to their fellows; look at these
> parents molesting their children; look at this landowner
> exploiting his workers; look at the violated women, the
> misused men, the abandoned children. Look, my soul, at
> the world; see the concentration camps, the prisons, the
> nursing homes, the hospitals, and hear the cries of the
> poor.

This grieving is praying. There are so few mourners left in this world. But grief is the discipline of the heart that sees the sin of the world, and knows itself to be the sorrowful price of freedom without which love cannot bloom. I am beginning to see that much of praying is grieving. This grief is so deep not just because the human sin is so great, but also—and more so—because the divine love is so boundless. To become like the Father whose only authority is compassion, I have to shed countless tears and so prepare my heart to receive anyone, whatever their journey has been, and forgive them from that heart.

The second way that leads to spiritual fatherhood is forgiveness. It is through constant forgiveness that we become like the Father. Forgiveness from the heart is very, very difficult. It is next to impossible. Jesus said to his disciples: "When your brother wrongs you seven times a day and seven times comes back to you and says, 'I am sorry,' you must forgive him."

I have often said, "I forgive you," but even as I said these words my heart remained angry or resentful. I still wanted to hear the story that tells me that I was right after all; I still wanted to hear apologies and excuses; I still wanted the satisfaction of receiving some praise in return—if only the praise for being so forgiving!

But God's forgiveness is unconditional; it comes from a heart that does not demand anything for itself, a heart that is completely empty of self-seeking. It is this divine forgiveness that I have to practice in my daily life. It calls me to keep stepping over all my arguments that say forgiveness is unwise, unhealthy, and impractical. It challenges me to step over all my needs for gratitude and compliments. Finally, it demands of me that I step over that wounded part of my heart that feels hurt and wronged and that wants to stay in control and put a few conditions between me and the one whom I am asked to forgive.

This "stepping over" is the authentic discipline of forgiveness. Maybe it is more "climbing over" than "stepping over." Often I have to climb over the wall of arguments and angry feelings that I have erected between myself and all those whom I love but who so often do not return that love. It is a wall of fear of being used or hurt again. It is a wall of pride, and the desire to stay in control. But every time that I can step or climb over that wall, I enter into the house where the Father dwells, and there touch my neighbor with genuine compassionate love.

Grief allows me to see beyond my wall and realize the immense suffering that results from human lostness. It opens my heart to a genuine solidarity with my fellow humans. Forgiveness is the way to step over the wall and welcome others into my heart without expecting anything in return. Only when I remember that I am the Beloved Child can I welcome those who want to return with the same compassion as that with which the Father welcomes me.

The third way to become like the Father is generosity. In the parable, the father not only gives his departing son everything he asks, but also showers him with gifts on his return. And to his elder son he says: "All I have is yours." There is nothing the father keeps for himself. He pours himself out for his sons.

He does not simply offer more than can be reasonably expected from someone who has been offended; no, he completely gives himself away without reserve. Both sons are for him "everything." In them he wants to pour out his very life. The way the younger son is given robe, ring, and sandals, and welcomed home with a sumptuous celebration, as well as the way the elder son is urged to accept his unique place in his father's heart and to join his younger brother around the table, make it very clear that all boundaries of patriarchal behavior are broken through. This is not the picture of a remarkable father. This is the portrayal of God, whose goodness, love, forgiveness, care, joy, and compassion have no limits at all. Jesus presents God's generosity by using all the imagery that his culture provides, while constantly transforming it.

In order to become like the Father, I must be as generous

as the Father is generous. Just as the Father gives his very self to his children, so must I give my very self to my brothers and sisters. Jesus makes it very clear that it is precisely this giving of self that is the mark of the true disciple. "No one can have greater love than to lay down his life for his friends."

This giving of self is a discipline because it is something that does not come spontaneously. As children of the darkness that rules through fear, self-interest, greed, and power, our great motivators are survival and self-preservation. But as children of the light who know that perfect love casts out all fear, it becomes possible to give away all that we have for others.

As children of the light, we prepare ourselves to become true martyrs: people who witness with their whole lives to the unlimited love of God. Giving all thus becomes gaining all. Jesus expresses this clearly as he says: "Anyone who loses his life for my sake . . . will save it."

Every time I take a step in the direction of generosity, I know that I am moving from fear to love. But these steps, certainly at first, are hard to take because there are so many emotions and feelings that hold me back from freely giving. Why should I give energy, time, money, and yes, even attention to someone who has offended me? Why should I share my life with someone who has shown no respect for it? I might be willing to forgive, but to give on top of that!

Still . . . the truth is that, in a spiritual sense, the one who has offended me belongs to my "kin," my "gen." The word "generosity" includes the term "gen" which we also find in the words "gender," "generation," and "generativity." This term, from the Latin *genus* and the Greek *genos*, refers to our being of one kind. Generosity is a giving that comes from the knowledge of that intimate bond. True generosity is acting on the truth—not on the feeling—that those I am asked to forgive are "kinfolk," and belong to my family. And whenever I act this way, that truth will become more visible to me. Generosity creates the family it believes in.

Grief, forgiveness, and generosity are, then, the three ways by which the image of the Father can grow in me. They are three aspects of the Father's call to *be* home. As the Father, I am no longer *called* to come home as the younger or elder son, but to *be* there as the one to whom the wayward children can return and be welcomed with joy. It is very hard to just *be* home and wait. It is a waiting in grief for those who have left and a waiting with hope to offer forgiveness and new life to those who will return.

As the Father, I have to believe that all that the human heart desires can be found at home. As the Father, I have to be free from the need to wander around curiously and to catch up with what I might otherwise perceive as missed childhood opportunities. As the Father, I have to know that, indeed, my youth is over and that playing youthful games is nothing but a ridiculous attempt to cover up the truth that I am old and close to death. As the Father, I have to dare to carry the responsibility of a spiritually adult person and dare to trust that the real joy and real fulfillment can only come from welcoming home those who have been hurt and wounded on their life's journey, and loving them with a love that neither asks nor expects anything in return.

There is a dreadful emptiness in this spiritual fatherhood. No power, no success, no popularity, no easy satisfaction. But that same dreadful emptiness is also the place of true freedom. It is the place where there is "nothing left to lose," where love has no strings attached, and where real spiritual strength is found.

Every time I touch that dreadful yet fruitful emptiness in

myself, I know that I can welcome anyone there without condemnation and offer hope. There I am free to receive the bur-
dens of others without any need to evaluate, categorize, or
analyze. There, in that completely non-judgmental state of
being, I can engender liberating trust.

Once, while visiting a dying friend, I directly experienced
this holy emptiness. In my friend's presence I felt no desire to
ask questions about the past or to speculate about the future.
We were just together without fear, without guilt or shame,
without worries. In that emptiness, God's unconditional love
could be sensed and we could say what the old Simeon said
when he took the Christ child in his arms: "Now, Master, you
can let your servant go in peace as you promised." There, in the
midst of the dreadful emptiness, was complete trust, complete
peace, and complete joy. Death no longer was the enemy. Love
was victorious.

Each time we touch that sacred emptiness of non-demanding
love, heaven and earth tremble and there is great "rejoicing
among the angels of God." It is the joy for the returning sons
and daughters. It is the joy of spiritual fatherhood.

Living out this spiritual fatherhood requires the radical
discipline of being home. As a self-rejecting person always in
search of affirmation and affection, I find it impossible to love
consistently without asking for something in return. But the
discipline is precisely to give up wanting to accomplish this myself as a heroic feat. To claim for myself spiritual fatherhood
and the authority of compassion that belongs to it, I have to
let the rebellious younger son and the resentful elder son step
up on the platform to receive the unconditional, forgiving love
that the Father offers me, and to discover there the call to be
home as my Father is home.

Then both sons in me can gradually be transformed into the compassionate father. This transformation leads me to the fulfillment of the deepest desire of my restless heart. Because what greater joy can there be for me than to stretch out my tired arms and let my hands rest in a blessing on the shoulders of my home-coming children?

LIVING THE PAINTING

W hen I saw the Rembrandt poster for the first time in the fall of 1983, all my attention was drawn to the hands of the old father pressing his returning boy to his chest. I saw forgiveness, reconciliation, healing; I also saw safety, rest, being at home. I was so deeply touched by this image of the life-giving embrace of father and son because everything in me yearned to be received in the way the prodigal son was received. That encounter turned out to be the beginning of my own return.

The L'Arche community gradually became my home. Never in my life did I dream that men and women with a mental handicap would be the ones who would put their hands on me in a gesture of blessing and offer me a home. For a long time, I had sought safety and security among the wise and clever, hardly aware that the things of the Kingdom were revealed to "little children"; that God has chosen "those who by human standards are fools to shame the wise."

But when I experienced the warm, unpretentious reception

of those who have nothing to boast about, and experienced a loving embrace from people who didn't ask any questions, I began to discover that a true spiritual homecoming means a return to the poor in spirit to whom the Kingdom of Heaven belongs. The embrace of the Father became very real to me in the embraces of the mentally poor.

Having first viewed the painting while visiting a community of mentally handicapped people allowed me to make a connection that is deeply rooted in the mystery of our salvation. It is the connection between the blessing given by God and the blessing given by the poor. In L'Arche I came to see that these blessings are truly one. The Dutch master not only brought me into touch with the deepest longings of my heart, but also led me to discover that those longings could be fulfilled in the community where I first met him.

It now has been more than six years since I first saw the Rembrandt poster at Trosly and five years since I decided to make L'Arche my home. As I reflect on these years, I realize that the people with a mental handicap and their assistants made me "live" Rembrandt's painting more completely than I could have anticipated. The warm welcomes I have received in many L'Arche houses and the many celebrations I have shared have allowed me to experience deeply the younger son's return. Welcome and celebration are, indeed, two of the main characteristics of the life "in the Ark." There are so many welcome signs, hugs and kisses, songs, skits, and festive meals that for an outsider L'Arche may appear a lifelong homecoming celebration.

I also have lived the elder son's story. I hadn't really seen how much the elder son belongs to Rembrandt's *Prodigal Son* until I went to Saint Petersburg and saw the whole picture. There I discovered the tension Rembrandt evokes. There is not only the light-filled reconciliation between the father and the younger son, but also the dark, resentful distance of the elder son. There is repentance, but also anger. There is communion, but also alienation. There is the warm glow of healing, but also the coolness of the critical eye; there is the offer of mercy, but also the enormous resistance against receiving it. It didn't take long before I encountered the elder son in me.

Life in community does not keep the darkness away. To the contrary. It seems that the light that attracted me to L'Arche also made me conscious of the darkness in myself. Jealousy, anger, the feeling of being rejected or neglected, the sense of not truly belonging—all of these emerged in the context of a community striving for a life of forgiveness, reconciliation, and healing. Community life has opened me up to the real spiritual combat: the struggle to keep moving toward the light precisely when the darkness is so real.

As long as I lived by myself, it seemed rather easy to keep the elder son hidden from view. But the sharing of life with people who are not hiding their feelings soon confronted me with the elder son within. There is little romanticism to community life. There is the constant need to keep stepping out of the engulfing darkness onto the platform of the father's embrace.

Handicapped people have little to lose. Without guile they show me who they are. They openly express their love as well as their fear, their gentleness as well as their anguish, their generosity as well as their selfishness. By just simply being who they are, they break through my sophisticated defenses and demand that I be as open with them as they are with me. Their handicap unveils my own. Their anguish mirrors my own. Their vulnerabilities show me my own. By forcing me to confront the elder son in me, L'Arche opened the way to bring him home. The same handicapped people who welcomed me home and invited me to celebrate also confronted me with my not yet converted self and made me aware that the journey was far from ended.

While these discoveries have profoundly impacted on my life, the greatest gift from L'Arche is the challenge of becoming the Father. Being older in years than most members of the community and also being its pastor, it seems natural to think of myself as a father. Because of my ordination, I already have the title. Now I have to live up to it.

Becoming the Father in a community of mentally handicapped people and their assistants is far more demanding than grappling with the struggles of the younger and the elder son. Rembrandt's father is a father who is emptied out by suffering. Through the many "deaths" he suffered, he became completely free to receive and to give. His outstretched hands are not begging, grasping, demanding, warning, judging, or condemning. They are hands that only bless, giving all and expecting nothing.

I am now faced with the hard and seemingly impossible task of letting go of the child in me. Paul says it clearly: "When I was a child, I used to talk like a child, and see things as a child does, and think like a child; but now that I have become an adult, I have finished with all childish ways." It is comfortable to be the wayward younger son or the angry elder son.

Our community is full of wayward and angry children, and being surrounded by peers gives a sense of solidarity. Yet the longer I am part of the community, the more that solidarity proves to be only a way station on the road to a much more lonely destination: the loneliness of the Father, the loneliness of God, the ultimate loneliness of compassion. The community does not need yet another younger or elder son, whether converted or not, but a father who lives with outstretched hands, always desiring to let them rest on the shoulders of his returning children. Yet everything in me resists that vocation. I keep clinging to the child in me. I do not want to be half blind; I want to see clearly what is going on around me. I do not want to wait until my children come home; I want to be with them where they are in a foreign country or on the farm with the servants. I do not want to remain silent about what happened; I am curious to hear the whole story and have countless questions to ask. I do not want to keep stretching my hands out when there are so few who are willing to be embraced, especially when fathers and father figures are considered by many the source of their problems.

And still, after a long life as son, I know for sure that the true call is to become a father who only blesses in endless compassion, asking no questions, always giving and forgiving, never expecting anything in return. In a community, all this is often disturbingly concrete. I want to know what is happening. I want to be involved in the daily ups and downs of people's lives. I want to be remembered, invited, and informed. But the fact is that few recognize my desire and those who do are not sure how to respond to it. My people, whether handicapped or not, are not looking for another peer, another playmate, nor even for another brother. They seek a father who can bless and forgive without needing them in the way they need him. I see clearly the truth of my vocation to be a father; at the same time it seems to me almost impossible to follow it. I don't want to stay home while everyone goes out, whether driven by their many desires or their many angers. I feel these same impulses and want to run around like others do! But who is going to be home when they return—tired, exhausted, excited, disappointed, guilty, or ashamed? Who is going to convince them that, after all is said and done, there is a safe place to return to and receive an embrace? If it is not I, who is it going to be? The joy of fatherhood is vastly different from the pleasure of the wayward children. It is a joy beyond rejection and loneliness; yes, even beyond affirmation and community. It is the joy of a fatherhood that takes its name from the heavenly Father and partakes in his divine solitude.

It does not surprise me at all that few people claim fatherhood for themselves. The pains are too obvious, the joys too hidden. And still, by not claiming it I shirk my responsibility as a spiritually adult person. Yes, I even betray my vocation. Nothing less than that! But how can I choose what seems so contrary to all my needs? A voice says to me, "Don't be afraid. The Child will take you by the hand and lead you to fatherhood." I know that voice can be trusted. As always, the poor, the weak, the marginal, the rejected, the forgotten, the least ... they not only need me to be their father, but also show me how to be a father for them. True fatherhood is sharing the poverty of God's non-demanding love. I am afraid to enter into that poverty, but those who have already entered it through their physical or mental disabilities will be my teachers.

Looking at the people I live with, the handicapped men and women as well as their assistants, I see the immense desire for a father in whom fatherhood and motherhood are one. They all have suffered from the experience of rejection or abandonment; they all have been wounded as they grew up; they all wonder whether they are worthy of the unconditional love of God, and they all search for the place where they can safely return and be touched by hands that bless them.

Rembrandt portrays the father as the man who has transcended the ways of his children. His own loneliness and anger may have been there, but they have been transformed by suffering and tears. His loneliness has become endless solitude, his anger boundless gratitude. This is who I have to become. I see it as clearly as I see the immense beauty of the father's emptiness and compassion. Can I let the younger and the elder son grow in me to the maturity of the compassionate father?

When, four years ago, I went to Saint Petersburg to see Rembrandt's *Return of the Prodigal Son*, I had little idea how much I would have to live what I then saw. I stand with awe at the place where Rembrandt brought me. He led me from the kneeling, disheveled young son to the standing, bent-over old father, from the place of being blessed to the place of blessing. As I look at my own aging hands, I know that they have been given to me to stretch out toward all who suffer, to rest upon the shoulders of all who come, and to offer the blessing that emerges from the immensity of God's love.

ACKNOWLEDGMENTS

When I think of the many people who have supported me during the writing of this book, the first two who come to mind are Connie Ellis and Conrad Wieczorek. Connie Ellis has lived through all the stages of the manuscript. Her enthusiastic, dedicated, and competent secretarial help has not only kept me moving during very busy times, but also kept me trusting in the value of what I was doing during moments of discouragement. Conrad Wieczorek has offered me indispensable assistance from the early beginnings of the book until its completion. I am deeply grateful for the generosity with which he made his time and energy available to edit the text and make suggestions for changes in form and content.

Many other friends have played an important role in the reworking of this book. Elizabeth Buckley, Brad Colby, Ivan Dyer, Bart Gavigan, Jeff Imbach, Don McNeill, Sue Mosteller, Glenn Peckover, Jim Purdie, Esther de Waal, and Susan Zimmerman have all offered significant contributions. Many of the refinements are the direct result of their advice.

A very special word of thanks goes to Richard White. The generosity with which he offered me his personal support and professional expertise gave me the necessary incentive to bring this book to its final form.

Finally, I want to express my special gratitude to three friends who died before the publication of the book: Murray McDonnell, David Osler, and Madame Pauline Vanier. Murray's personal and financial support, David's friendship and warm response to the first draft, and Madame Vanier's hospitality during the time of writing, all have been a source of great encouragement to me. I miss their presence very much, but know that their love is much stronger than death and will continue to inspire me.

It fills me with great joy that I can think of this book as a true fruit of friendship and love.

NOTES

and Through Peasant Eyes: A Literary-Cultural Approach to the Parables (Grand Rapids, Mich.: William B. Eerdmans, 1983), 161–62

41   "After signing over . . . underlies both requests": Ibid., 164

42   "The moment of . . . but lasts forever": Christian Tümpel (with contributions by Astrid Tümpel), Rembrandt (Amsterdam: N. J. W. Becht-Amsterdam, 1986), 350. Author's translation.

42   "The group of . . . death into life": Jakob Rosenberg, op. cit., 231, 234

43   "fashioned me in . . . my mother's womb" (Psalm 139:13–15)

43   "I can walk . . . would I fear" (Psalm 23:4)

43   "cure the sick . . . cast out devils" "received without charge" "give without charge" (Matthew 10:8)

45   "They do not belong . . . consecrated in truth" (John 17:16–19)

46   Sensing the touch . . . touch was voice (See I Kings 19:11–13)

CHAPTER 3

58   "I am offering . . . holding fast to him" (Deuteronomy 30:19–20)

59   "it was very good" (Genesis 1:31)

60   ". . . grace is always greater" (See Romans 5:20)

62   "Unless you turn . . . Kingdom of Heaven" (Matthew 18:3)

64   "In all truth I tell you . . . born from above." (John 3:3)

64   "lamb of God . . . of the world" (John 1:29)

64   Isn't he the innocent . . . for us (II Corinthians 5:21)

65   "cling to his equality . . . human beings are" (Philippians 2:6–7)

65   "My God, my God . . . forsaken me?" (Matthew 27:46)

65   The one who told the story . . . made us part of his fullness (See John 1:1–14)

65   drawn all people . . . home to his heavenly Father (See John 12:32)

65   "God wanted all . . . everything on earth" (Colossians 1:19–20)

65   He, who is born . . . blood of the Lamb: Pierre Marie (Frère), "Les fils prodigues et le fils prodigue," Sources Vives 13, Communion de Jerusalem, Paris (March 87), 87–93. Author's translation.

67   ". . . we are already . . . he really is" (I John 3:2)

CHAPTER 4

74   Barbara Joan Haeger, "The Religious Significance of Rembrandt's Return of the Prodigal Son: An Examination of the Picture in the Context of the Visual and Iconographic Tradition.": Ph.D. diss., University of Michigan (Ann Arbor, Mich.: University Microfilm International, 1983), 173

74   "not to the . . . the biblical text": Ibid., 178

75   "inner drama of the soul": Ibid., 178

76   "bitter, revengeful person ... in his way": Gary Schwartz, *Rembrandt: zign Leven, zign Schilderijen* (Maarsen, Netherlands: Uitgeverij Gary Schwartz, 1984), 362. Author's translation.

76   "collect testimony ... an insane asylum": Charles L. Mee, *Rembrandt's Portrait: A Biography* (New York: Simon and Schuster, 1988), 229

76   "Rembrandt hired ... stay locked up": Ibid.

CHAPTER 5

88   "Do not be ... 'born from above' " (John 3:7)

CHAPTER 6

90   "Rembrandt does not ... to the viewer": Haeger, op. cit., 185–86

91   The father loves ... "it alteration finds": Arthur Freeman, "The Parable of the Prodigal," unpublished manuscript

92   "How blessed are ... who are weeping" (Luke 6:20-21)

92   "I bless you ... and the clever" (Luke 10:21)

93   "say their prayers ... for people to see them" (Matthew 6:5)

93   "In truth I ... had their reward" (Matthew 6:5)

93   "an affectionate form of address": Joseph A. Fitzmyer, *The Gospel According to St. Luke*, Volume 2, Cc.x-xxiv. In *The Anchor Bible* (Garden City, N.Y.: Doubleday, 1985), 1084.

94   "In the house ... places to live" (John 14:2)

97   "Father from whom all fatherhood takes its name" (Ephesians 3:14-15)

99   "Everything you ask ... will be yours" (Mark 11:24)

101   all the glory ... the Son too (John 1:14)

102   All the Father does, the Son does too (John 10:32)

102   "The Father and I are one" (John 17:22)

102   "The Father loves ... everything to him" (John 3:35)

102   "I have made ... from my Father" (John 15:15)

102   "The Son can ... the Father doing" (John 5:19)

102   "You must believe ... is in me" (John 14:11)

102   To believe in ... love is revealed (John 5:24; 6:40; 16:27; 17:8)

CHAPTER 7

107   "Parable of the Father's Love": See Joseph A. Fitzmyer, op. cit., 1084

108   "The spiritual in ... from the flesh": Paul Baudiquet, op. cit., 9. Author's translation.

108   "Since his youth ... to grow old": Ibid.

109 "grasp, conquer . . . of the artist": René Huyghe, cited in ibid.
110 while their hearts are far from him (See Matthew 15:8; Isaiah 29:13)
110 "deceitful tongues" and "disloyal hearts" (Psalm 78:36-37)
111 "feeding his flock . . . against his breast" (Isaiah 40:11)

CHAPTER 8

115 *The Jewish Bride,* also called *Isaac and Rebecca,* painted around 1688, Rijksmuseum, Amsterdam
115 "Can a woman . . . of my hands" (Isaiah 49:15-16)
116 "Jerusalem, Jerusalem . . . and you refused" (Matthew 23:37-38)
116 You who dwell . . . shall find refuge (Psalm 91:1-4) *The Grail Psalms* (Collins)
121 . . . parable of the laborers in the vineyard (Matthew 20:1-16)
122 . . . only true response can be deep gratitude: I owe much of this insight into the parable of the laborers in the vineyard to Heinrich Spaemann's very moving study, "In der Liebefern der Liebe, Eine Menschheitsparabel (Lukas 15, 11-13)" Kapitel V in *Das Prinzip Liebe* by Heinrich Spaemann (Freiburg im Breisgau: Verlag Herder, 1986), 95-120.
123 "in the shadow of God's hand" and "engraved on his palm" (Isaiah 49:2,16)
123 "forms . . . textures us" (Psalm 139:15)
123 "knits us . . . mother's womb" (Psalm 139:13)
123 See "first" (1 John 4:19-20)

CHAPTER 9

129 . . . God who is rich in goodness and mercy (See Romans 2:4 and Ephesians 2:4)
129 . . . the richness of his glory (Romans 9:23)
129 . . . life in abundance (John 10:10)
129 "All of God's chillun . . . ovah God's heab'n" "All God's Chillun Got Wings," St. 10: See *The Interpreter's Bible* (New York and Nashville: Abingdon Press, Vol. 8, 1952), 277
130 "Yahweh showed me . . . and your fig tree" (Zechariah 3:1-10)
131 "Many will come . . . in the Kingdom of Heaven" (Matthew 8:11)
131 "Look, my banquet is . . . to the wedding" (Matthew 22:4)
132 "From now on . . . of my Father" (Matthew 26:29)
132 "The reign of . . . of the Lamb" (Revelations 19:6-9)
137 "Everything the Father has is mine" (John 16:15)
137 "I have loved you . . . your joy be complete" (John 15:9-11)

139 "Be compassionate as your Father is compassionate" (Luke 6:36)
142 "The Spirit himself . . . share his glory" (Romans 8:16–17)
144 "The tax collectors . . . eats with them" (Luke 15:1–2)
145 "[Father,] they do not . . . you who sent me" (John 17:16–21)
145 "If you love . . . Father is compassionate" (Luke 6:32–36)
146 "Anyone who has . . . the Father" (John 14:9)
146 "In all truth . . . honor the Father" (John 5:19–23)
150 "When your brother wrongs you . . . you must forgive him" (Luke 17:4)
151 "All I have is yours" (Luke 15:31)
152 "No one can . . . for his friends" (John 15:13)
152 "Anyone who loses . . . will save it" (Mark 8:35)
153 "nothing left to lose": See song "Me and Bobby McGee," by Janis Joplin, with the sentence "Freedom's just another word for nothing left to lose"
154 "Now, Master, you can . . . as you promised" (Luke 15:10)
154 "rejoicing among the angels of God" (Luke 15:10)

EPILOGUE

156 "little children" (Matthew 11:25)
156 "those who by . . . shame the wise" (I Corinthians 1:27)
159 "When I was . . . all childish ways" (I Corinthians 13:11)
161 It is the joy of a fatherhood . . . from the heavenly Father (See Ephesians 3:14)

HOME
TONIGHT

ARE YOU HOME TONIGHT?

We are not human beings on a spiritual journey. We are spiritual beings on a human journey.

—Teilhard de Chardin

When Henri Nouwen first arrived at L'Arche Daybreak in 1986, he was asked to share a home with several people with intellectual disabilities, one of whom was John. Having lived many years in the community John is a rooted, grounded, middle-aged man in his group home of ten persons and his first question to any stranger is "So, where's your home?" Also wide-awake to the movements of each person around him, John daily asks assistants in his home and in the community a second, more immediate question: "Are you home tonight?" Henri, with his frenetic schedule, was not excused, especially from the second of these penetrating questions, and he very often had to falteringly explain to John why he would again be absent from the table that evening. Even though Henri initially came to Daybreak in search of a home, he needed more than the first year to discover the multifaceted meaning of "Where's your home?" and "Are you home tonight?" He needed this father figure, John, to firmly and consistently remind him that he was on a journey—home.

In the midst of his second year in the community Henri suffered a breakdown that took him away from L'Arche Daybreak for a period of seven months. He lived that time mostly in solitude and with the support of two friends from the Homes for Growth team in Winnipeg, Manitoba. I had the privilege of visiting him during his time there, and while sharing about his recovery he spoke movingly of his solitude and of his reflective "encounters" with the people in Rembrandt's painting of the prodigal son.

His experience was raw and deeply personal.

Fresh from his time in Winnipeg prior to his return to L'Arche Daybreak and more than three years before the publication of his classic book *The Return of the Prodigal Son*, Henri gave a three-day workshop about what had happened to him in his solitude with the Gospel story and the painting. Despite his struggle to put this experience into words, Henri took a risk and "found his voice" to describe what may be his best articulation of accepting himself as God's beloved son. He told this group of caregivers from L'Arche communities worldwide that his one desire in sharing as he did was to help each one of them to discover *their* personal connection between the parable and *their* own lives. Just as he had done in his solitude, he urged each one to make the prodigal son story his or her most intimate story.

The marvellous thing about learning from a story is that a story never ends, so our learning from it need not end either.

—From *The Active Life* by Parker J. Palmer, 1990, Harper and Row, San Francisco, p. 98.

Henri believed in his listeners and trusted their ability to move beyond his experience to a personal, unique, and precious engagement with the parable on their own. That same confidence in the reader of this manuscript is evident even from beyond the grave, as he points the way for each of us to deeply and uniquely encounter Unconditional Love through the Scripture parable.

His conferences at the workshop were not taped professionally, but since his death, extracts from them have been reproduced and distributed. Henri seems to have prepared his first conference with more attention than the second or third, and for this reason the exact transcription of the tapes has not been published. John Mogabgab and Robin Pippin from Upper Room Ministries in Nashville, Lindsey Yeskoo, a friend from Toronto, Trace Murphy at Doubleday in New York, and I accepted the challenge of editing the material in a way that gives Henri his authentic voice, captures his compelling testimony, and maps a way for each of us to an encounter of deep consequence.

Henri gave a talk each morning of the three-day workshop at the end of which he directed the participants to enter into quiet time and the practice of three ancient spiritual disciplines: listening, journaling, and communing. This personal spiritual workout was designed to enable each one to personally embrace and enter into the story and the painting for themselves. Later in the day in small groups, people listened to and shared their workout experiences with one another. Optional times of personal meditation and common worship were part of the schedule.

I would like to beg you . . . as well as I can, to have patience with everything unresolved in your heart and to try to love the questions themselves as if they were locked rooms or books written in a foreign language. Don't search for the answers, which could not be given to you now, because you would not be able to live them. And the point is to live everything. Live the questions now. Perhaps then, someday, far into the future, you will gradually, without even noticing it, live your way into the answer.

—From *Letters to a Young Poet* by Rainer Maria Rilke.

In keeping with this pattern, *Home Tonight* is designed to offer you the opportunity to step into the workshop experience and thus to hear the same voice that was more compelling than all of Henri's excuses, fears, and resistance.

It took a certain amount of courage for Henri to communicate his return *home* in spirit but somewhere he knew that his story carried the potential to bear fruit in the lives of others. What he didn't realize at the time, but what becomes more and more obvious as the talks unfold, is that Henri is gradually being transformed into the father figure he speaks about—the one who longs and hopes for our return as well.

So now, with Henri's "voice" to guide you and the living Spirit of Love to enflame you, it's your turn to listen personally to John's insightful questions, "Where's *your* home?" and "Are *you* home tonight?"

Sue Mosteller
Henri Nouwen Legacy Trust
August 2007

WALK WITH ME INTO THE STORY

Read with a vulnerable heart. Expect to be blessed in the reading. Read as one awake, one waiting for the beloved. Read with reverence.

—From *A Tree Full of Angels* by Macrina Wiederkehr, 1991, Harper and Row, San Francisco, p. 53.

F rom the outset I encourage you to allow the Scripture story of the return of the prodigal son to descend into you—to move from your mind into your heart—so that images in this story become etched in your spirit. I trust that something new will be born in you that is very different from what happened in me; something that is yours alone. Simply know that *how* you receive this parable is truly important. The parable and the painting are inviting you in, calling you to enter and participate as one of the characters. Choosing to be *part* of the story will allow you to become conscious of new connections with your own personal life journey, so I urge you to gradually allow the story to become your own most intimate story.

Furthermore, I urge you not to walk into the story alone, just in your own name. Rather, enter into the story in solidarity with all your brothers and sisters in the human family on earth. I honestly don't say this lightly, because I truly feel that you will enter into it well if you enter in the name of all those who share your humanity. Your desire to participate with those in the parable is not just good for you alone, but it is also good for many others because your personal life is a gift for the people immediately around you and beyond. We know now, especially from scientific research, that you and I are intimately related to everything and everyone in the universe. This is an invitation, then, to see yourself right here and right now "in the name" of many brothers and sisters, believing that as something moves in you, something may also transpire in those in whose name you live.

This may be new for you, but I encourage you to imagine yourself surrounded first by family and then by loved ones, relatives, friends, acquaintances, business associates, those in your neighborhood, church, culture, continent, and world. Perhaps some of the circles nearest you aren't easy for you. There are family struggles with spouses, parents, children, brothers, and sisters. There are many painful memories and feelings around breakages, losses, and communication struggles. Also, many other people near and far are in your consciousness; some doing well while others languish in poverty, sickness, abuse, violence, loneliness, famine, refugee camps, and despair. Bring them all around you, claim your humanity with them, never thinking or growing or speaking or acting just for yourself.

*As we feel the pain of our own losses, our grieving hearts open our
inner eye to a world in which losses are suffered far beyond our
own little world of family, friends, and colleagues. It is the world
of prisoners, refugees, AIDS patients, starving children, and the
countless human beings living in constant fear. Then the pain of
our crying hearts connects us with the moaning and groaning of
a suffering humanity. Then our mourning becomes larger than
ourselves.*

—From *With Burning Hearts,* by Henri J. M. Nouwen, 1999,
Orbis Books, Maryknoll, NY, p. 28.

As you progressively become opened to others, allow all you
choose in the most hidden places of your heart to be lived for all
those who are alive *and* for those who have died. Gather them
and keep them around you. You belong to every other person
and to every particle of the universe. Like a stone thrown in
the water, your life has ever-widening circles of relationship
surrounding it. Enter the parable with all people in your heart.
Call them around you, identify yourself with them, and let your
thinking be deeply one with them as you journey with me into
the story.

Throughout this book, where I often paraphrase when quot-
ing from Scripture, I write of my personal experience *in* the parable of the prodigal son. If you understand my suffering and
the joy out of which my words are born, you may then be able
to take enough distance to say, "My life is different, but I find
connections between those in the story and *my* story just as he
did with his." I trust that as you engage the scriptural story you
will let all my words go except what is relevant for you and your
sacred relationship with God's creative Spirit.

Since I was very young my life has been dominated by two strong voices. The first said, "Make it in the world and be sure you can do it on your own." And the other voice said, "Whatever you do for the rest of your life, even if it's not very important, be sure you hold on to the love of Jesus." My father was a little more inclined to say the first and my mother the second. But the voices were strong. "Make your mark. Be able to show the world you can do it by yourself and that you are not afraid. Go as far as you want to go and be a man. Be a good older son and brother, and be sure you really do something relevant." And the other said, "Don't lose touch with Jesus, who chose a very humble and simple way. Jesus, by his life and death, will be your example for living."

I've struggled because one voice seemed to be asking me for upward mobility and the other for downward mobility and I was never sure how to do both at the same time.

I suppose that being the eldest son and part of a very ambitious family, I let the voice of upward mobility quickly win out. I initially *did* want to show the world I could do it, so I became a hyphenated priest. Do you know what a hyphenated priest is? Priest-psychologist. It wasn't enough to just be a priest. I wanted to be a psychologist too. Then if somebody didn't like priests, they might at least like psychologists! Thus I went on my upwardly mobile way. From Holland I went to the United States and soon went on to teach at Notre Dame. Then I went from Notre Dame to Yale, and from Yale to Harvard, and my father said, "Henri, you are doing very well!"

My mother, on the other hand, was asking, "Yes, but are you losing your connection with Jesus?"

> *. . . I have entered deep waters,*
> *and the flood sweeps over me.*

I am exhausted from weeping;
I thirst as in a desert.
I no longer see the path while
  Waiting for your return.

—From *Psalms for Praying* by Nan C. Merrill, 1996, The Continuum
International Publishing Group, New York, Psalm 69, p. 134.

Through it all, I've carried within me the pain of loneliness
and a nagging need for affection. Although I loved teaching in
the universities I was always yearning for intimacy in my life.
I found this special love to a certain degree in my relationship
with my mother. She loved me in a particular way, followed my
every move, faithfully corresponded with me, expressing a love
that was tangible, full, and close to being unconditional. When
she died in 1978 during my time at Yale, I grieved her absence
in a very profound place inside. Her love had always "held" me
safe, but now it was gone. Her death was a double loss for me
of both her person and also my whole sense of "home." Her
absence plunged me into a downward spiral so that my final
teaching years at Harvard in the early 1980s were some of the
unhappiest of my life. It was there that I began an important
life passage, from loneliness to L'Arche.

For the past year, I've been called into another, more challenging passage, from L'Arche to the second loneliness, and the
parable of the prodigal son has companioned me along the way
to a homecoming of large proportions. Now, quite simply, I desire to walk into this story with you as a potential entrance into
a new passage of reclaiming something precious for you in your
own life.

This story has the potential to be your most intimate story. It
holds unique insights for you in this moment of your life. I only

offer you my story to encourage you to claim your story, and to more seriously embrace your humanity in relationship with the One who created you. It is a call to engage your heart as well as your mind, and your life experience as well as your beliefs, to turn inward toward the unique "presence" that offers you safety, healing, forgiveness, and other important gifts.

. . . our familiarity may pose problems. These are stories from the Christian Scriptures that some of us have been hearing all our lives. They have been interpreted for us so often that our minds may be closed to new meanings.

—From *The Active Life* by Parker J. Palmer, 1990, Harper and Row, San Francisco, p. 99.

To enable you in all of this you are invited to stop at certain intervals to engage in the practice of three ancient spiritual disciplines: listening, journaling, and communing. Each "spiritual workout" is a potential gateway for you to move beyond my story and more personally enter into the parable and the painting yourself. Similar to physical workouts that limber the body, spiritual disciplines support your fragile heart to bypass mere reading and to accept that you are being spoken to by the text in a most personal and specific way. Spiritual disciplines allow you to let the words descend from your mind into your heart, possess you, and live in you. They move you from learning about spiritual realities to encountering the living Spirit of Love. Regular spiritual workouts enliven you for the journey to integrity, the journey home.

The following story from Luke 15:11–32 provides the complete backdrop to my own story. Find a quiet, comfortable space, put aside preoccupations, and trust as you embark on the adventure of the spiritual disciplines. Read slowly. Drink it in. Let it soak into your bones. Allow it to flow freely from your mind into your heart.

Then [Jesus] said, There was a man who had two sons. The younger one said to his father, "Father, let me have the share of the estate that will come to me." So the father divided the property between them. A few days later, the younger son got together everything he had and left for a distant country where he squandered his money on a life of debauchery.

When he had spent it all, that country experienced a severe famine, and now he began to feel the pinch; so he hired himself out to one of the local inhabitants, who put him on his farm to feed the pigs. And he would willingly have filled himself with the husks the pigs were eating but no one would let him have them. Then he came to his senses and said, "How many of my father's hired men have all the food they want and more, and here am I dying of hunger! I will leave this place and go to my father and say: I have sinned against heaven and against you; I no longer deserve to be called your son; treat me as one of your hired men." So he left the place and went back to his father.

While he was still a long way off, his father saw him and was moved with pity. He ran to the boy, clasped him in his arms and kissed him. Then his son said, "Father, I have sinned against heaven and against you. I no longer deserve to be called your son." But the father said to his servants, "Quick! Bring out the best robe and put it on him; put a ring on his finger and sandals on his feet. Bring the calf we have been fattening, and kill it; we will celebrate by having a feast because this son of mine was dead and has come back to life; he was lost and is found." And they began to celebrate.

Now the elder son was out in the fields, and on his way back, as he drew near the house, he could hear music and dancing. Calling one of the servants he asked what it was all about. The servant told him, "Your brother has come, and your father has killed the calf we had been fattening because he has got him back safe and sound." He was angry then and refused to go in, and his father came out and began to urge him to come in; but he retorted to his father, "All these years I have slaved for you and never once disobeyed any orders of yours, yet you never offered me so much as a kid for me to celebrate with my friends. But for this son of yours, when he comes back after swallowing up your property—he and his loose women—you kill the calf we had been fattening."

The father said, "My son, you are with me always and all I have is yours. But it was only right we should celebrate and rejoice, because your brother here was dead and has come to life; he was lost and is found."

Consider what you have read as a sacred trust, as the gift of a fertile field full of yet-buried tiny seeds that need to be tended and watered so as to grow and bear fruit in you. Move forward in stillness.

LISTENING

You have read many words. Try not to be overwhelmed but rather focus on the one detail from the story that touches you more than the rest. Who is voicing that message? Why do you think it is meaningful for you? Stay attentive only to these stirrings in your heart.

But it's not so simple, that sort of "quiet hour." It has to be learned. A lot of unimportant inner litter and bits and pieces have to be swept out first. Even a small head can be piled high inside with irrelevant distractions. True, there may be edifying emotions and thoughts, too, but the clutter is ever present. So let this be the aim of the meditation: to turn one's innermost being into a vast empty plain, with none of that treacherous undergrowth to impede the view so that something of "God" can enter you, and something of "Love," too.

—From *An Interrupted Life, and Letters from Westerbork* by Etty Hillesum, 1996, Henry Holt and Company, New York, pp. 27–28.

JOURNALING

Mindful of what you feel, look at Rembrandt's masterful depiction of the parable on the cover of your book. Give your attention to how the light falls on the scene. Record in your journal all that you observe about the light. Stay with it, and write what you heard when you listened and what the light in the painting is saying to you. Take special note of the shadows and the darkness and write about them in contrast to the light. Find the words that express your thoughts and feelings about light, darkness, and shadows in your own life.

COMMUNING

The exercise doesn't end at the tip of your pen, so put it down and allow yourself to move on. Imagine yourself before the One who loves you more than a daughter or a son, and speak your thoughts and feelings without fear. Lay them out as you would with a most trusted and cherished friend. Try to pinpoint your feelings and beliefs in terms of the light, darkness, and shadows you've encountered. It may be painful, but resolve to be completely honest, trusting that all you articulate will be heard without judgment and with loving compassion. Remain and be quietly present in the moment.

Heart speaks to heart.

PART I

LEAVING
AND
RETURNING
HOME

CHAPTER I

FROM LONELINESS TO L'ARCHE

Suffering is a dreadful teacher but often the beginning of the best in us. Suffering and creativity are often interdependent. Pain produces a terrible tension released in our creative response. Suffering can be like a grain of sand in an oyster: it can create a magnificent pearl.

—From *Straight from the Heart: Reflections from Twentieth-Century Mystics* by Dick Ryan, ed., 2001, Crossroad Publishing Company, New York, p. 158; quoted from *Teresa of Avila* by Tessa Bielecki, 1994, Crossroad Publishing Company.

W hen I was at Harvard teaching about Jesus to hundreds of people from all over the world, I was miserable. It was then that I unconsciously touched the strong voice from my childhood that spoke to me about the simple way of Jesus. I began to wonder if my proclaiming the Gospel wasn't the best way of losing my very spirit and my connection with the Divine in my life. Harvard is a very ambitious institution, interested in the best and the brightest, in power, upward mobility, political influence, and economic success. Talking about Jesus there wasn't easy and I felt pressure to adopt the model of the university, to become more competitive and to "make it" as a professor in that environment. Separated by death from the loving relationship with my mother, I also felt very lonely, detached in prayer, unable to respond to those who wanted to become my friends, and without a community around me. I knew that I *had* to do something, but I felt desperate because I didn't know what to do. I began to ask Jesus in times of prayer for directions out of my pain.

One morning in my little apartment a knock came at the door. The little woman standing on the step smiled at me. "Hello," I said. "What are you doing here so early in the morning?"

"Well," she answered, "my name is Jan Risse."

"What can I do for you?"

"Well, I've come to bring you greetings from Jean Vanier."

Now the name Jean Vanier was just a name for me. I admired his communities, called L'Arche, that welcomed people with disabilities, and I had even mentioned Jean Vanier in one of my books. But I had never met him. So again I said to Jan Risse, "What can I do for you?"

She continued to smile and replied, "Well, I come to bring greetings from Jean Vanier."

"Thank you so much. I really appreciate that. So, what is it that you really come for?" I asked.

"Well, I come to bring greetings from Jean Vanier."

Conscious of my busy day ahead and hoping to bypass the small talk, I said, "Did you want me to give a lecture somewhere, or give a seminar, or a talk? What can I do for you?" She looked at me and suggested that I invite her to come in! I stood aside and said, "Sure, you can come in, but I have a class and then I have a meeting and I'm completely tied up until suppertime."

In my living room she turned and said, "OK, that's fine. You go off and I'll be fine right here until your return." Thus, she came in and I left for the better part of the day. Upon my return in the early evening I gazed at my room. The table was covered with a white linen cloth and beautifully set with candles, a bottle of wine, fine china, and flowers in the center. Astonished I exclaimed, "What's this?"

"Oh, I thought you and I could have dinner together," she casually replied.

"But where did you find all these beautiful things?" I asked.

"From your own cupboard!" she said, pointing to the buffet. "You must not look around your own house very often!" She had created this wonderful dinner for the two of us with candles and wine—from my own house!

I found her a room on campus and she stayed for three days. We had a few visits and she came to my classes and then she left. Her last words to me were "Remember, Jean Vanier sent his greetings."

I sat in my chair and said to myself, "Something is happening. This visit wasn't for nothing." But then nothing happened for many, many months until the phone rang one day and Jean Vanier was on the other end of the line. "Henri," he said, "I'm on a retreat here in Chicago and I was thinking of you. Is there any chance you could come and join us here?"

Whatever happens to me in life,
I must believe that somewhere,
In the mess or madness of it all,
There is a sacred potential—
A possibility for wondrous redemption
In the embracing of all that is.

—From *Straight from the Heart: Reflections from Twentieth-Century Mystics*
by Dick Ryan, ed., 2001, Crossroad Publishing Company, New York,
p. 85; quoted from *A Mystical Heart* by Edwina Gateley, Crossroad
Publishing House.

I hastened to reply, "Jean, I have already given a number of
retreats this year."

Jean answered, "I'm not asking you to give the retreat. I'm
here on a retreat with a number of people from L'Arche worldwide, and I just thought you might like to be here to pray with
us. We're all in silence, so you don't have to worry about talking
to lots of people. You and I could visit and it might be a rest for
you."

Almost immediately the same sense that something important was happening prompted me to drop everything and go to
Chicago for several days. Nobody was talking, but more than
fifty people were together there for conferences, meals, sharing,
and worship. Apart from a daily visit with Jean in which I shared
my angst in Harvard, I enjoyed a silent retreat with people from
L'Arche around the world. When it was time to leave I felt rested
as well as challenged by something Jean Vanier had said to me
in passing at one point: "Perhaps our people [i.e., people with
disabilities who live in L'Arche] could offer you a home."

That one sentence touched a chord in me and seemed like a

prophetic call, so I visited Jean in his L'Arche home just north of Paris the next time I went to Europe. I felt relaxed with the people with disabilities and in general I experienced peace, rest, and safety in the community. I knew Harvard wasn't the place for me, so I resigned at the end of the year and took a writing sabbatical in Jean's community at Trosly. While I was there, the L'Arche Daybreak community in Toronto, Canada, called me to come there for three years as their pastor and I said "yes" to their invitation.

Bit by intelligible bit, a vocation lets us express our healthiest instincts, our noblest desires. . . . In small things and in large, we can attend to the haunting inner summons of our soul.

—From *Straight from the Heart: Reflections from Twentieth-Century Mystics* by Dick Ryan, ed., 2001, Crossroad Publishing Company, New York, p. 85; quoted from *Holy Work,* by Marsha Sinetar, 1989, Crossroad Publishing House.

The following year I found a wonderful home at Daybreak, and there completed the first part of my journey from loneliness to L'Arche. But it was a surprise to discover that there was still a way to go. A long way.

In my L'Arche formation the word most used was the word "home." L'Arche is a home. Jean had said to me, "Maybe our people can offer you a 'home.'" Daybreak was saying, "Our community wants you to be pastor, and we think we can offer you a 'home.'" Because my life had always been lived alone and because of inner loneliness, that word, "home," touched me in my heart. In the competitive world of the university, "home" was not a significant word. "Institution," "success," "financial gain," and "power" obliterate the concepts of "community," "intimacy," and "togetherness."

Because I was longing for belonging and a sense of home, I came to L'Arche filled with new hope of finding fulfillment. It was a shock for me during the first three years at L'Arche to gradually realize that "home" might mean something other than what my heart craved and my flesh desired. I was under the illusion that home was the pure experience of warmth, intimacy, and affection, and at the beginning there was a lot of that. But the longer I lived at Daybreak the more I realized that I might have to give up home in order to find it. While living with handicapped people and their assistants at Daybreak I sensed that the Lord was inviting me to something that I was certainly not ready to live.

As I lived longer in the Daybreak community old demons around my need for affection revisited me, and I began to find it difficult to love freely without being selfish and demanding. I sensed myself going into a dark tunnel leading to a second loneliness unlike anything I had ever lived before. I don't have many words to describe what happened to me, but the story of the prodigal son will help me unwrap for you the gift and spiritual significance of this, my journey.

Healing begins when, in the face of our own darkness, we recognize our helplessness and surrender our need for control . . . we face what is, and we ask for mercy.

—From *Straight from the Heart: Reflections from Twentieth-Century Mystics* by Dick Ryan, ed., 2001, Crossroad Publishing Company, New York, p. 78; quoted from *Prayer and the Quest for Healing: Our Personal Transformation and Cosmic Responsibility* by Barbara Fiand, 1999, Crossroad Publishing Company.

Reading the story and studying the painting of the prodigal son brought me to recognize that there is a younger child in me that needs conversion, and there is an elder sibling in me that needs conversion as well. Most importantly, however, I realized there is a father, a parent, that needs to be first revealed in me and then claimed by me, in order for *me* to receive the younger and the elder children that long, like me, to come home. Because of this experience with the parable, I feel more confident that a time will come when we will all share the celebration— not only of the return of many younger prodigals, but also the return of the elder daughters and sons to the home of their true identities as siblings and parents around the table with the Father-Mother-God. The word "home," more than anything else, called me to move forward on my journey to share my life with others in L'Arche.

So on my journey from loneliness to L'Arche I was finally paying attention to my life and to the internal and external "happenings and events" that pointed me to life changes. "Being attentive to the signs" is a wisdom practice handed down through the generations from our very wise and holy ancestors.

LISTENING

These exercises happen within the sacred context of your life. You are invited to listen with your heart as well as with your mind.

Find a quiet space and become comfortable. Look at Rembrandt's painting and gently step into the painted scene as an invisible guest. Situate yourself in the place in the room where you feel most comfortable as an onlooker. Close your eyes and become aware of the sounds in the room. What noises are you hearing? What voices do you hear? Take time to listen to the unfolding scene—from within.

JOURNALING

Still in the portrait, open your journal and write what you see and hear. Take your time. Then focus and take note of the feelings your presence there evoked in you. Write how each person and their words affected you. Write what you feel and how your heart responds.

> *We know that there is an enormous power inherent in each of us, at every moment in time, to experience the unbounded love and deep joy which is potentially our inheritance.*

—From *Always We Begin Again: The Benedictine Way of Living* by John McQuiston II, 1996, Morehouse Publishing, Harrisburg, PA, p. 80.

COMMUNING

Go to the privileged place in your heart where no one but you and your God have access. Articulate to the One who fashioned you and who is with you always, even to the end of time, your experience as participant in the parable. Stop and listen for the still, small voice of Love. Speak again, then wait and listen. Remain. Abide. Rest.

Heart speaks to heart.

A WISDOM PRACTICE FOR THOSE ON
A SPIRITUAL JOURNEY

Practice #1—BE ATTENTIVE TO THE "SIGNS"

Feeding the pigs and close to despair, the runaway prodigal knew that his life *had* to change. A certain hope was born when he considered going home, but that was soon replaced by shame, fear, and the utter impossibility of such a simple move. But his options were limited, so glimmerings of excitement around thoughts of "home" persisted. Because he listened, he was one day able to turn with uneasy confidence and begin his journey home.

> *Don't surrender your loneliness so quickly.*
> *Let it cut more deep.*
> *Let it ferment and season you,*
> *As few human or even divine ingredients can.*
> *Something missing in my heart tonight*
> *Has made my eyes soft,*
> *My voice, so tender,*
> *My need for God,*
> *Absolutely clear.*

—Shams al-Din Hafiz

In those final years at Harvard I also "knew" that teaching in the university was deadening. I prayed, sought advice, and tried to be attentive to inner movements indicating what was to be next for me. Connecting first with Jan Risse and then with Jean Vanier moved me in my heart, and I knew that our meetings were not accidental. I listened. Although the initial idea of moving to L'Arche excited me, it was still with reluctance, fear, and uneasy confidence that I left the university and haltingly stepped into the impossible.

To live authentically each of us must be aware of our "within." We need to become conscious of feeling content, safe, and in the right place, and of feeling lonely, disillusioned, or mildly depressed. In front of turmoil, what do we do? Wise teachers tell us to be *very* attentive at these moments, to be open to "signs," feelings, comments, a line in a book, unexpected meetings or events that may move us to consider new directions, to refind balance, and to remain fully alive. Spiritual signs usually have four characteristics: They are simple not complicated, persistent, seemingly impossible, and always about others as well as ourselves. Be attentive when you experience these on your journey. Try to recognize an opportunity as well as a difficulty. Try not to respond too quickly. Pray for wisdom. Seek advice and refuse to act until you have external affirmation for your direction. Take time to believe in your free choice before you move forward in a new direction.

CHAPTER 2

THE YOUNGER SON

*All artists must learn the art of surviving loss: loss of hope, loss of
face, loss of money, loss of self-belief . . . Artistic losses can be turned
into artistic gains and strengths—but not in isolation of the belea-
guered artist's brain. . . . We must acknowledge it and share it.*

—From *The Artist's Way: A Spiritual Path to Higher Creativity* by Julia
Cameron, 1992, Jeremy P. Tarcher/Putnam, New York, p. 129.

I am a Dutchman. Rembrandt is a Dutchman and van Gogh
is a Dutchman. These Dutch painters have entered into my
heart in a very deep way, so I have them in mind as I speak
to you. They have become my consolation and when I find I
have nothing else to say, when I have only tears for what is happening in my life, I look at Rembrandt or at van Gogh. Their
lives and their art heal and console me more than anything else.

Rembrandt painted the picture of the prodigal son between
1665 and 1667, at the end of his life. As a young painter, he was
popular in Amsterdam and successful with commissions to do

portraits of all the important people of his day. He was known as arrogant and argumentative, but he participated in the circles of the very rich in society. Gradually, however, his life began to deteriorate:

First he lost a son,
then he lost his first daughter,
then he lost his second daughter,
then he lost his wife,
then the woman he lived with ended up in a mental
   hospital,
then he married a second woman who died,
then he lost all his money and fame, and
just before he himself died, his son Titus died.

It was a man who experienced immense loneliness in his life that painted this picture. As he lived his overwhelming losses and died many personal deaths, Rembrandt could have become a most bitter, angry, resentful person. Instead he became the one who was finally able to paint one of the most intimate paintings of all time—*Return of the Prodigal Son*. This is not the painting he was able to paint when he was young and successful. No, he was only able to paint the mercy of a blind father when he had lost everything: all of his children but one, two of his wives, all his money, and his good name and popularity. Only after that was he able to paint this picture, and he painted it from a place in himself that knew what God's mercy was. Somehow his loss and suffering emptied him out to receive fully and deeply the mercy of God. When Vincent van Gogh saw this painting he said, "You can only paint this painting when you have died many deaths." Rembrandt could do it only because he had died so many deaths that he finally knew what the return to God's mercy really meant.

We can look back over Rembrandt's life and witness his personal and artistic transformation. If it touches us, it is important for us to consider our own story, and to take our own lives very seriously.

I became aware of how important the Rembrandt painting was for me when, just prior to my becoming pastor at L'Arche Daybreak in 1986, a friend called me and said, "I'm going to Russia. Would you like to come with me?" My immediate response was, "Oh, how amazing! I'm going to see Rembrandt at the Winter Palace of Peter the Great!" I didn't say anything about Moscow or the Kremlin. I'm ashamed to say that I wasn't even thinking of Russian people, or Russian culture, or even Russian icons. I was thinking about Rembrandt because I knew this painting was in the Hermitage Museum in Leningrad and I knew I wanted to see the real thing.

After we arrived in Russia and with some effort, I finally connected with the restorer in the Hermitage Museum. I told him, "I want to see that painting. That's all. I don't want to pass by it in a line of people but I want to sit in front of it for as long as I want to sit there! I don't want anything else!" He kindly took me directly to the painting, eight feet high and covering one wall of the museum, and he put me right in front of it. I sat in one of the three velvet chairs before the painting and I stared to my heart's content. I studied the painting carefully and then began making notes while whole crowds of people came, stopped for a moment, and passed by.

All life is a beginning. I need an open, spontaneous, joyful attitude that knows it does not know. I need an emptiness in me . . . I need

*to find the part in my soul still empty, still able to be surprised,
still open to wonder.*

—From *The Finding Stone* by Christine Lore Weber, 1995, Lura Media,
San Diego.

By two o'clock in the afternoon when the sun on the painting caused a glare, I took my chair and shifted it to another
position. Before I could sit down the guard approached me and
in a commanding way said in Russian something like, "This
chair goes *there!*" He picked it up and put it in its original spot.
I tried to tell him, distinctly moving my lips and pointing to
the window, "But I can't see anything. Look, can't you see the
glare? I *have* to sit here!" He shook his head, stating again, "No,
the chair goes *there!*" Finally, in desperation, I said to myself,
"Forget about it," and I sat down on the floor. To the guard
this move turned out to be a much greater sin than moving the
chair in the first place. So he came racing back, looked down
at me on the floor, and said, "You can't sit on the floor!" He
pointed and said, "Sit on the radiator!" I got up and settled
myself uncomfortably on the radiator.

Soon the next large group of people appeared, and when the
tour guide saw me on my perch she looked aghast and hastened
to indicate to me, "You're not allowed to sit on the radiator!"
But then the guard jumped back in and told her in no uncertain terms, "I gave him permission to sit on the radiator!" Fortunately, while the two of them were fighting it out, Alexi, the
restorer for the whole museum, came by to see how I was doing.
He recognized my confusion and entered into conversation to
quiet the guard and the guide. Then, without speaking to me,
he left, followed by the guide and the tour group. After about

ten minutes Alexi returned carrying a velvet chair, which he set down before me, saying, "This is your own chair! You can move it wherever you like."

I sat before the painting for three days, two or three hours a day, pondering, studying, reflecting, and making notes. The more I looked, the more I became part of the story, and I began to make connections between the Gospel parable and my own personal life. I was deeply aware of the return; the return to the womb of the Divine Creator.

All human nature vigorously resists grace because grace changes us and the change is painful.

—From *The Habit of Being* by Flannery O'Connor, 1979, Vintage Books, New York. p. 307.

The life force I saw was more than a father. The Divine I saw was also a Mother. I knew in my heart how the reminder by Jesus to become like a child, so as to enter into the kingdom, was portrayed as a return to the womb of God. I also felt that my whole future would depend on my willingness to reenter the womb of my Creator-God and to find my home there. This was a welcome confirmation of my decision to allow the people of L'Arche Daybreak to help me make my return home in body and spirit.

After my return from Russia I began my life as pastor at L'Arche Daybreak—my choice of home. I had made a conscious decision that my spiritual focus for the first year would be finding my center and home in the One who had created me and who loves me with unfathomable love. I began to reflect on my life with the painting and the parable as my context.

Although I myself am the oldest child in my family, I still feel there is a lot of that young man in the painting in me. There's a part of me that always wants to break away from a good thing, to break away from home. Although I've always had a good home and an OK father and mother, there remains in me a young adolescent urging me to cut loose. "I want to break out, discover forbidden things for myself and I don't want to hear forbidding voices. I want to get what belongs to me and run with it."

So here is the paradox: as humans we are caught between competing drives, the drive to belong, to fit in and be a part of something bigger than ourselves, and the drive to let our deepest selves rise up, to walk alone, to refuse the accepted and the comfortable, and this can mean, at least for a time, the acceptance of anguish. It is in the group that we discover what we have in common. It is as individuals that we discover a personal relationship with God. We must find a way to balance our two opposing impulses.

—From *Becoming Human* by Jean Vanier, 1998, House of Anansi Press, Toronto, pp. 18–19.

This adolescent attitude of wanting to find my own answers, solve my own problems, and discover my own truth is natural, so people who try to give me answers before I'm even looking for them irritate me. The parental voices speak, "This is how to behave. This is how to relate. This is how to worship. This is how to do this and not do that. This is the school for you." To hell with all that!

I want to live my own life without parental voices.
I don't want to have answers before I even raise the questions.

I don't want to have religion before I even have a need
for it.

I don't want to be given all the right ways before I've
learned on my own about wrongdoing.

I don't want answers coming to me from a place that is
pre-given.

How can something really become mine when I haven't accepted it from within? How can I appreciate home when I
wasn't looking for home because I have no other options than
the home I already have? I hear myself complaining, "Don't you
know that my life is full of questions? Can't you see that I want
to say 'yes' to my own truth from within? I don't want what is
premade. I want to build my own home and I don't want a pre-
fab home that someone who doesn't even know me has made."
My psychological training made me know very well what that
was all about.

This phase is about self-discovery and self-expression. Because adolescence holds all the dangers of getting lost, the parents become justifiably afraid. *They* know what is right. They
know how I should eat. They know how I should talk. They know
how I should walk. They know what I should and shouldn't do.
And it's true. They do know a lot because they have lived longer
than I have. So their concern is natural and good. At the same
time everything in me is saying, "Forget it! I no longer want all
that. It's my life, not yours. Let me go free." And I know that my
feelings are natural and good.

*I do not act as I mean to, but I do things that I hate . . . for though
the will to do what is good is in me, the power to do it is not.*

—From the Jerusalem Bible, Romans 7:15–18.

I come from a background that is very traditional Catholic. Everything in our home was crystal clear. Nothing was ambiguous. We were well taught all the essentials: how we socialized, how we met new people, how we prayed, how we worshipped, and how we studied! I remember very vividly at the time how jealous I was of those who had no religion. They could do anything they wanted and they didn't even feel guilty about it! All I could do was say, "Hell, I've already been told I'm not to do this and I should do that, I'm not allowed to go there and I'm supposed to go here, this is the way to behave and that is not!" Meanwhile I saw people who couldn't care less. They did everything and anything with their minds, with their bodies, with other people, and they seemed perfectly free. So I was jealous. I wanted to be a pagan so I could do all the things I wanted to do and not feel guilty.

But that wasn't for me. I can thank my parents for my education, for encouraging me to make good friends, for a healthy body, and for a good and true family. But every time I did something wrong, I ended up feeling guilty! I didn't want to feel guilty, but damn it, my parents raised me with so much clarity around right and wrong that whatever I did I was always in trouble and full of bad feelings besides. I vividly remember the inner dialogue:

"OK, I want to become a Christian, but first I want to do all the things I'm not supposed to do so that I can be converted. OK, I'm willing to discover that maybe some things are questionable, but let me find that out by myself. I don't want anyone to tell me what is good and what is no good. What I need is to go out, to travel, and to move. So just give me my stuff, let me go, and trust that I can discover what I need to know on my own. Why, since I was a little baby, did I already have to be a little priest?"

I really wish my parents had recognized how natural it is to want to cut loose and to travel and to do something other than what they consider to be decent or appropriate.

I live in confusion and despair
because of my anguish;
My body responds with illness
because of my stubbornness,
Ignorance casts me into darkness, and
I grope in every direction,
searching in vain.

—From *Psalms for Praying* by Nan C. Merrill, 1996, The Continuum International Publishing Group, New York, Psalm 38, p. 72.

Much of my adolescent "breaking out" bothered my conscience with feelings of guilt and fear as to how to get back on track as soon as possible. I began my return as well as I could and in faith but I continued to slip backwards: "I'm a beloved child, returning home where I belong, but my Maker will probably be furious and never want to see me again." I imagined being shouted at for having been given so much, for not becoming a lawyer or getting a real job. I projected that I'll be told to get out and never come back! Finally, I began to prepare my speech. "I'm just your miserable little child, and maybe you can give me a little morsel of food because I'm so miserable." I revert to old patterns of projecting God's reaction from the place of my failure. That is my repeated experience of trying to return home.

Perhaps you who read this book can identify with my wavering returns. You believe you have an identity and you know who you are, but you don't know, either, because you feel so insecure.

Perhaps you, too, run for affirmation, affection, or success. Perhaps you don't know clearly what exactly you seek, but you experience an angst that holds you back from feeling truly free. You, too, may be afraid to open yourself to the unconditional love of the One who "formed you in your mother's womb." You might ask yourself why you are always busy and seldom still, always running and complaining at the same time of having no time to simply be.

There are psychoanalytic theories about why Christians become violent against others. It is as if we are angry that we haven't really chosen or experienced or integrated our faith for ourselves. We received it often as a burden that is difficult to reject because of the learned consequences.

The Scripture story of the prodigal son recounts his taking his inheritance and leaving home to spend it all on women, games, and gambling. He's going to test drive the pleasures of life in a foreign land and away from familiar teaching voices. In the secret of his heart he's probably saying to himself, "Whatever am I doing? This isn't very smart. In fact, it's ridiculous." As he loses it all, he knows how stupid he is. On the other hand, isn't this exactly what he has to do in order to finally claim what for himself is truly real? And isn't he learning about his false and his true self?

Rabbi Levi saw a man running in the street, and asked him, "Why do you run?" He replied, "I am running after my good fortune!" Rabbi Levi tells him, "Silly man, your good fortune has been trying to chase you, but you are running too fast."

—From *Sabbath: Restoring the Sacred Rhythm of Rest* by Wayne Muller, 1999, Bantam Books, New York, p. 48.

Perhaps each of us might take a moment to identify with the prodigal. Perhaps we are able to remember times when we consciously knew the truth of what our parents, teachers, and friends were saying, but we said it was dumb and stupid and we rationalized, "Well, you can all tell me that, but right now I need to find out for myself."

While the young man in the story seemingly left his home and lost everything, one possession remained. He was still a *member* of his family. He *belonged* to those people and to that homestead. As he moved through the pain of his disillusionment with life and himself to the awareness that there was something that could never be lost, he began his actual return. "I'm still the child of my father and of my mother. I still *belong* to my family. I still have a home where people who know me are alive." Hidden below all these thoughts is an enormous load of confusion, guilt, and shame because he knows he has acted stupidly and is now at the bottom. He has few options. He can only choose to live in despair or to reach out to reclaim his truth. From deep within he opts to turn and to return. "Let me go back to my father's house."

He's not immediately able to claim the whole truth however. While he is saying "I'll go home," he is not saying "My parents will be happy to see me back and will receive me with open arms." Not even close! The most he is able to say is "I'm going home to the place where I belong and my family has servants who have more food than I'm getting here. I will just say, 'Father, I've sinned against you, and so why don't you treat me at least like you treat the servants.'" So on one hand he claims his truth about having a true home and turns back, but on the other hand, confused and blinded with guilt, he hasn't much freedom at all. At least he claims it, though, and it is enough for him to turn and return.

I hear my Beloved.
See how he comes leaping on the mountains,
Bounding over the hills,
My Beloved is like a gazelle, like a young stag.

See where he stands behind our wall.
He looks in at the window,
He peers through the lattice.

My Beloved lifts up his voice, he says to me,
Come then, my love, my lovely one, come.
For see, winter is past, the rains are over and gone.

—From the Jerusalem Bible, Song of Songs, 2:8-11.

Jesus made the connection about his belonging in his baptism when he heard the Father's incredible affirmation of his person. "You are my favorite son. In you I am well pleased." This knowledge of his primal truth made it possible for him to live his life and to accept his death in a world of both acceptance and rejection, without ever losing his deep affiliation with the One who sent him into the world. He knew the truth. He claimed himself in truth so that whether people wanted to be with him, listen to him, make him king, reject him, beat him, spit on him, or nail him to the Cross, he never lost the truth that he was God's beloved child.

This same connection and lack thereof is demonstrated as well in the stories of Peter and Judas. Both were given a place in the company of Jesus and it was, for them, an identity. They were chosen and they knew it. Yet both left their truth through denial and betrayal. At the moment of realization, Peter reclaimed his identity as friend of Jesus and wept in sorrow. Judas, however, unable to claim equality with people who hadn't been overtly sinful, became suicidal, renounced his inheritance, and hanged himself.

You and I know spiritually about belonging, leaving, and returning. We, like the young prodigal, can learn to act ahead of our feelings, trust that love is there, and make our shaky return. And we will do it more readily if we come to know the God figure in the story. Before now I was never able to see how the love of the father embraced not just the return of his younger child but also his running away from home. That is an enlightening consideration prompting me now to question, "Do you mean you were actually *there* in my leaving?" and "Does this mean that I can come home and you'll still be there for me?"

Perhaps the whole movement of leaving and returning is only one movement rather than two, especially as it is experienced in the loving heart of the father. This is not a parent who says, "Don't go." That kind of statement is not in keeping with the spirit of this story. The spirit of the story is different. It reads, "Yes, son. Go. And you will be hurt and it will be hard, and it will be painful. And you might even lose your life, but I will not hold you back from taking that risk. When and if you come back, I am always here for you. But I'm also here for you now in your leaving. Yes, we belong together and I am never separated from you." This aspect of Love Divine is, for me, a critical life-connection.

> *Teach me, that I may know my weaknesses,*
> *the shortcomings that bind me,*
> *The unloving ways that separate me,*
> *that keep me from recognizing your life in me.*

For, I keep company with fear, and
   dwell in the house of ignorance.
Yet, I was brought forth in love,
   and love is my birthright.

—From *Psalms for Praying* by Nan C. Merrill, 1996, The Continuum
International Publishing Group, New York, Psalm 52, p. 102.

I feel that in our hearts it's good to be convinced somewhere
of the merciful One's love and to risk leaving occasionally. Isn't
it true that there are times for us, as in the life of the younger
son, when we simply need to go off for a while? I believe the
Giver of Life loves each of us as a daughter or a son who is leaving and returning constantly. The more we become sensitive to
our own journey the more we realize that we are leaving and
coming back every day, every hour. Our minds wander away but
eventually return; our hearts leave in search of affection and
return sometimes broken; our bodies get carried away in their
desires then sooner or later return. It's never one dramatic life
moment but a constant series of departures and returns.

Having lived my own encounter with the story and the painting, I feel empowered to invite you to claim your leaving and
returning home with compassion. We are beloved children of
our Maker. We are held safe by everlasting and unending love.
It's normal, then, for us in growing up spiritually to live according to our nature. "Yes, I'm loved, even when I take a risk
to satisfy my desire to claim my life. I'm loved, even if I make
mistakes. I may have acted badly but I didn't have any other way
to do it at that moment. People have hurt me and I've suffered
unjustly, but I am loved before anything happened to me." This
is important so as not to judge ourselves more harshly than the
One who loves us.

A spiritual discipline . . . is the concentrated effort to create some
inner and outer space in our lives . . . A spiritual discipline sets
us free to pray, or to say it better, allows the Spirit of God to pray
in us.

—From *Making All Things New* by Henri Nouwen, 1981,
HarperSanFrancisco, San Francisco, p. 68.

When we do not claim the presence of love in our departures,
we experience a guilt-ridden return to a dark God, reprimand-
ing us, saying, "I always knew you would fail. I could have told
you that you would need me again." This is not the image of
the Great Creator in the prodigal's story. God is not laughing
because we couldn't do it on our own. The Spirit is not demanding that we finally confess in guilt and shame as a condition of
our return. The God in the parable is a personal, intimate, and
loving Presence who lets each of us go and welcomes each one
home, all in amazing generosity and forgiveness. This reflection
isn't an intellectual exercise about right and wrong. More, it is
an opening of ourselves to gradually let go of fear, to trust anew,
and to make space for the love of the One who both blesses our
leaving and waits to celebrate our return.

LISTENING

In a quiet moment open yourself to listen to the story in a whole
new way. This time approach the written parable from the perspective of posture. Ready yourself to be surprised and listen
for what the given positions suggest to you.

Reflect on each main character in the painting and ask yourself what you learn about these individuals from the way the

artist portrayed them in that one moment in time. Ponder what Jesus may be trying to convey in the story. Read your own meaning into the characters.

JOURNALING

Again let pen meet paper and take time to describe your portrayal of the younger son's position in the painting and in the story. What does his posture tell you about the condition of his heart? Write any feelings of inner or outer identification with him. Continue to write, mindful of some of your own leavings and returnings, even if they are painful. Try to capture your experience and your feelings in words without looking for perfection. Stay with the real question and write. As a daughter or son, what is stirred in you because of this young man?

> *I learned to get out of the way and let the creative force work through me. I learned to just show up at the page and write down what I heard. Writing became more like eavesdropping and less like inventing a nuclear bomb. . . . I didn't have to be in the mood. I didn't have to take my emotional temperature to see if inspiration was pending. I simply wrote. No negotiations. Good? Bad? None of my business. I wasn't doing it. By resigning as the self-conscious author, I wrote freely.*

—From *The Artist's Way: A Spiritual Path to Higher Creativity* by Julia Cameron, 1992, Jeremy P. Tarcher/Putnam, New York, pp. xiv–xv.

COMMUNING

Voice your heart's response to the One who, no matter how great the ache, allowed you the space to leave without revoking the blessing. And if you are still away, voice the feelings evoked in your heart right now.

If you remember the ever-outstretched arm extended to you in unrestrained welcome, and if you ever feel the hand of Unconditional Love set itself securely on your back, give thanks for being safely *home* once again.

Heart speaks to heart.

We keep silence. Help us to save ourselves by forgetting ourselves. In every experience and thought, bring us to the certain knowledge that we are children of the infinite.

—From *Always We Begin Again: The Benedictine Way of Living* by John McQuiston II, 1996, Morehouse Publishing, Harrisburg, PA, p. 74.

A WISDOM PRACTICE FOR THOSE ON
A SPIRITUAL JOURNEY

Practice #2—CELEBRATION

"A festival is a sign of heaven. It symbolises our deepest aspiration—an experience of total communion" (Vanier, Jean. *Community and Growth*, London: Darton, Longman, and Todd, 2nd revised edition, 1989). The old father in the parable spontaneously knew the appropriate response to a long-desired homecoming. He ordered the servants to "kill the fatted calf and prepare a feast." We aren't told whether or not the contrite runaway was ready to be celebrated as "a beloved with whom there is total communion." But we often can identify with a certain shameful reluctance in ourselves to be celebrated with similar unconditional affection.

In the university setting I lost the real meaning of "festival," but the simple gestures of love and affirmation at Daybreak remind me that celebration is much more than a party or a spectacle. I'm touched when we pause at the end of a delicious, noisy birthday meal and each one announces to the celebrant unique gratitude for his or her life. I'm moved when following a death we gather to tell stories, laugh, cry, and remember together. I'm touched each spring when Ellen's parents arrive with several others from the Khahila to share the Seder supper and point us to God's presence through the history of the "chosen people." And there is real joy when Friday night worship ends and people spontaneously begin to dance during the final hymn! Celebrating is rejoicing in friendship, lifting a glass because of it, affirming each other, and knowing gratitude in our hearts.

As a spiritual discipline of love, celebration is, beyond partying and entertaining, a well-prepared meeting of wonderment and friendship. Utilize your creativity to fashion simple "fiestas" to overtly affirm, bless, and lift up a loved one. And when you are the one being celebrated, really try to be simple and receive true nourishment for your unsteady heart.

CHAPTER 3

FROM L'ARCHE TO
A SECOND LONELINESS

Sing and dance together and be joyous,
but let each one of you be alone.
Even as the strings of a lute are alone
though they quiver with the same music.
Stand together yet not too near together
for the pillars of the temple stand apart,
and the oak tree and the cypress
grow not in each other's shadow.

—From *The Prophet* by Kahlil Gibran, 1951, Alfred A. Knopf,
New York, pp. 15–16.

My honeymoon at L'Arche lasted a little more than a year. Then the old demons returned and I began to struggle with the knowledge of how I was clinging to my selfish needs. I yearned to live my affective life in a new way, as an expression of something beyond, something bigger and wider than my own little life, but there was a huge resistance within me to let go of old patterns. I slowly became aware, but only in my head, of something about "the first love" and "the second love." Let me explain.

I became more and more intellectually clear that the first love comes from the ultimate life force we call God, who has loved me unconditionally before others knew or loved me. "I have loved you with an everlasting love." And I saw that the second love, the love of parents, family, and friends, was only a modified expression of the first love.

I reasoned that the source of my suffering was the fact that I expected from the second love what only the first love could give. When I hoped for total self-giving and unconditional love from another human being who was imperfect and limited in ability to love, I was asking for the impossible. I knew from experience that the more I demanded, the more others moved away, cut loose, got angry, or left me, and the more I experienced anguish and the pain of rejection. But I felt helpless to change my behavior.

I had never been clear about all this before my time with L'Arche. I always knew that my lifelong struggle was a cry for affection but I didn't realize that I was expecting a first love from those who could only respond with a second love. Clinging to this way of emotional survival at L'Arche Daybreak I sought warm, intimate friendships with people as a way of finding "home." I invested myself in the community and in relationships with people and it worked for a while. During my second year, however, I experienced a very concrete breakage with my best friend. At that moment my whole world came crashing down and it seemed as though all the losses of my whole life came back to haunt me. I completely lost all my bearings as well as my sense of personal integration in Church and community. I cannot express to you how hard it was to suddenly realize that precisely where I had begun to find home, I suddenly discovered a profound loneliness and anguish.

Life may be brimming over with experiences, but somewhere, deep inside, all of us carry a vast and fruitful loneliness wherever we go.

—From *An Interrupted Life, and Letters from Westerbork* by Etty Hillesum, 1996, Henry Holt and Company, New York, p. 93.

I was in agony, shut down, and unable to function. As much as I wanted to work this out in the context of my newfound home, I knew from my training as a psychologist that the community was unable to give me needed professional support and distance to see my situation more clearly. So I left Daybreak to live and come to grips with my struggle in another therapeutic community, in Winnipeg, Manitoba. I was deeply convinced that I was there in order to deepen what it meant for me to be in L'Arche. It was a very, very hard time for me, alone and away from my community while desiring to be there more than ever. This experience would gradually put me in touch with the search for home that was much deeper than friends, intimacy, and safety.

Struggling with this whole thing of having passed from loneliness to L'Arche and now being called from L'Arche to a second loneliness to be able to live in L'Arche, I clearly remembered my first experience of seeing Rembrandt's painting of the prodigal son. I knew then that this painting was to have enormous meaning for my life, and so now, in my solitude in Winnipeg, I began to look at and study the painting for long periods of time.

I'm unable to articulate well what happened to me. I was in so much pain and agony, so utterly lonely, but right there I saw before me this father touching his errant child in a way that was a blessing. I identified with the young man and felt how the father touched him with the same affection that I longed for in my heart. That touch of Love was one of recognition by hands, and not so much by eyes or mind but more by heartfelt love. Those hands on my shoulders had something to do with having been known before speech. Living by imagination in the painting moved my grieving heart.

My face is a mask I order to say nothing
  About the fragile feelings hiding in my soul.

—Glen Lazore (Mohawk)

I've been looking at this picture for many years now and it has accompanied me through all the passages I've spoken about: from the loneliness to L'Arche and from L'Arche to the second loneliness, as well as from the second love to the first love. And with my growing awareness, I still believe that this painting holds more for me that is yet to be fully revealed. These insights are in the world of the intellect, but I do believe they help me live the deep emotions of my life.

Primal love, the first unconditional love of the Source of all life, is only reflected to me through limited people: a human mother and father, grandparents, siblings, and mentors. Even though I know that I was knitted together in my mother's womb and totally loved by God, my father was very authoritarian and my mother was terribly scrupulous. Although my parents graced me with enormous love throughout their lives, my initial experiences of the Creator's unconditional love came to me from a nervous, scrupulous woman whose many fears prevented her from freely holding and touching me, and from a father who gave me the strong message that I was to make it in the world and become a professor. God's first unconditional love doesn't radiate too well through two such parents. They were both wonderful people for whom I am eternally grateful, but they were nevertheless broken people and limited people. They loved me with all their ability and they also wounded me. Their love is but a reflection of that unlimited love that already embraced me prior to their knowledge or love of me.

> *Here is the insight most central to spiritual experience: we are known in detail and depth by the love that created and sustains us, known as members of a community of creation that depends on us and on which we depend. This love knows our limits as well as our potential, our capacity for evil as well as good, the persistent self-centeredness with which we exploit the community for our own ends. Yet, as love, it does not seek to confine or manipulate us. Instead, it offers us the constant grace of self-knowledge and acceptance that can liberate us to live a larger love.*
>
> —From *To Know as We Are Known: Education as a Spiritual Journey* by Parker J. Palmer, 1983, HarperCollins, New York, p. 11.

Parental love is a limited reflection of an unlimited love. In the experience of parental love I was wounded as were you, and every other human being. Most parents are the best and the greatest, but in the human experience, parents are also very, very broken people. As much as they desire to give their children the very best, their own brokenness prevents them from being able to do it, and against their own desires they communicate limited love.

Partly for this reason all of us feel the desire to search beyond home for our belovedness, and we generally get caught in many of the cultural movements that exist around us. A dissipated life is one in which we consciously or unconsciously live with the questions "What do you think of me? Look at me! Look at what I'm doing! Look at what I have! Aren't I great? Do you think I'm OK? Do you accept me? Do you see me as good? Do you like me? Do you love me?"

We work tirelessly to present ourselves in a good light before others in the false belief that our identity comes from who we are in *their* eyes, or from what we do or what we have. We look to people outside ourselves to tell us if we are unique, acceptable, and good. We need to know from those around us if we pass the test of being someone unique and lovable. This thinking is encouraged by the world in which we live: How much money does he make? What does she own? Who does he know? Is she famous? What can he do for me? What are they writing about her? Whose arm can he twist? If I don't *do* well or *have* enough money, success, or a good reputation, then I am nothing.

These cultural illusions fill the world in which we live and profoundly influence how we feel about ourselves. They warn us:

> You are what you *do* (lawyer, mother, CEO, teacher, caregiver, scientist, or unskilled laborer), so do something relevant!
>
> You are what you *have* (wealth, education, power, popularity, handicap, nothing), so get busy and acquire all you can!
>
> You are what *others think of you* (kind, mean, saintly, loving, stupid), so act properly and gain respect!

Movies, art, and entertainment support these illusions and are forms of manipulation. We are treated endlessly to visions of people who don't know who they are, acting out their dreams for acceptance. We watch as caressing degenerates into grasping, and kissing evolves to biting. Sexual violence follows from the need we have for others to conform to our out-of-control human needs. Seldom is there free giving and receiving but rather we cling to the selfish and possessive expression of our personal needs. The whole area of body and of sexuality is at the center of our search for our true self. That's why we're challenged to gradually move from a dissipated life to a more contained life, not in a prudish way, but because a true identity begets the precious gift of true intimacy.

> *We too often feel that God's love for us is conditional like our love is for others. We have made God in our image rather than seeing ourselves in God's image. . . . Ours is a culture of achievement, and we carry over these attitudes to our relationship with God. We work ourselves to a frazzle trying to impress everyone including God . . . We can believe that our relationship with God, our standing before God, has got nothing to do with our performance, our works.*

—From *God Has a Dream: A Vision of Hope for Our Times* by Desmond Tutu, 2004, Image Doubleday, New York, p. 32.

The life of Jesus refutes this dark world of illusion that entraps us. To return home is to turn from these illusions, from dissipation, and from our desperate attempts to live up to others' expectations. We are not what we do. We are not what we have. We are not what others think of us. Coming home is claiming the truth. I am the beloved child of a loving Creator. We no longer have to beg for permission from the world to exist.

I was fired from a job when I was sixteen years old and was devastated. My entire personal worth was laid waste. My mother found me crying in my upstairs room. . . . I told her what happened. . . . She sat down on my bed and took me into her arms. "Fired? Fired?" she laughed. "What the hell is that? Nothing. Tomorrow you'll go looking for another job. That's all." She dabbed at my tears with her handkerchief. ". . . Remember, you were looking for a job when you found the one you just lost. So you'll just be looking for a job one more time." She laughed at her wisdom and my youthful consternation. "And think about it, if you ever get fired again, the boss won't be getting a cherry. You've been through it once, and survived."

—From *Wouldn't Take Nothing for My Journey Now* by Maya Angelou, 1993, Random House, New York, p. 80.

Our choices for a life of either dissipation or containment make a huge difference when it comes to our experience of undeserved suffering. Living our truth in containment allows us to suffer in a whole new way. If, for example, my heart is broken in a relationship, I naturally feel very insecure and I tend to have feelings of low self-esteem and failure as well as hurt and disillusionment. I may want to die, which says much about how I value my life. I have many mixed feelings of the good and the ugly, and my feelings are real. But even when it hurts immensely and I move toward depression, this amazing truth about who I really am remains. I am loved. I know this not because of an intellectual or psychological experience, but I know it from a place deep within. I am a good person, known and cherished by the One who brought me to my existence. Before I was hurt, I was a beloved. I always have the option, despite my wounded feelings, to turn and reclaim who I really am. This truth about myself that I claim has been constant, a given, since before I was born. I *am* the favored child of a loving Creator.

Jesus knew who he was and was thus able to live the days of his passion in agony and peace. He didn't need to blame others or himself, because he understood the brokenness of those who caused him pain. Jesus, in the knowledge that he was loved, was able to stand in his pain and forgive those who wounded him.

For me the experience of homecoming is around my deep need for affection, which expresses itself in many ways in my heart and body. This human longing often projects me into the world of fantasy where yearning, loneliness, lust, anger, hurt, and revenge overwhelm me. Because of what I know to be true, and in the midst of my pain, I may reflect, "Right here is my opportunity to return. Right at this point I can gently turn back to the truth. I haven't come home yet. Yes, I have a body and my body is good and I can touch people and be touched. But I have to touch and be touched from the place of my belovedness more than from the place of my need."

Jesus said, "As the Father loves me, so I also love you." Clinging to the knowledge of being first of all a beloved son who is not fully home yet holds me from slipping into a life of total dissipation. I may not yet be fully contained, but that doesn't change the fact that my body is a temple where the creative Spirit resides. It doesn't change the fact that, like Jesus, I am a beloved son of God. That is the truth.

A contained life is returning to and living this primal truth. It's a real struggle to bring our whole selves home and it is best accomplished gently and gradually. Jesus tells us it is a narrow path, meaning that we slip off occasionally, and that is OK. The whole course of the spiritual life is falling off, and returning, slipping away from the truth and turning back to it, leaving and returning. So in our leaving, as much as in our returning, we must try to remember that we are blessed, loved, cherished, and waited for by the One whose love doesn't change.

> *Dear Child of God, in our world it is often hard to remember that God loves you just as you are. God loves you not because you are good. No, God loves you, period. God loves us not because we are lovable. No, we are lovable precisely because God loves us. It is marvellous when you come to understand that you are accepted for who you are, apart from any achievement. It is so liberating.*

—From *God Has a Dream: A Vision of Hope for Our Time* by Desmond Tutu, 2004, Image Doubleday, New York, pp. 31–32.

Loving our incarnate selves, body and heart, is all about homecoming. It is the gathering of everything into oneness. As body, mind, and heart become one, the dissipation falls away and we feel more whole, more contained, more one with self and the universe. It is from there we tenderly touch another, embrace her, wash and care for his body, hold her, love him, kiss her, and feel free. In that place we no longer need the other to tell us who we are or to give us an identity. Like Jesus, we know who we are, children forever loved by our personal God.

Returning, then, is moving toward containment, toward home, holding fast to our true identity as the beloved of Love Divine. We might know it with our minds, but our bodies often take us by another way, running around out of control and all over the place. The spiritual life is a life in which we continually turn toward the truth, toward home, and hopefully those who love us help us turn back to ourselves, as the favored daughters or sons of the Spirit of Love.

When you go back to South Africa and stand up to preach and teach, remember always that each person sits next to their own pool of tears.

—From *Listening to the Ground* by Trevor Hudson, 2007, Upper Room Books.

My crisis with my friend precipitated my entry into a new loneliness unlike my former loneliness at Harvard and Yale. This second loneliness was much more radical and existential; something about going beyond the interpersonal into the mystical, and trusting that by giving over my specific attachment and need for my friend, something larger would be given. It was really about the Divine becoming the center of my life. It had to do with Jesus' invitation in Scripture, "Leave your father, leave your mother, leave your brother, leave your sister, leave your friends, and you will have a hundred brothers, and sisters, and friends." I must dare to speak of it because "the second loneliness" is a contemporary way to describe the oldest mystical traditions about the spiritual life. The dark night of the soul is another image of the second loneliness. In the experience of the dark night, Saint John of the Cross gradually understood that the Spirit will never be owned or grasped in the affections of the human heart because God's Spirit is so much greater than our human capacity.

My most profound learning from this time was about the

passage from that first loneliness of emotionally unsatisfying friendships to the second loneliness of a demanding intimacy with Love Itself. This deeper communion with God did not invite me to renounce friendship altogether, but it challenged me to let go of certain emotional, intellectual, and affective satisfactions. This second loneliness is not something for me to overcome but to live, standing up and as a full human being. This second loneliness is one that sets me interiorly on the road to communion with the Divine and at the same time brings me in touch with my deepest self in relationship with brothers, sisters, and good friends.

> *The first call is frequently to follow Jesus or to prepare ourselves to do wonderful and noble things for the Kingdom. We are appreciated and admired by family, by friends, or by the community. The second call comes later, when we accept that we cannot do big or heroic things for Jesus; it is a time of renunciation, humiliation, and humility.*
>
> —From *Community and Growth* by Jean Vanier, 1979, Darton, Longman, and Todd, London, p. 139.

It is paradoxical but real. The more I find intimacy with the Creator of my life, the more loneliness I experience. And at the very same time this loneliness offers me a new sense of belonging to the family of Divine Love that is much greater and more intimate than any belonging that the world can offer. The world of communion with the Great Spirit that is truly experienced as a world of loneliness and the highest level of separation from my human yearning to be loved, is also revealed to me as the highest level of belonging to the Creator of the galaxies and being part of the human race.

In the second loneliness, the greatest loneliness and the greatest solidarity with the Divine Lover and with the human condition are coming together. Once I accept this passage as a call to be deeply, deeply connected with Unconditional Love, with my own fragile humanity, and with brothers and sisters everywhere, something shifts within. Allowing God's first love to be primary for me changes the way I live my existential loneliness, mainly because I am more rooted in the truth, and thus more able to live my suffering while standing as a full, human person.

In the deeps are the violence and terror of which psychology has warned us. But if you ride these monsters down, if you drop with them farther over the world's rim, you find what our sciences cannot locate or name, the substrate, the ocean or matrix or ether which buoys the rest, which gives goodness its power for good, and evil its power of evil, the unified field: our complex and inexplicable caring for each other, and for our life together here. This is given. It is not learned.

—From *Teaching a Stone to Talk* by Annie Dillard, 1982, HarperCollins, New York, pp. 94–95.

This is the reason I suggested earlier that we not enter the story of the prodigal son alone, but rather bring others with us into it. Each of us is conscious that we are surrounded by a lonely, suffering world of people. If we are to touch our own, unique second loneliness, we need to be in touch with the larger picture of the human condition of which we are part. So, once again, let me ask you to try to see yourself and your unique life as one that is in solidarity with many others in the world. Otherwise your life remains small, isolated, uninteresting. You and I, in our limited communities of family and church, are broken, little people. Somehow, with our more scientific and cosmic worldview, we are invited to break through to a broader communion with others in the world and with the holy One of the universe.

If I encourage you to live the great struggle of your life and your pain standing up, I do so trusting that we are in solidarity with something larger than our individuality. Mary stood under the Cross. *Stabat mater* is the Latin for "the standing mother." Under the Cross she didn't faint but stood with her son and with the world in her suffering. I confess to you that I cannot fully do it, but I know for sure that I'm called to stand, to look upon the world and proclaim what our humanity is really about. We are very small and little—that's the mystery. Hopefully my personal experience and the many reflections that follow in this book will generate in you the desire to make your own personal connection with the Gospel story.

I remember the day a young engineer came to me and said, "Henri, something really powerful happened to me. I was driving on the highway in a car and I felt terribly lonely and then an inner voice, perhaps the voice of Jesus, seemed to say to me, 'Why don't you take this dirt road, then step out of your car, and we'll walk together.' So I left my car behind and I was feeling very alone. I tried to imagine that Jesus and I were walking together, but I felt incredibly lonely. At the very same moment I knew that he was speaking to me in my heart. And I also knew in a flash that I was closer to him than ever before. It's hard to explain but that encounter was so real for me. I know I'll never be the same because of it."

This little story reminds me of how a human life is a life that moves from the first loneliness of driving on the highway in alienation to the second loneliness of walking alone with Jesus, trusting that He is enough. Unmet needs continue to scream from within but we no longer demand healing from lovers and friends.

My life in L'Arche became the way for me to encounter the central struggle of my life, namely the second loneliness revealed to me by experience and by the parable of the prodigal son. Through them I've touched God's first, unconditional love. The story and the painting reveal to me that it is possible to experience goodness, friendship, and affection without my whole life becoming dependent upon it. It is also possible to feel rejected and abandoned without being destroyed. There's nothing as painful as being rejected, but if it is lived against the background of the first love, it becomes possible to survive. This is a story of the spiritual life.

As a heart longs for flowing streams,
so longs my soul for You
O Beloved.
My soul thirsts for the Beloved,
for the Living Water.
When may I come and behold
your face?
Tears have been my only nourishment
day and night
While friends ask continually,
"Where is the Beloved of your
heart?"

—From *Psalms for Praying* by Nan C. Merrill, 1996, The Continuum International Publishing Group, New York, Psalm 42, p. 81.

Look closely at Rembrandt's painting and study it, alone and with other spiritual searchers like yourself. Try to grasp that this practically blind father, who recognizes his beloved child not so much by seeing as by touching, has something very primal to do with real human loving and being loved. It has nothing to do with declarations or statements or arguments. The father's love is before speech. This intimate connection with unconditional love sends us back to our very first experience of being loved by the way we were touched. The initial touch by Divine Love and by our parents entered into our consciousness and offered us our first sense of being loved uniquely, and it gave us our first experience of home, of belonging, of safety and protection. Throughout our lives it seems we continue to yearn for that first touch that reassured us that we were indeed beloved.

> *It doesn't interest me what you do for a living. I want to know what you ache for, and if you dare to dream of meeting your heart's longing. . . . I want to know if you will risk looking like a fool for love, for your dream, for the adventure of being alive. . . . I want to know if you have touched the center of your own sorrow, if you have been opened by life's betrayals or have become shrivelled and closed from fear of further pain. I want to know if you can sit with pain, mine or your own, without moving to hide it or fade it or fix it. . . . I want to know if you can disappoint another to be true to yourself.*

—From *The Invitation* by Oriah Mountain Dreamer, 1999, HarperSanFrancisco, San Francisco, p. 1.

As I've "lived" these past years with the painting, I read hundreds of exegetical stories about it. The variations of people's interpretations, from the most sociological to the most intimate, are legion, and some of them boggle the imagination. Because it is so open-ended, this is one of the greatest stories in the Gospel and in literature as a whole. That's encouraging because it implies that each one of us is also free to make our own exegesis. I'm trying to explain mine in what I've already written about my experience, and that's also why my comments about the prodigal son have a lot to do with me. But the beauty is that there is meaning for your life and your story, too, because every human life has its own exegetical possibilities. Your life is profoundly important, so I beg you to take yourself very seriously in the light of this exegetical story that has meaning for your most intimate human journey.

LISTENING

Become still. Listen to the hearts of the people in the parable and become conscious of their loneliness. Move slowly back to the painting, asking for new eyes to see and new ears to hear the heart-cries of each one. Look and listen with your heart and feel their individual pain. Perhaps their loneliness reaches into yours. In this sacred context don't be afraid to give yourself time to feel your own existential loneliness as a full member of the human family.

JOURNALING

With pen in hand, attempt to translate your thoughts and feelings into words for your journal. Move deeply into your heart and write of your experiences of loneliness in relationships and in the absence of relationships. How does loneliness affect your sense of yourself? Dare to express yourself and don't stop until you do. Finish by expressing how the story and the painting give light to your precious life.

COMMUNING

Imagine yourself in the very presence of your loving Creator and let your heart speak. Name your aloneness and your struggle to find love, to give love, and to love yourself. Honestly identify yourself as a victim of not having been loved perfectly, and ask for help to reclaim your lovableness. Honestly identify how you have wounded others, and with confidence ask pardon. Express your heartfelt longing to rest secure again in the embrace of the One who loves you with an everlasting love. Be still, and listen for the response.

Heart speaks to heart.

The word humility, like the human, comes from humas, *or earth. We are most human when we do no great things. We are not so important; we are simply dust and spirit—at best, loving mid- wives, participants in a process much larger than we. If we are quiet and listen and feel how things move, perhaps we will be wise enough to put our hands on what waits to be born, and bless it with kindness and care.*

—From *Sabbath: Restoring the Sacred Rhythm of Rest* by Wayne Muller, 1999, Bantam Books, New York, p. 176.

A WISDOM PRACTICE FOR THOSE ON
A SPIRITUAL JOURNEY

Practice #3—CLAIM YOUR TRUE IDENTITY

The whole parable is about the journey of an arrogant, lost, and set-free adolescent finding the path to mature adulthood. He thinks he knows the way to unlimited pleasure but gets painfully lost along the way. The story ends as he falteringly "claims" his true belonging and "tastes" the truth of who he really is—a beloved child.

Personally, as my struggle reveals, I don't often "feel" like a beloved child of God. But I *know* that that is my most primal identity and I know that I must choose it above and beyond my hesitations.

Strong emotions, self-rejection, and even self-hatred justifiably toss you about, but you are free to respond as you will. You are *not* what others, or even you, think about yourself. You are *not* what you do. You are *not* what you have. You are a full member of the human family, having been known before you were conceived and molded in your mother's womb. In times when you feel bad about yourself, try to choose to remain true to the truth of who you really are. Look in the mirror each day and claim your true identity. Act ahead of your feelings and trust that one day your feelings will match your convictions. Choose now and continue to choose this incredible truth. As a spiritual practice claim and reclaim your primal identity as beloved daughter or son of a personal Creator.

PART II

THE
INVISIBLE EXILE
OF
RESENTMENT

CHAPTER 4

THE ELDER SON

A s I said earlier, I knew that besides the runaway, there was also an elder son in me that needed to return home. It is my belief that the eldest in the story of the prodigal son is the figure standing to the right of the father in the painting. Once again I invite you to situate yourself in the small center where you live your unique life, with all your family, friends, brothers, and sisters on the planet around you. Now listening from your deepest heart, journey with me into the story of the other sibling as paraphrased from the parable. (The full text is in Luke 15:11–32.)

The elder son, returning from his work in the fields, heard a commotion.

When he inquired, one of the servants told him, "Your brother is home, safe and sound. Your father has killed the fatted calf and ordered a celebration."

The elder son was angry and refused to go in.

His father came out and urged him to attend the feast.

When we listen to a sentence, a story, or a parable not simply to be instructed, informed, or inspired but to be formed into a truly obedient person, then the Book offers trustworthy spiritual insight. The daily practice of lectio divina (sacred reading), over time, transforms our personal identity, our actions, and our common life of faith. . . . Scripture does have a personal word for us, yet knowledge of historic Christian teaching helps us avoid the easy trap of wanting scripture to support our own designs.

—From *Spiritual Direction: Wisdom for the Long Walk of Faith* by Henri J. M. Nouwen, 2006, HarperSanFrancisco, San Francisco, p. xviii.

But the young man retorted, "All these years I have slaved for you and never once disobeyed you. Yet you never offered me so much as a kid for me to celebrate with my friends. Now, for this son of yours, coming home after swallowing up your property—he and his loose women—you kill the fatted calf?"

The father responded, "My son, you have always been with me. All I have is yours. And it is also right to celebrate and rejoice, because your brother was dead, and has come to life. He was lost and is found."

I'm happy to reflect with you what I'm learning about the elder son and all he represents for us in our own lives. His most visible characteristic is that he did not run away but stayed home. Consider this carefully. This young person is the one who, from an objective perspective, did everything right. He did not take off, but rather he worked hard and took care of his father's estate. He was obedient and dutiful, committed and faithful. It is obvious that the gift of the eldest was his faithfulness. The father relied on him and on his steady, hard work to keep the estate going. Undoubtedly, because of this work, the family prospered.

However, all was not as perfect as it seemed. I say this because even though he did stay home, it is apparent that he had wandered far away in his mind and heart. Listen carefully to his words: "All these years I have slaved for you and never once disobeyed any of your orders. And yet you never offered me so much as a kid for me to celebrate with my friends." Hear his "earning" as opposed to "intimacy" mentality. Hear his bitterness and resentment.

You don't choose your family. They are God's gift to you, as you are to them. Perhaps if we could we might have chosen different brothers and sisters. Fortunately or unfortunately we can't. We have them as they have us. And no matter how your brother may be, you can't renounce him. . . . Can you imagine what would happen in this world if we accepted that fact about ourselves—that whether we like it or not we are members of one family?

—From *God Has a Dream: A Vision of Hope for Our Time* by Desmond Tutu, 2004, Doubleday, New York, p. 22.

This was not a happy young man. He harbored dark feelings as well as angry thoughts about the one in the family who had grabbed the inheritance and run off to satisfy selfish desires. We quickly see that the faithfulness of this stay-at-home adult child wasn't entirely pure. On the contrary it was loaded. I can imagine his inner monologue directed toward his father: "Why on earth would you give that worthless good-for-nothing so much of *our* money? How could you bow to such arrogance and disrespect? Don't you even 'get it' that he's a loser? Can't you appreciate that I am here working my head off for you while he goes out and does all those despicable things? Why should I have to stay and work while he spends our money to dissipate himself? You have no expectations of him, whereas you and everyone else *expect* me to be dutiful."

It is interesting to note right here how the younger son got lost in quite a spectacular way. He was completely open about his desire to move far away into a dissipated lifestyle of greed and lust, having his women, gambling, and finally losing everything including himself. His departure implies that he knew he was lost and so did everybody else! And in the end, he was also overt about his return home. He seemed unashamed about his choices and felt no need to hide his adulterous lifestyle. Family image and a good reputation weren't priorities for him.

On the other hand, the elder son's story that looks so righteous on the surface was far from peaceful. Yes, he *was* obedient, but his actions were tempered with reticence, and without any real interaction with his father. His relationship to his father showed no signs of being free or flowing, nor was it really safe either. Listen very carefully to his words about his younger brother: "This son of yours who lived a loose life with those women." He doesn't say, "my brother." He says, "this son of yours."

And the father answers, "Your brother has returned."

Note how one of the characteristics of the elder's resentment is separation from any identification with his younger sibling. He is not even close to accepting his brother as his own flesh and blood, nor as the one with whom he grew up, played, and shared a significant history. No, he's inwardly raging with anger and judgment: "that son of yours. *I* am not that way. *He* is that way. And yet you throw *him* a big party and invite lots of people, but *I* do all the hard work around here. All our other siblings with their families and friends will arrive and party and have a wonderful day without ever knowing how much *I* had to do to make the whole party possible. After they talk and party they'll leave the place in a mess and *I'll* do the clean-up, because *I'm* the one who's responsible for it all."

Rembrandt sensed the deepest meaning of this when he painted the elder son at the side of the platform where the younger son is received in the father's joy. He didn't depict the celebration, with its musicians and dancers; they were merely the external signs of the father's joy. . . . In place of the party, Rembrandt painted light, the radiant light that envelops both father and son. The joy that Rembrandt portrays is the still joy that belongs to God's house. . . . The elder son stands outside the circle of this love, refusing to enter. The light on his face makes it clear that he, too, is called to the light, but he cannot be forced.

—From *The Return of the Prodigal Son: A Story of Homecoming* by Henri J. M. Nouwen, 1992, Doubleday, New York, p. 69.

The father did not react to the darkness in his eldest son but rather approached him in a spirit of collaboration for the building up of the estate over many years. "All that is mine is yours," says his father. There is a wonderful intimacy here, an affection and gratitude on the part of the father for his eldest son. Of course it was difficult for the young man to stay in the family home, but being there was also an opportunity for him to cooperate with his father and to become an equal player in carrying responsibility. Surely there were differences between the two of them. Like life, it wasn't simple, but the partnership held potential for growth and fulfillment at the same time. Instead, this son looked away from his privileged partnership, gave resentment a place in his heart, and was less and less able to situate himself uniquely in the family. No wonder he was unable to celebrate his brother's return!

Resentment is one of the most pervasive evils of our time. Resentment is rampant in our society. Resentment is very pernicious and very, very destructive, and you and I are seldom free from it.

I know a really wonderful teacher who's done wonders with some of the children she's taught. She's experienced, dedicated, and excellent in the classroom. In any setting with peers, however, she's the one who is always busy, always doing for others, and always fussing about details around the gathering. It's clear that she doesn't feel comfortable as part of a circle of equals. This lady transforms every social situation into a job by bustling about in the group, helping people with their coats, seeing that everyone has something to eat or drink, tidying up, doing the dishes, but never taking time to really be relaxed and present to others or enjoy herself. I hear people say of her, "She's so good, always sacrificing herself and helping get things done!" The difficulty is that that kind of affirmation never allows her to become aware that she is being praised for actions that stem from not feeling equal to others in the group, and possibly from deep-seated resentment.

Resentment, the curse of the faithful, the virtuous, the obedient, and the hardworking, settles itself in the human heart and causes havoc. That is why it's important to think and reflect upon it. All of us who give our lives for loved ones, work hard, and objectively have many virtues to be praised, are sometimes not really free from the burden of resentment in our hearts.

Belonging calls forth what is most beautiful in our capacity to love and accept others but it also can awaken anger, jealousy, violence, and the refusal to cooperate.

—From *Becoming Human* by Jean Vanier, 1998, House of Anansi Press, Toronto, p. 58.

Each of us knows anger, and anger is real. We are powerless to simply turn it off and it fills our inner space with added distress. So, what can we do about our anger? Psychology tells us that if we are in touch with our angry feelings, name them, and even perhaps lash out, the anger loses some of its power over us. We are encouraged to "work with" our anger, enter into our reasons for being upset, and try to engage with those who wound us. "Damn it! I'm furious with you! But I beg you to talk with me about what has happened. Should we invite someone to help us talk to each other? How can we come to terms with this upset so we can each get on with our lives?" This type of action prevents resentment from building a home in our hearts.

But when, in our efforts to be pious, we eat up the angry feelings and do not make them known, resentment begins. One begins feeling a little angry but does nothing about it. With time, as unattended anger builds in a given relationship or life situation, one becomes progressively more irate. The constant swallowing of negative feelings causes them to pervade the inner universe and usurp one's power to relate in a truly loving way. Gradually it is no longer hot anger, but it grows cold and settles itself deep into the innermost heart. And over the long term, resentment becomes a way of being.

*A brother who was insulted by another brother came to Abba
Sisoes, and said to him: "I was hurt by my brother and I want to
avenge myself."*

*The old man tried to console him and said: "Don't do that, my
child. Rather leave vengeance to God."*

But he said: "I will not quit until I avenge myself."

*Then the old man said: "Let us pray, brother"; and standing
up, he said, "O God, we no longer need you to take care of us
since we now avenge ourselves."*

*Hearing these words, the brother fell at the feet of the old man
and said: "I am not going to fight with my brother anymore.
Forgive me, Abba."*

—From *Desert Wisdom*, by Yushi Nomura, ed., 1982, Orbis Books,
Maryknoll, NY, p. 53.

Resentment is cold anger. That's what it is. The greatest difficulty with resentment is that it's very hidden and interior as
opposed to being overt. It has the potential to present itself as
holiness and that makes it even more pernicious. Resentment
resides in the very depths of our hearts, sitting in our bones and
our flesh while we are mostly unaware of its presence. Whereas
we might imagine that we are faithful and good, we may in fact
be very lost in a much deeper way than someone who is overtly
acting out. The younger son in the story goes out, makes a fool
of himself, and then returns. That's a very clear-cut movement.
But the resentful person objectively never gets lost in the first
place, so what does returning look like for such a one? Perhaps
it is much harder to heal from resentment than from dissipation.

The elder son epitomizes something important in his response to his life situation. Without appreciation for his good

fortune and the promise of a secure future as overseer of the land, he's basically a frustrated, angry, and unhappy young man. He's oblivious to the fact that he probably feels insecure outside the safety of his own home. In the harshness of his judgments, he's not conscious that he probably would be threatened to face his father and ask for money to travel and see the world. He's blind to the way in which he stayed home, worked hard, and acted politely enough, but without his heart being engaged. And he's probably the only one who hasn't recognized his frozen smile as a cover-up for the anger that seeps out in all his interactions.

So the one in the story who in many respects did the objectively good thing, the person who was praised as the "good son" as compared with the "bad one," the one who stayed home, worked hard, was obedient to the old father, and was faithful, ended up being as lost spiritually as the younger guy who ran off and dissipated his inheritance. But the elder was lost in a very different and complex way. Unlike the dissipation of the younger, the elder was far away from home emotionally because of resentment.

What would constitute his return? What if he experienced a breakthrough and on the other hand said, "I'm so glad I was always obedient and I listened to you, and never once disobeyed your wishes. It's been hard but I've learned so much and I recognize how fruitful our collaboration has been." I can only imagine how differently he would approach his life. When the story ends, it seems that he remains full of angry virtue, but there is always hope of his possible return.

Where do people find the courage to live divided no more . . . ? In the Rosa Parks story, that insight emerges in a wonderful way. After she had sat at the front of the bus for a while, the police came

*aboard and said, "You know, if you continue to sit there, we're
going to have to throw you in jail." Rosa Parks replied, "You may
do that . . . ," which is a very polite way of saying, "What could
your jail of stone and steel possibly mean to me, compared to the
self-imposed imprisonment I've suffered for forty years—the prison
I've just walked out of by refusing to conspire any longer with this
racist system?"*

—From *Let Your Life Speak: Listening for the Voice of Vocation* by Parker J.
Palmer, 2000, Jossey-Bass, San Francisco, p. 34.

LISTENING

In your quiet space take a moment to inhale outer and inner
silence, while you exhale outer and inner noise. Gradually focus
your attention on the elder son in the parable. Listen to what
you are thinking when you look at him. What do his words and
his silence say to you? Consider if the bitterness in his heart
touches something in yours. Converse with him and discover
how he thinks and feels. Listen and be open to the ways that
you and he are alike.

JOURNALING

Begin by listing everything in Rembrandt's painting that distin-
guishes the elder sibling from the others in the parable. Pause.
Now venture back into Chapter Four and complete your list
with any other insights about him that are there. Pause again.
Next, slowly reread the list, point by point, from the position of

your hidden, inner life. Begin to list the characteristics about yourself that mirror his. Dare to confront yourself in honesty, unarmed and unafraid of your truth. Write what you see in yourself and how you feel about what you see.

> *A period of rest . . . is a spiritual and biological necessity. A lack of dormancy produces confusion and erosion in the life force.*

—From *Sabbath: Restoring the Sacred Rhythm of Rest* by Wayne Muller, 1999, Bantam Books, New York, p. 7.

COMMUNING

Surrender. Speak slowly of all you have written to the Presence of Love that is with you. Point by point give everything into the hands that hold you. Offer your thanks for what you are learning about yourself and about being loved without having to earn it. Ask for the strength to become more aware of the hidden exile of your self-righteousness and judgments. Ask for wisdom and courage. Listen for the response.

Heart speaks to heart.

A WISDOM PRACTICE FOR THOSE ON A SPIRITUAL JOURNEY

Practice #4—LOVE THOSE WHO ARE DIFFERENT

Prevented by resentment from any identification with his younger sibling, the firstborn son indignantly refers his father to "That son of yours . . ." The loving father, without judging either child, gently reminds the elder of his important connection with the younger:

Your *brother* was lost.

I'm getting the message that I'm a beloved child so it's time for me to stop offering friendship to my friends and withholding love from my "enemies." Now I want to recognize many real sisters and brothers from the place of my own acting shamefully and also leaving home. I want to grow in likeness to the father figure in the parable.

Jesus teaches us in the Sermon on the Mount, "Love your enemies." Rationally that makes no sense at all since the enemy is, by definition, the one that we do not love. But Jesus not only spoke this wisdom. He lived it. As disciples, we try to follow his teaching and see ourselves as brothers and sisters in the human family, no better and no worse than any other person. Let us look at the life of Jesus and learn the meaning of his teachings about difficult relationships.

> Do good to those who hate you, bless those who curse
> you, and pray for those who treat you badly.
> Treat others as you would like people to treat you.
> If you love those who love you, what credit can you ex-
> pect? Even sinners love those who love them.
> Instead, love your enemies, and do good to them, and
> lend without any hope of return. You will have great
> reward, and you will be children of the Most High.
> God is kind to the ungrateful and the wicked.
>
> (LUKE 6)

CHAPTER 5

THE HIDDEN EXILE OF RESENTMENT

Once, in talking about the parable to a friend, I was confiding how I sometimes felt a desperate urge to run away to a life of self-indulgence and freedom from commitments. I confessed how, like the prodigal, I longed to break free from places of being known and go off to a foreign land where I could indulge myself and let loose.

Abba Poemen said:
"There is one sort of person
who seems to be silent,
but inwardly criticizes other people.
Such a person is really talking all the time."

—From *Desert Wisdom* by Yushi Nomura, ed., 1982, Orbis Books, Maryknoll, NY, p. 83.

I remember my friend looking at me and saying with great compassion, "Henri, it may be that you think your problem is that of the young runaway in the story, but I'm sitting here listening to you and wondering if you aren't much more like the elder son rather than the younger!" I was shocked! In all my reading of the story I had hardly noticed the elder brother and had never once considered any identification with him as a possibility. But that observation by my friend opened a door for me and allowed me to touch a whole different set of questions from the point of view of the one who was obedient, dutiful, and the eldest in the family. My process of identifying with this person in the story has truly become a source of new, important, and painful memories as well as connections with my own life, beginning in my family of origin.

My own father was one of eleven children, all of whom got married but one. As in many families at that time, there were named or unnamed expectations on the unmarried daughter, the one who stayed home. I can still hear my aunt reiterating how she was giving her life to take care of her aging mother, and I recognized that that was an honorable thing to do. However, it seemed to me as though she wasn't enjoying herself. I know now that she was a very intelligent and articulate woman, and I feel that she had many reasons to be angry. I also believe that she interiorized her anger, eating it up more and more as time went on. Externally she tried to be sweet about it, but meanwhile most of us could see that she wasn't feeling well. Resentment grew in her because in those days there were few ways for her to express herself or to be helped in her lonely journey. All of us knew but no one asked or provided an opening for her to explode, "Yes, I feel used and abused, and furthermore I'm as angry as hell. You people are busy and fulfilled and you never really listen to *me*. Did you ever imagine how hard my life is and how tired I am? Are you aware that I have no privacy and no life of my own? Can you not see that I'm exhausted, upset, frustrated, and angry?"

On the one hand my aunt was generous, but on the other hand her sacrifice was so enormous that she eventually suffered from a buildup of resentment inside. She *was* giving her whole life and we all knew she was determined to do it until her mother died. I remember hearing family members say, "Look how Aunt Clara is doing it all. Isn't that wonderful?" She *was* fulfilling family expectations, but she was also feeling desperate and isolated with her lot in life. I believe she wasn't free or able to find people to help her deal with her lack of freedom and her feelings of being used. Whereas I used to look at my aunt with scorn, today I feel a deep compassion for her and for all she lived in those years with my grandmother.

> *The artistry of the trapeze troupe emerges from a cooperative*
> *effort to create something of fleeting and fragile beauty. It knows*
> *danger but not violence, courage but not conquest, striving for*
> *excellence but not competition, the joy of achievement but not*
> *victory.*
>
> —From *Learning to Fly: Reflections on Fear, Trust, and the Joy of Letting Go*
> by Sam Keen, 1999, Broadway Books, New York.

Furthermore, I personally identify with her as I also identify with this elder brother in the story because I recognize how, over time, there has been a buildup of resentment in me. I am the oldest in our family and I suspect that since my time in university resentment has claimed a piece of my heart, especially in my relationship with my dad. You see, he accomplished his goals late in life by becoming a successful professor of law, and based on his background this rise to fame was quite unusual in his day. My dad was very bright and able to function well in the world of competition. I, as the oldest in our family, seemed to be programmed to believe that I had to be at least as good as my dad. Thus began a sort of lifelong competition with respect to our careers and to most other subjects as well. When I started to study for the priesthood, he began to read theology. Then, when I went into psychology, he began to acquaint himself with that discipline. I felt by the way that he questioned and challenged me, he was vying with me to have the last word on the subject. On the one hand my father was a very loving person, but on the other hand it was as if he most often responded to me with "I could have told you that long ago!" This observation was unique between my father and me and made me frustrated, especially because it wasn't like that between him and my other siblings. I often felt angry, but I swallowed it and never spoke about it to anyone. Today I can speak of it, but while I was in it, I kept it to myself because that is what I thought I should do. It didn't fill my consciousness but the relationship between us wasn't free and flowing either, and I know now that resentment was at work in me.

I also know that since I was a child my heart has consistently yearned for intimacy, and I've always lived as though I had to earn it. Failing to claim so much of what I desired that was actually abundantly present to me, I worked hard to prove myself deserving of the love that I felt I needed to live. So in many respects I identify strongly with the experience of the elder son's work-to-earn-love patterns.

Abba Mios was asked by a soldier whether God would forgive a sinner. After instructing him at some length, the old man asked him: "Tell me, my dear, if your cloak were torn, would you throw

*it away?" "Oh no!" he replied, "I would mend it and wear it
again." The old man said to him: "Well, if you care for your cloak,
will not God show mercy to his own creature?"*

—From *Desert Wisdom* by Yushi Nomura, ed., 1982, Orbis Books,
Maryknoll, NY, p. ii.

When the time came to leave home I happily departed, but I
also very consciously took the time to stay connected, be obedient to my parents' expectations, and be sure that the family
remained as one of my priorities. I was choosing to do what
was *right* and that is why I understand this resentful mentality.
My younger siblings were entirely different from me. They left
home to pursue their goals with much more freedom than me.
At one point one brother went into an incredible crisis, and he
did something that I never could have done. He just let it all
fall apart right in front of our father. I remember how fully he
shared everything with my dad, everything in a most devastating crisis. And there the two of them sat, loving each other with
enormous intimacy like two brothers. My dad spoke so lovingly
about him, and seemed to have no need to compete with him at
all, ever. You can imagine that I had a hard time with that, but
because I was pious, I simply ate it up and never dealt with it.
Now I can say that my faithfulness wasn't free and had little to
do with piety. Despite my angst, I clung to this safe way of looking good and being unfree in my ability to relate easily. Besides
that I harbored jealous and bitter feelings toward my siblings'
ability to act with much more freedom than me, and that had
a profound impact on the way I related with them. Only now I
realize that I can't change that past, but I can respect the individual histories and claim my own freedom in response to my
family now.

I offer this personal struggle simply to demonstrate how hard it was for me to trust my unique place as the eldest son in my family. I seem to have lived my life convincing myself that the work-to-earn-love ethic is what a good life looks like. However, this image for my life has been consistently interrupted, and my ideals torn to shreds. I hear myself complaining, "Why is it that all those damn things keep happening within and around me and I can't live my ideal?" Personal failure, family tragedy, financial struggles, historical disasters, and political disillusionments have each, in time, interrupted my ideal life and caused me grief. Meanwhile, over the course of all these disillusionments, I continued to eat up the anger and allowed resentment to find a perfect home in my heart.

My friend inviting me to focus on the elder sibling led me to the realization that this person lives inside of me, so I understand his experience from within. The eldest child in the parable believed that he had to earn his father's love. "I've done this for you and I've done that, and you haven't recognized me. You haven't given me anything in return." He sees himself in relationship to his father as a boss is with a worker or slave. I also assumed his twisted logic and I know that in doing so I wounded my father and prompted his angry sentiments. "Really, were you expecting a little present from me to prove to you that I love you? Why don't you look at me and trust that I rejoiced in your coming before you were even born? Don't you know that I recognize you as my flesh and blood, that I know you well, and that I love you deeply? Can't you even see that my love has nothing to do with whether you work hard or not? Whether you stay home or not, act faithfully or not, slave for me or not? I love you because you are my firstborn child. You don't have to earn points with me and afterward be rewarded by having a little party. The thought that you have to deserve being my son wounds me. You *are* my son and I love you!"

Thank you, Lord, for the gift of my life thus far. Thank you for your teaching in this parable that opens me to new possibilities for my own life. Send me your loving Spirit of Wisdom to help me listen and identify my resentments with those of the elder son. Show me the signs of my hidden exile from fulfillment because of my self-righteousness and judgments. Help me to not be afraid to seriously consider what I can do about my angers and my fears. I desire to grow in love and acceptance of all my brothers and sisters, as well as of myself, as I am. But I need wisdom, strength, and courage. Please come to me and remain close to me.

—From the tapes of Henri Nouwen's workshop.

Strange how the need to earn love dies hard in me, even though the more I cling to it, the harder it is for me to live my life journey without bitterness. I can't seem to stop working hard to prove something and then search for a rationale that will help me understand "Why do they treat me like that?" or "What more can I do to prove that I deserve more?" or "Why do I have to work so hard to be in this relationship?" I simply don't understand why people don't appreciate how hard I'm trying to be worthy.

Reading often means gathering information, acquiring new insight and knowledge, and mastering a new field. It can lead us to degrees, diplomas, and certificates. Spiritual reading however, is different. It means not simply reading about spiritual things but also reading about spiritual things in a spiritual way. . . . As we read spiritually about spiritual things, we open our hearts to God's voice. Sometimes we must be willing to put down the book we are reading and just listen to what God is saying to us through its words.

—From *Bread for the Journey: A Daybook of Wisdom and Faith* by Henri J. M. Nouwen, 1997, HarperSanFrancisco, San Francisco, entry for April 15.

My identification with the elder son has made me aware of the enormous spiritual difference between working my whole life long to earn the equality, love, and friendship that I need in my primary relationships and of living these relationships out of gratitude for the boundless, gratuitous gifts that continuously shower down upon me in my life. In the former, my refusal to accept that I am already lovable destroys trust and corrodes my heart, while in the latter, my difficulties become opportunities to trust even more that love will carry me toward my mature humanity. I have the ability to respond to my relational difficulties from two points of view and I must choose my direction. Either I say, "Watch me, God, and see how much I'm working for you. Don't you think you should finally love me?" or I say, "Oh loving Creator, thank you for gifting me with life and with unconditional love. Help me to continuously be grateful for your generosity and trust that you are always with me to help me to love." Either I am the victim of others' cruelty or my pain is the impetus for my transformation. This distinction and my freedom to respond shape the unfolding of my spiritual life. Choosing to act from the love that is always present with me in my suffering I become grounded in my identity as a beloved son of God. This is the path to greater and greater freedom and intimacy with the first love, the One who chose me before I was born.

Earlier in this work I reflected with you about the distinction between the first love and all other loves in the spiritual life. At this point in my spiritual journey I choose to claim the first love, independent of what I do, what I have, or what others think of me. I am a beloved son of God who was loved since before time began. Claiming this truth is the inner work that I commit to today and it leads me to see that I must respond to life's interruptions from a new perspective. It is radical for me, involving an almost constant effort to overcome my resistance to old patterns. That is why I have resolved to give time to reflect on this invitation, to pray often in gratitude and petition, and to find the necessary support and accountability for my commitment.

I have learned through bitter experience the one supreme lesson to conserve my anger, and as heat conserved is transmuted into energy, even so our anger controlled can be transmuted into a power which can move the world.

—Mohandas Gandhi

LISTENING

Take some time to breathe deeply and to calm yourself. Bring yourself back to your identification with the resentful one. Listen and acknowledge that you try to be dutiful. Invite your heart to speak to you about your feeling inadequate before others. Listen and identify who you've given the power to upset you and hold you hostage in angry feelings. Stay, listen, and give time to hear all that your heart wants to say.

Try to see if there isn't also a cry in your heart to believe "I am a sister. I am a brother. I'm not better or worse than anyone else." Hear that cry as a true call to claim yourself as a full member of the human family. Listen to your true heart telling you that you are a precious and cherished person, among so many other wonderful people, who search and struggle like you, and who one day will die, like you. Listen and try to plumb the depths of your truth.

JOURNALING

Try to put into words the inner dialogue that took place during your listening time. Perhaps zero in on some of the people or events that destroyed your image of yourself as enough. Give yourself freedom to express the burden that you carry.

Move slowly to write your insights into the truth about you and about your amazing life. In this sacred space, question how you can reclaim the truth and move away from feeling inadequate. Write your gratitude for those beautiful gifts that have been showered upon you in the course of your years. Finally, express your desire to stand fully in the true beauty of who you are.

COMMUNING

Abide with the Presence of the Sacred with you in this time and place. Speak of all you have heard and written. Ask to be mindful of the words of Jesus, "My Father and I will come to you and we will make a home in you." Ask to be empowered to believe, to feel at home with Love present, and to live from that sacred place. Speak your heart and listen for the response.

Heart speaks to heart.

You who live in the shelter of the Most High and who abide in the shadow of the Almighty, will say to the Lord, "Oh Lord, you are my refuge in whom I trust. . . . You will conceal me with your pinions and under your wings I will find safety. . . . I shall not fear the terror of the night nor the arrow that flies by day, nor the plague that stalks in the darkness, nor the scourge that wastes at noon. A thousand may fall at my side, ten thousand fall at my right, but all this will never approach me. . . . Because I have made the Most High my dwelling place, no evil shall befall me. . . . For God will command the angels concerning me, to guard me in all my ways. On their hands they will bear me up. . . . "Those who love me, I will deliver," says the Lord. "I will protect those who know my name. When they call to me, I will answer them; I will be with them in trouble. I will rescue them and honor them. With long life I will satisfy them, and show them my salvation."

—Psalm 91, paraphrased.

A WISDOM PRACTICE FOR THOSE ON
A SPIRITUAL JOURNEY

Practice #5—BEFRIEND THE POOR

In the parable there were two very different perspectives about the young runaway. The elder child was scandalized and broke relational ties with a younger brother. But the brokenhearted father never lost hope for the return of a beloved child. The former maintained his illusions of a perfect world and refused permission to his sibling to experiment or to fail. The latter with more life experience accepted the mystery of human suffering with compassion and tenderness.

At L'Arche Daybreak I initially felt exhilarated in an environment acceptable for people with disabilities to *not* have their lives totally together! But not long afterward my own life fell apart and I was the one who was suddenly and totally unable to function! Heartfelt prayers with gestures of love were heaped upon me from some of the weakest members of the community, a few of whom gently put a hand on my shoulder and said, "Don't worry, Henri. You're going to be OK." With the outpouring of this genuine tenderness in my weakest hour, I began to penetrate Jesus' words, "Blessed are the poor."

As a spiritual practice consider fostering a real relationship with one who is visibly marginalized. Look beyond bizarre behavior, unfamiliar humor, or a broken body and offer mutual friendship. Step beyond fear, beyond being a do-gooder, beyond controlling the relationship, and discover beyond the handicap a precious sister or brother. From your unlikely friend you may be surprised to feel that you, too, are truly lovable and blessed just as you are.

CHAPTER 6

HOMECOMING TO GRATITUDE

The first rule is simply this:
Live this life and do whatever is done, in a spirit of thanksgiving.
Abandon attempts to achieve security, they are futile,
give up the search for wealth, it is demeaning,
quit the search for salvation, it is selfish,
and come to comfortable rest in the certainty that those who
     participate in this life
with an attitude of thanksgiving will receive its full promise.

—From *Always We Begin Again: The Benedictine Way of Living* by John
McQuiston II, 1996, Morehouse Publishing, Harrisburg, PA, pp. 17–18.

M oving away from resentment requires moving toward something more positive, and that something is thankfulness. Why? Because gratitude is the opposite of resentment and gratuity moves us away from the world of earning-and-repayment in love.

Listen to what Jesus says to Peter: "When you were young,

you girded yourself and went where you wanted to go. When you grow old, you will stretch out your hand and someone else will gird you and lead you where you rather would not go." Jesus' way is the opposite of psychological teaching. That way of the world proposes that in our youth we are dependent and others tell us what to do, while as older adults we can go our own way, be independent, and do what we want.

Jesus, however, invites us to a *new* way, the opposite of this shallow way of living. He is saying, "When you were young in the spiritual life you were in control and made your choices about what you believed or did not believe. But when you grow older and more mature spiritually, you are to allow those around you to gird you and lead you where you rather would not go! Jesus' path leads toward an intimacy with the Divine that supports the growth of faithful, unconditional love in our primary relationships, as well as growth in respectful care for those beyond our inner circles with whom we are interrelated in the human family. "Love your enemies" is tough love and it is the path of our return from the corrosion of resentment to the joy of gratitude. Relinquishing the need to control and dominate family members, colleagues, and friends is "the way, the truth, and the life" that Jesus speaks about. Jesus lovingly challenges us, saying, "Give up shaping and controlling events and people, and be willing to be girded and led."

Jesus' invitation is a call to abandon relational safety zones and become vulnerable, interdependent, and obedient to the voice of unconditional love. It implies living gratefully and finding an intimate solidarity with brothers and sisters in the human family. This identification with people so different from ourselves is really wonderful but also extremely difficult, because instead of claiming control in these relationships we open ourselves to an unknown future with many surprises. Solidarity with others requires attitude changes, acceptance of difference, and the struggle to live humbly and respectfully with them. It urges us to put aside self-righteousness and become equal in our relationships.

Adam was one of my housemates. . . . He was the first person I was asked to care for when I joined the L'Arche Daybreak community in Toronto where he lived. . . . Adam was my friend, my teacher, and my guide: an unusual friend, because he couldn't express affection and love in the way most people do; an unusual teacher, because he couldn't think reflectively or articulate ideas or concepts; an unusual guide, because he couldn't give me any concrete direction or advice. . . . Adam's death touched me deeply because for me he was the one who more than any book or professor led me to the person of Jesus.

—From *Adam: God's Beloved* by Henri J. M. Nouwen, 1997, Orbis Books, Maryknoll, NY, pp. 15–16.

Who, then, girds us and leads us to be transformed into loving human beings? Our loved ones, spouses, partners, and children, as well as our leaders and those marginalized by society who are also the instruments of our transformation—all lead us in certain aspects of our lives. Each one wraps us in the swaddling bands of commitment before taking us far beyond our expectations of love to the path of greater and great intimacy and gratitude. Married life is wonderful but it is also a furnace of transformation. Family demands fidelity that hurts, friendships test our ability to love beyond our feelings, world events call us to more compassion than we think we have, and death is an invitation to hope beyond what we see and feel. Jesus came among us and lived the way of gratitude through his communion with the one he called "Father." He entered into his passion, lost control of his life, and walked the narrow path of return while forgiving his enemies.

He told his disciples, "To you I open the Psalms and Prophets in Scriptures so that you will understand that I had to struggle and suffer and then later enter into glory." Jesus' whole life is a life that moves from action, control, preaching, teaching, and performing miracles to passion where everything is done to him. He's arrested, flogged, spit upon, crowned, and nailed to the Cross, and he doesn't control any of it. The fulfillment of Jesus' whole life is not in what he did, but in what was done to him. Passion. Action is control. Passion is allowing ourselves to be emptied out at the hands of others, so that the glory of God can be revealed in us.

It is obvious that the turning away from resentment for those who, like me, identify with the elder son is probably much more difficult than returning from a life of dissipation displayed by the young prodigal, because resentment is much less overtly obvious than dissipation. Most often, the resentful person is not even aware of being lost in the first place.

Identifying with the elder son in the story revealed to me my profound sorrow and how I have spent a good deal of my life building a stone wall of protection around my heart. Now, when I actually *hear* the truth about my hardness of heart, it seems as though one of the stones is being taken out of my protective wall. This wounds me and makes me frightened and then angry. It's a big struggle. I'm trying to become much more aware and less fearful. I'm consciously trying a different response: "Don't be afraid. Let the stones be taken away and be grateful. Go beyond your comfort zone and trust. Have courage and open yourself to your heart's deeper desire, and let the wall fall down."

But if you do not clear a decent shelter for your sorrow, and instead reserve most of the space inside you for hatred and thoughts of revenge—from which new sorrows will be born for others—then sorrow will never cease in this world and will multiply. And if you have given sorrow the space its gentle origins demand, then you may truly say: life is beautiful and so rich. So beautiful and so rich that it makes you want to believe in God.

—From *An Interrupted Life, and Letters from Westerbork* by Etty Hillesum, 1996, Henry Holt and Company, New York, p. 97.

Far from making me feel safe, this practice frightens me. But at the same time space is opening up within me like a hollow cave that allows me to receive other people with acceptance and wonder. My faltering efforts to be grateful for my loved ones in family and community give me energy and a real joy. I tend to sense the voice of Love Divine whispering in my heart, "Be thankful and find more room for joy in your life. Recognize everything in your life as a gift and consciously give thanks. Open yourself and allow me to remove your heart of stone and give you a heart of flesh."

I'm having to name my fear of the implications of being equal with others. I'm having to acknowledge my attitude of superiority and self-righteousness. I'm coming face-to-face with my anger, my unresolved conflicts, my unwillingness to engage emotionally, and my lack of forgiveness of those I am committed to love. I'm so aware that my return is impossible without

God's help, because it is so hard for me not to act from my angry feelings, my jealousy, and my enormous fear of losing myself if I become one with others. To live gratefully I need to talk about my difficulties and become more accountable to my mentor. I need solitude to reflect on my relationships, and I need time to ask God to help me by giving me the love I lack.

> *Overcome any bitterness because you were not up to the magnitude of the pain entrusted to you. Like the mother of the world you are carrying the pain of the world in your heart.*
>
> —A Sufi saying

Finally, let me give one more scriptural example. Perhaps you are familiar with the parable of the eleventh hour, paraphrased below. The full text may be found in Matthew 20:1–16.

The owner of the vineyard goes out early in the morning and asks people to work the day for him for a just wage.

They come, and then he similarly recruits new people three or four more times as the day progresses, promising a just payment for work done.

At the end of the day the owner of the vineyard gives each worker the same wage, beginning with those he hired last.

Honestly, this treatment of the workers by the master is very hard to accept. I think it is terribly unfair. The people who came and worked only for the last hour get as much money as those who worked the whole day in the vineyard.

I am still running, running from that knowledge,
that eye, that love from which there is no refuge.
For you meant only love, and love,
and I felt only fear, and pain.

—From *Teaching a Stone to Talk* by Annie Dillard, 1982, Harper and Row, New York, p. 141.

On reflection, though, the workers' and our reaction to this behavior is very interesting indeed! We feel angry and we rationalize by our "justice" mentality. At least the landowner could have paid the early-comers first and sent them away so that they wouldn't see what the latecomers got! But no! Right in the face of those early-comers who worked the whole day the master pays a day's wage to the latecomers. It follows that those watching are expecting to receive more, but they don't get it! That's offensive. It not only insults all *their* feelings of justice but ours as well!

Do not judge, and you will not be judged; because the judgements
you give are the judgements you will get. . . . Why do you observe
the splinter in your brother's eye and never notice the great log in
your own? . . . Hypocrite! Take the log out of your own eye first,
and then you will see clearly enough to take the splinter out of
your brother's eye.

—From the Jerusalem Bible, Matthew 7:1–5.

Our reaction is so interesting. This same parable was adapted for a group of children and went like this:

There was a father who had many children and he went to the oldest and said, "I want you to help me out today."

The child worked hard for the father the whole day. Later the father called the second child, who was younger, and later still a third.

By midafternoon all the children were engaged in the task with the exception of the two-year-old baby. At the end of the day, the father called all the children together and began by giving the little two-year-old the same reward that he gave to each other child.

In the group of children to whom the story was told, *nobody* thought the father was unfair. They responded, "Wasn't it fun that the toddler got the same as everyone else?" Isn't it something to think about that; children enjoyed that everyone got the same from the funny father who was so good with the kids! Indeed, I had never even considered working in the vineyard as an enormous privilege. To work for my dad the whole day together with my brothers and sisters . . . isn't that wonderful? And isn't it great that those who came only at the last minute and couldn't work the whole day received so much?

> *O, that I might walk in the Light with a grateful heart,*
> *And radiate peace to the world.*

—From *Psalms for Praying* by Nan C. Merrill, 1996, The Continuum International Publishing Group, New York, Psalm 101, p. 207.

This makes me realize how self-righteous I am and what a weird way of thinking I have adopted because I resent the latecomers receiving the same as me. I wonder why I forget how great a privilege it is to spend the day with brothers and sisters doing what I was asked to do by the one who loves me most. What prevents me from rejoicing in my father's generosity with those I love the most?

So, too, when the father of the prodigal son calls for a party he's far from considering that his eldest child will feel excluded. Rather he is saying, "Come in, one and all, because your brother has returned! Be grateful with me for his return! See my goodness toward the one in the family who hasn't made it easy for me. Note that I celebrate my child's return. Come, join the party, and learn to be grateful like me!"

This movement to be grateful rather than judgmental of others is a real turning and a profound conversion. The wonderful side of it is that we discover not only how much we need the unconditional Lover to give us love but also how deeply we are connected with others as brothers and sisters. This passage from resentment to gratitude confirms us in our humanity.

And in the passage of return there is a further step to be taken. The return is not just about you and me, but it has to do with our response to another person's resentment. Seeing what we do, and working to change, there is an urge to critically judge resentment seen in others. This is important because we each must choose our reactions to the anger and pain of others. It is when we are primarily giving thanks for our lives that we have the potential to receive another's anger and judgment while remaining upright and letting it move through us. When we are looking for occasions to be grateful we hear anger and pain in a new way and can more readily accept it as being theirs and not ours. It is in that spirit that we try simply to receive it without judgment. This is only possible as we adopt thanksgiving as our way of living. Otherwise *their* resentment connects with *ours* and that only makes things worse. In the grateful life we no longer listen to another's resentment as an affirmation of our own. Nor do we judge. We simply receive it in love.

*To understand the enemy both within us and outside of us is an
important part of forgiveness.*

—From *Becoming Human* by Jean Vanier, 1998, House of Anansi Press,
Toronto, p. 162.

To be able to lovingly receive the dark judgments of another
is a painfully slow process with many ups and downs and much
learning. There is a fine line between accepting another's anger
and accepting abuse, and each of us must know the difference
and not accept abusive treatment. You and I do not have to
agree with another's ways, nor do we have to pretend that that
person's treatment of us was not wrong. But it is important to
objectively acknowledge the other's unique story and especially
the suffering of the one who offends us. When I feel hurt I must
try to stand up for myself and at the same time try not to project judgment. I must work to accept how the other person's
individual story is a whole world of joy and pain just like mine.
I know this is the way for a growing solidarity between us.

Ever so gradually I'm learning to offer my neighbor permission to be different from me and to make unique choices that
are different from the ones that I would make. My awareness of
how each one has an irreplaceable position in the human family is opening me to allow space for the beauty of the differences
that exist between us. It's my firm conviction that returning
from resentment to gratitude offers me a sense of deep belonging in our vast and precious human family as well as with the
One who created us in all our beauty and diversity.

*Dear Lord, having been plunged into this solitude and with my
hands outstretched, I become more accustomed to the darkness.*

More alone than I could ever be, I'm learning to live the death that you have chosen for me. It is more painful than any other death but my eyes are adapting in the darkness. I begin to distinguish the disguises of your love, deeper than any love I've ever known. And slowly it dawns on me that my loneliness is turning me towards you. The death is very deep, but within it is also joyous life. In this darkest darkness I am finally aware of light, your light. I begin to see where "home" is for me. Love is being born in me over and over again. Thank you, Lord. Thank you.

—From the tapes of Henri Nouwen's workshop.

LISTENING

Find space and time for stillness within and around you. Wait. Without going back to read, simply listen for the images or insights that struck you while reading this chapter. What are these passages saying to you about your present life? Listen and allow your heart time to express its yearning for wholeness, for integrity, and for transparency. Try not to fear the silence and wait with stillness for your heart to articulate the deep stirrings within. Listen for your heart cry to come home to yourself.

JOURNALING

Begin by writing something wonderful that happened to you in your life. Perhaps it was an experience with one of your parents, or when you fell in love, or meeting someone who impacted your life journey. What else happened that was important for you? Continue to write about the valued meetings, the important insights, the unexpected "miracles," and the surprises that brought you joy.

Write in a spirit of gratitude for people and moments of import. Write about good things in your life that you take for granted—including life itself! Let your pen describe your treasured history.

If there be anywhere on earth a lover of God is always safe, I know nothing of it, for it was not shown to me. But this was shown: that in falling and rising again we are always kept in the same precious love.

—Julian of Norwich

COMMUNING

Remember you are surrounded by the presence of the divine Breath who communicates with you in the deep recesses of your heart. Enter and speak into that presence the honest gratitude for all the good things you have received. Try to go beyond your hesitations with belief and unbelief, beyond the ambiguities of your life, and entrust all to the One who knows and loves you most completely. Allow yourself to give thanks with joy.

Heart speaks to heart.

A WISDOM PRACTICE FOR THOSE ON
A SPIRITUAL JOURNEY

Practice #6—CLAIM HOME ON THE WAY HOME

In reality or in spirit, each of the young adults in the parable left in disillusionment but was later received home. Conforming or not, polite or not, contrite or not, each sibling belonged in the family and each was entitled to unique love without condition. Jesus points toward such a home for us when he says, "I am going to prepare a place for you."

Meanwhile, however hard I try, I do not find a *permanent* home of safety, acceptance, and creative caring. Only occasionally in the smile, the kind word, the embrace, or the gift of friendship do I have a fleeting taste of "home on the way home." But my months in solitude made me grateful for such unique gifts of caring. They reminded me of another, greater Love. Now I feel called to receive any momentary affirmation simply and with gratitude. Further, I'm challenged to freely confirm others by saying in so many words, "I'm so glad *you* are here and we are together."

Jesus teaches us "Love your neighbor as yourself." If we are too preoccupied and too busy, we fail to connect in simple exchanges of love with others. Love doesn't need long speeches. Rather, love is attentive to fleeting moments of peace, kindness, friendship, and compassion. Love invites us as a spiritual discipline to communicate with our loved ones more and more from hearts broken open by compassion.

PART III

HOME IS
RECEIVING LOVE
AND
GIVING LOVE

CHAPTER 7

THE PRIMAL RELATIONSHIP

But look, I am going to seduce her and lead her into the desert and speak to her heart.

—From the Jerusalem Bible, Hosea 2:16.

J esus' life is an invitation for us to believe, not primarily in him but in the *relationship* between himself and the God whom he names "Father." Furthermore, Jesus comes into the world to communicate to those of us who are listening that this very same *relationship* is uniquely available to each one of us. By his life and death Jesus announces the yearning in the heart of Love Divine, to be in relationship with each individual person. For you or I to engage this primal encounter is for us to return "home."

This *relationship* between Jesus and the One who sent him into the world is *the* central focus of Jesus' whole life and teaching. He urges us to see how he comes to us not on his own but sent and in *relationship* with God the Creator-Spirit. Jesus' whole mission, his life, words, works, disgrace, and glory, are only relevant because of his *relationship* with the One who sent him. Everything about his life is forever in *relationship* with the One he calls Father. He is passionate when he says, "Believe in me," which means "Believe that I am sent by the One who calls me Beloved." It means "Believe every word I speak, because I heard these words in *relationship* with my Father." "Believe in me" means "Believe that every work I do is not mine alone but is also my Spirit-Father-God working through me." It means "Believe that the glory I receive does not belong to me but is given to me by the One with whom I am intimately united in my spirit."

This is a union so total and so full that there is not even the slightest place for an experience of absence or separation. To be *in* that relationship is to be home in the deepest possible sense of the word.

Hold tightly to the hand of faith
For strength through deep valleys;
Learn to trust in the One,
Who is ever your companion and guide.

—From *Psalms for Praying* by Nan C. Merrill, 1996, The Continuum International Publishing Group, New York, Psalm 119, p. 264.

This is new for me, that my following of Jesus calls me to believe not only in the full communion between Jesus and the One who sent him into the world but to believe in *my* communion with the One who sent *me* into the world. Jesus says, "Philip, how can you say 'Show us the Father'? Don't you know that when you see me, you see the Father also?" Jesus is one who is never alone, but always bonded in love without the slightest distance, the slightest fear, or the slightest hesitation between himself and the One who sent him into the world.

Jesus the man mirrors an "enfleshed" relationship with Unconditional Love to reveal how to "be home" in our humanity. "Who sees me, sees the Father. Who believes in me, believes in the Father. I and the Father are one. I am in the Father and the Father is in me." At his baptism, Jesus and others heard the voice of Love Divine: "You are my beloved son. My favor rests on you." Later Jesus says, "As the Father has loved me, so I also love you. The Father and I are one." The words "My favor rests on you" are said to us. The relationship is available to us and to see Jesus is to know the relationship.

I call you friends, because I have made known to you everything I have learned from my Father.

—From the Jerusalem Bible, John 15:15.

Jesus never, never, never makes a distinction between his relationship with Unconditional Love and ours. Jesus never says, "I know the great Spirit fully and you can know a little bit about the Holy One." He doesn't say, "I can do great things in the name of God-Mother, and you can maybe do a few things." No. Jesus instead tells us, "All the things I've heard because of my communion with the Indwelling Beloved I tell you because I want you to have the same experience of knowing Love that I have. All the things I do in the name of the One who loves me so much, you have power to do, too. In fact, you will accomplish even greater things than me. And all the glory I receive from the One who affirms me in my humanity is available for you to receive as well. You are to be as fully the adult child of

Unconditional Love as me. You are to live a communion with Love itself that is so intimate that you also become the visibility of Love's Spirit present in the world."

I really need to hear this, and I believe that you do, too. Jesus came not simply to tell us about a loving Creator who is far away and who, from there, cares for us. Not at all! Jesus came to offer us the same full communion with the Spirit-Father-Mother-Lover that he enjoys, where he is in no way smaller than the One who sent him.

> *Dear Child of God, all of us are meant to be contemplatives. Frequently we assume that this is reserved for some rare monastic life, lived by special people who alone have been called by God. But the truth of the matter is that each one of us is meant to have that space inside where we can hear God's voice. God is available to all of us. God says, "Be still and know that I am God."*
>
> —From *God Has a Dream: A Vision of Hope for Our Times* by Desmond Tutu, 2004, Doubleday, New York, p. 101.

The word for that intimate communion between Jesus and God is "Spirit." It captures an affiliation that is so total, so loaded, so holy, so sacred, so complete that it lacks absolutely nothing. The Greek word for "spirit" is *pneuma*, which means "breath." The bond between Jesus and the One he calls Father is like breathing. Breathing is so central and intimate that we aren't even aware that we're breathing. If we become aware of it, it's because something is wrong. Otherwise we are simply breathing and no one comments on it by saying, "Oh my, you're breathing!" or "I notice you're breathing really nicely today!" No. We don't ever talk about it. It is just part of our lives and we just breathe and our breath is life.

The relationship between Jesus and the Father, like our breathing, is immediate, urgent, and near. Jesus tells us after his resurrection, "It's good for you that I'm going, because if I go, I will then send you my breath, my Spirit. Then you will fully live in me as I live in you."

The parable of the prodigal son invites our reflection on this great, great revelation of amazing good news. The story embodies the *relationship*. Look again at the Rembrandt painting of a father laying hands on his young son. Feel those hands and remember how such loving tenderness affects us and makes us live. We may know the anguish of not being touched with love, but these incredible hands lift us from our knees in total forgiveness while healing our broken hearts.

The eyes, the hands, and the cape image the profound blessedness, lasting love, and "home" to which we can return again and again. Claim the words celebrating *your* return: "Quick! You are to have the best robe; here is a ring for your finger and sandals for your feet." Saint Paul tells us, "You will receive a new garment of the children of God and you will be like God." That is the best robe. The ring is the ring of the inheritor, the ring that is given to the inheritors of the kingdom. And the sandals ensure that we walk in safety. Lastly, "The calf we have been fattening will be killed in your honor; we will celebrate by having a fiesta." The banquet is a celebration of heaven where our differences bless us as family, and where we feast together from the same table.

Jesus "did not cling to his equality with God, but emptied himself," for an experience of total communion. He uses these images for a *relationship* that is, in fact, much, much more than the human images of daughter, son, mother, or father. What is so compelling is that we become like the one we love. Our return "home" is to relate intimately in spirit with Love and also to *become* Love for others: compassionate, forgiving, creative, spirit-filled lovers in the best sense of the word.

LISTENING

Breathe deeply and find a still rhythm for exhaling preoccupations and for inhaling peace. In your imagination take your place silently beside Jesus and walk together up the mountain in the evening. Sit apart and watch him situate himself to pray. Watch him enter into communion with the One who sent him into the world. Imagine his communion with Love Divine. Stay and listen.

> *The desert fathers counselled, "Go into your cell, and your cell will teach you everything." Set aside a period of time in nature or at home, at a church or temple, a library or anywhere you will not be disturbed. Sit, walk, meditate, pray, read, whatever pleases you. Pay attention.*
>
> —From *Sabbath: Restoring the Sacred Rhythm of Rest* by Wayne Muller, 1999, Bantam Books, New York, p. 178.

Now go alone to the mountaintop and imagine yourself in the presence of the One who sent you into the world. Be still. Wait. Don't speak but rest in the presence. Listen.

JOURNALING

Write what you witnessed on the mountaintop. Note your feelings while you were present there with Jesus in communion with Love Unending. What was difficult for you? Write what you heard in your imagination. What were you feeling as you ascended the mountain alone? Write what transpired as you tried to imagine yourself in communion with God's Spirit. Write your emotions, what you heard, your thoughts, and your feelings.

COMMUNING

Quietly enter into that privileged place in the depths of your heart and abide with Love. Give yourself permission to rest there with or without words. Commune.

Heart speaks to heart.

A WISDOM PRACTICE FOR THOSE ON
A SPIRITUAL JOURNEY

Practice #7—CLAIM YOUR INNER "SPIRIT" LIFE

In the parable both siblings are preoccupied with themselves because neither has inwardly matured enough to feel responsible for belonging in this, their family of origin. The mature one, the father figure, lives with a deep interiority and is fully composed, fully accepting of his position in the family, and uniquely committed to each family member.

Unfortunately my interiority up to now has been to claim my many disturbing "spirits"; angry feelings, painful dreams, troubling fantasies, and hurts around unresolved relationships, more than to be attentive to the Spirit of Jesus, who also occupies my inner landscape. Now I'm working to adopt the practice of speaking directly and often to the God-Spirit living within me.

Jesus announced the availability of the Giver of Life for an inner relationship of communion with each one of us. He said,

"If you love me you will keep my word, and my Father will love you and we shall come to you and make a home in you." (John 14:23)

"I shall ask the Father, who will give you another Paraclete to be with you for ever, the Spirit of Truth whom the world can never accept since it neither sees nor knows God; but you know the Spirit with you and in you." (John 14:16–17)

In the Scripture Jesus is very often found to be in communion with the Divine Love. He goes to the mountain and spends the whole night in prayer to God. He speaks his inner union aloud on the Cross: "Father, forgive them, for they know not what they do."

CHAPTER 8

TOUCH AND BLESSING

We always want someone else to change so that we will feel good. But has it ever struck you that even if your wife changes or your husband changes, what does that do to you? You're just as vulnerable as before; you're just as idiotic as before; you're just as asleep as before. You are the one who needs to change, who needs to take medicine. You keep insisting, "I feel good because the world is right." Wrong! "The world is right because I feel good." That's what all the mystics are saying.

—Anthony de Mello

There was a time in my life when I became focused on how my parents had wounded me and I remember wishing that they had behaved differently. Listening to others, however, I saw how they too experienced times of feeling primarily hurt by parents, partners, relatives, friends, or those in their church community. Isn't it true that we have been hurt because parents and others were unable to reflect unconditional love to us? Perhaps they held on to us too tightly or seemed to push us away. They wounded us not because they wanted to wound us, but because they also were people who were loved imperfectly by others. Each one of us, as well as all who went before us, share the human condition and suffer from being loved imperfectly. We are not meant to stop at simply feeling the pain of these wounds, nor are we to become stuck in guilt or accusations. Rather this whole experience is to move us toward accepting a relationship with God's living Spirit of Unconditional Love. Our spiritual journey is nothing more than a return to the intimacy, the safety, and the acceptance of that very first relationship with Love, that is uniquely present and at home within each one of us.

I am aware that I have been deeply loved and enabled in my life. I move and speak to you, I relate with many people, I walk and smile because I've been loved so immensely. I owe a debt of gratitude to many, many people for loving me into this, my existence, despite knowing that those very same people who loved me were also wounded and broken people like me. I acknowledge that I am sometimes surprised to still feel pain because of those old hurts, and when I do, I have a hard time claiming the immense love that I've been given. When I live from the pain I doubt myself and have trouble in relationships. My difficulty is that when I feel the hurts I go looking for love externally from other wounded people instead of claiming and communing with the One who knows me, loves me as I am, and makes a home in my heart.

Jesus taught us about the whole movement of God's love with bread. His actions with bread in Scripture image his and our lives as beloved children of God. In the multiplication of the loaves at the Last Supper, Jesus took the bread first. Bread was chosen as God chooses each one of us uniquely as a beloved daughter or son. After the bread was in his hands Jesus blessed it, just as our Creator confirms each of us as beloved children. The bread is broken as Jesus was broken on the Cross and as we are broken because of undeserved suffering in our lives. Finally, the bread was given for the life of others, just as Jesus' life was given, and ours is to be given. Jesus does this many, many times: taking, blessing, breaking, and giving. We experience the joys of being chosen and blessed. And we are broken not because we are cursed but because, like Jesus, passion moves us to *com*passion and to be given for others who suffer.

> *We who lived in concentration camps can remember the men who walked through the huts comforting others, giving away their last piece of bread. They may have been few in number . . . but they offer sufficient proof that everything can be taken from a man but one thing: the last of his freedoms—to choose one's attitude in any given set of circumstances, to choose one's own way.*

—From *Man's Search for Meaning* by Viktor E. Frankl, 1963, Washington Square Press, New York, p. 104.

The first biblical story about the garden in Eden describes how God walked with Adam and Eve in a relationship of unconditional love. When they doubted and turned away from God's word toward each other's word, they experienced nakedness, anxiety, and fear. Adam responds to God's "Where are you?" in the garden with "I was afraid because I was naked, so I hid." Original sin names this failure to trust the original relationship. Original sin is following the temptation to experience the first love from other people and things. Fortunately Adam and Eve's pain and anxiety touched the very heart of God, who sent Jesus into the world to personally witness to the first-love relationship.

Working occasionally with prisoners in the past, I was humbled to realize how those deeply wounded individuals became criminals because of their desperate need to be noticed, respected, heard, or free from their sense of total alienation. Most of them were frantic to feel loved. Being rejected plunged them into terror and to believing it is better to kill than to be killed. I truly feel that many acts of killing are not primarily because people are evil but because they are desperate. So often I have found so-called "felons" to be hungry for the safety of committed relationships with love and care. I saw how easily they cried and I heard them say, "What have I done? I only wanted to be recognized as someone of value. I longed to be part of a family with my wife and my children." Many of these brothers and sisters have never known or felt the safe touch of a loving hand.

> *With pain and gratitude O Divine Spirit, I come to you*
> *with all my brothers and sisters on the planet,*
> *I pause with them to receive your love.*
> *Help each one of us to know truth, and to more fully claim our*
> *individual belovedness.*
> *May your Spirit be in each one to accomplish new miracles.*

—Adapted from Henri Nouwen's original manuscript of his workshop.

Perhaps you and I need to look at suffering people in our world from a new perspective. We all know the lonely person in others or ourselves who, through so many disturbing behaviors, is asking, "Please recognize me, please love me." Human suffering is so often an expression of our extreme need to feel genuinely loved, and when we know nothing about the first love, we turn to others who cannot offer us the love we need. It is then that the cry moves us toward violence. "I can't do without you. You must stay with me." Suddenly instead of caressing we grab and that frightens the other person away. It's daunting to see how the grabbing, the slapping, the biting, the violence, and sometimes the rape are really the other side of our desperate need to love and be loved.

Soul of Christ sanctify me
Body of Christ save me
Blood of Christ inebriate me
Water from the side of Christ wash me
Passion of Christ strengthen me
O good Jesus hear me
In your wounds hide me
Suffer me not to be separated from thee
From the malicious foe defend me
In the hour of my death call me
And bid me come to thee
That with the saints I may praise thee
Forever and ever. Amen

—Prayer of Saint Ignatius, quoted by Henri Nouwen in original tapes of his workshop.

Rembrandt was able to paint the prodigal's return only after a long life of immense suffering. Few people have cried as many tears as Rembrandt, for his children who died and for his wives

who died. His tears and suffering opened his eyes to understand the love of a God who wept so much for a lost child as to
become almost blind, but with a blindness that reveals inner
light. Rembrandt understood and could paint the one whose
love does not prevent his child leaving for a foreign land where
he will suffer. Rembrandt used a human image to illustrate
how the One who relates intimately with us offers us freedom,
is conscious of our suffering as a beloved child, and watches for
our return. Nothing, neither tears nor near blindness, prevents
the recognition of the favored one returning home.

> For wisdom is quicker to move than any motion;
> she is so pure, she pervades and permeates all things,
> She is a breath of the power of God,
> pure emanation of the glory of the Almighty;
> so nothing impure can find its way into her.
> For she is a reflection of the eternal light,
> untarnished mirror of God's active power,
> and image of his goodness.

—From the Jerusalem Bible, Wisdom 7:24–26.

Look at the hands of the father in the painting. Very few
people notice at first glance that there are two different hands,
one of a man and the other of a woman. Rembrandt knew that
the Divine was not merely a man looking upon creation from
the sky, and he understood something about the Creator that
Jesus wanted us to know. He experienced the God of Jesus as
One with all the best characteristics of mothers and fathers
and more. Rembrandt painted the hand of the woman from an
earlier painting of the Jewish bride. She has very delicate, gen-

tle, and tender hands that speak about who she is as woman— protecting, caring, and inordinately in love. The hand of the man is Rembrandt's own hand. It speaks of who he is as father, supporter, defender, and giver of freedom. After a long life and having lived the death of both of his wives and all of his children, Rembrandt understood the depths of holding and letting go, of offering protection and freedom, of maternity and paternity. That's how he was able to paint this image of God toward the end of his life. His suffering had somehow not made him bitter or resentful but had rather opened him to recognize Love's yearning heart for intimate, unique relationships with daughters and sons. Rembrandt was able to paint the Giver of Life as a most compassionate and loving Counselor, holding, blessing, letting go, and receiving back into safety the immature but emerging adult children of creation. Look at the cape. It is like a Gothic arch, very protecting. It is like the wings of a mother bird surrounding her children. "In the shadow of your wings I take refuge till the storms of destruction pass by" (Psalms 57:1). The touch of blessing on the shoulders of the adult child is the touch of maternity and paternity in its perfection.

Once I heard Jean Vanier, founder of the communities of L'Arche around the world, speak about hands. He described the hands that gently encircle a wounded bird as being hands that are also open to allow movement and freedom to fly. Jean believes that each of us needs to have both these hands around us. One says, "I've got you and I hold you safe because I love you and I'll never be apart from you. Don't be afraid." The other says, "Go, my child, find your way, make mistakes, learn, suffer, grow, and become who you need to be. Don't be afraid. You are free and I am always near." Jean Vanier imagines these two hands as the hands of Unconditional Love.

The word blessing in Latin is *benedicture. Bene* means "good," and *dicture* means "to say." *Benedicere,* and likewise, "blessing," means "to announce good things and to confirm one another." In the picture, the touch of hands is the blessing of the one who passionately affirms and loves the child that he and his wife brought into the world. If he is listening at all, this young prodigal can only hear "I'm so thankful you are home. I've watched you grow and I've always wanted you close to me as an adult. I've missed you terribly and I've been waiting for you. You are my cherished one, beloved of my heart." This blessing must have pierced the heart of the young adolescent.

Jesus' whole mission was to witness to our participation in this blessed relationship with the One who breathes love without conditions. When he told the parable of the prodigal son he was aware of how this sacred, sacred event of parent blessing the child was engraved in the history of God's people. Abraham blessed Isaac, and later Isaac blessed Jacob. In giving us this story Jesus wanted each of us to see, to understand, and to believe that loving hands of blessing are forever resting upon us. The Creator of the galaxies lives, whispers uniquely good things about us in our hearts, and urges us to rise up and use our freedom to become compassionate peacemakers in our world. This bond of love that touches each one of our lives from the very beginning of our creation to the very end of time and beyond is our original blessing.

When you and I are home in this relationship, we find ourselves in the heart of the One that Jesus addresses as Father. We reside in the intimacy of the womb of Love Itself. Looking out from the heart of Love, our own hearts bleed with compassion, because from there we are seeing as God sees. From this intimate connection with God we grow to become like the One we love. You and I, along with all members of the human family, are blessed people with the blessing of unconditional love that will never be taken away. We are also people who offer compassion to those who suffer.

How glorious is your dwelling place
  O Loving Creator of the universe!
My soul longs, yes, aches for
  the abode of the Beloved;
All that is within me sings for joy
  to the living Heart of Love!
Even as the sparrow finds a home,
  and the swallow a nesting place,
  where its young are raised within
    Your majestic creation,
You invite us to dwell within
    Your Heart.

—From *Psalms for Praying* by Nan C. Merrill, 1996, The Continuum International Publishing Group, New York, Psalm 84, p. 174.

Jesus tells us that he is our way. We find the way when we follow him through the pages of Scripture. There we see how he was constantly communing and in relationship with the One who sent him into the world. When suffering was part of the way, Jesus chose not to ask "Why?" He chose not to blame those who hurt him. He stood in his agony, intimately connected with the One who loved him and also forgiving and caring for those who so cruelly tortured and killed him. This is the way, and by offering us this way, Jesus gives us new eyes to look into our experience of suffering and of life.

True homecoming is choosing the way of Jesus, where we acknowledge the good and painful in our lives and we ask for patience and courage to forgive all those who have wounded us on the journey. Their love was limited and conditional, but it set us in search of that unconditional, unlimited love. This way takes us on a path through the desert of suffering to our hidden wholeness and to our utter beauty in the eyes of the One we name God.

LISTENING

In your stillness, listen and respond to the question "Who is your God?" Listen deeply for what you believe are the characterics of the very Source of your life. Listen to how your heart relates to your God. Next look again at the painting of the meaningful but limited image of the One Jesus calls God. Listen to the Heart of all hearts longing for intimacy and togetherness. Imagine the eyes of the father figure moving from the son to embrace you and to invite you to take the place of the adult child. When you are ready, put your head on Love's breast and allow the tender female hand to touch you in gratitude for your return. Feel the strong male hand caress you with joy and thoughts of celebration. Listen to words of tenderness, welcome, and unconditional love directed toward you.

JOURNALING

Write of your mixed emotions under this embrace of welcome.

Be content with what you have;
rejoice the way things are.
When you realize there is nothing lacking,
the whole world belongs to you.

—From *Sabbath: Restoring the Sacred Rhythm of Rest* by Wayne Muller, 1999, Bantam Books, New York, p. 82; quoted from Lao-Tzu with no reference.

COMMUNING

In awe and reverence listen to the words of affirmation and welcome. Take the Beloved's hands in yours and get to your feet. Look into the eyes of love and speak. Commune in love.

Heart speaks to heart.

A WISDOM PRACTICE FOR THOSE ON A SPIRITUAL JOURNEY

Practice #8—RECEIVE MERCY

Neither of the young men in the parable had lived long enough to know about giving or receiving mercy. However, after suffering separation in their own unique ways, they were each offered a unique return from isolation into the family fold.

With no conditions, the love figure at "home" blesses each of the children with forgiveness, mercy, and unconditional welcome.

I enjoy being strong and able to support those who feel vulnerable. I'm also a generous giver, but in my ever-present "earning" mentality, I feel nervous to receive kindness from others in view of having to always repay. I have mixed emotions about being welcomed home when I know this has not been my first leaving and will probably not be my last. But my life and my suffering are opening me to receive care, kindness, and support, with gratitude, and to feel worthy of love.

Let us be aware of small gestures of love offered us by others that remind us of our unique beauty. Let us try to gratefully accept the smile, the tender word, the caring embrace, and the recognition that affirms our personhood. These are but reminders of the overwhelming reception awaiting our every return to communion with God's Spirit, and that mercy is always available and always confirming the truth of our belovedness.

CHAPTER 9

UNCONDITIONAL LOVE

*Liberation of the human heart . . . opens us up and leads us to the
discovery of our common humanity . . . a journey from loneliness
to a love that transforms, a love that grows in and through belonging. . . . The discovery of our common humanity liberates us from
self-centered compulsions and inner hurts; it is the discovery that
ultimately finds its fulfilment in forgiveness and in loving those who
are our enemies. It is the process of truly becoming human.*

—From *Becoming Human* by Jean Vanier, 1998, House of Anansi Press,
Toronto, p. 5.

It is a fact that we live because of being touched by the love
of parents and others that is only a reflection of an even
greater love. And there is no question that our relationships
with family and others contributed to our feelings of being
lovable or not so lovable. Our sense of ourselves was enhanced
by true love and diminished because the love from family was
imperfect. It seems to me that it is the limited experience of

unlimited love that awakens us to the deep inner cry for someone to love us unconditionally.

Personally I know I need healing in my relationships with family and especially with my father. I remember him once saying to me, "I know you see me as authoritarian, and that is true. I am. But my question is, why can't you let me be that way?" He laughed as he went on, saying, "You are a psychologist. You have Freud and others who help you understand authoritarian personalities, and here you have one right in your own family. I do not understand how you have always lived your friendships with freedom but you cannot allow me to be free in the way I live my relationships." I answered, "You're absolutely right. Why not?"

However, deep inside I still feel a need for him to be different, because I read into his behavior that he tries to manipulate me by instructing me on how to make coffee, ordering me to get a haircut, insulting me by saying I am not old enough to drive his car, and by insisting on having the last word in almost every conversation. We do not understand each other at many levels, and I, at fifty-seven years of age, feel injured by the way he relates to me. So I know that I have to make many more concessions, accept him more as he is, and try harder to relate lovingly with him.

Because of this struggle, I *know* there has to be more, a higher love that sets me free from my need to change my father. Perhaps I'm not completely there yet, but I do believe that from the perspective of being fully loved by God it's possible for me to let go of those things that distress me about my father so as to be able to laugh with him and to be more grateful for who he is. Knowing I am loved prior to my father loving me inspires me to see him as he is: simply a man with a good and loving heart, important and little, like everyone else. Yes, he's a bit of a character, but why can I not smile when he is telling me how to make the coffee? I have a good feeling about giving my father permission to be who he is without conditions, even though I'm not yet fully able to do so. After all, I, too, am just a little man with many foibles and a loving heart trying to find my way. Claiming God's first love helps me enormously to surrender my unrealistic expectations and to really be grateful for the father I have.

As for the future, your task is not to foresee, but to enable it. It is not for us to stalk the vision, the vision is stalking us.

—A Native American saying

It is good for us to "be with" and to forgive family members, partners, and children without needing to shape them in a violent way. It is liberating to accept that they are different from us, that they think and act in their own ways, and that they make different choices than we might make. It is important to liberate them to make their own mistakes and to learn life's lessons at their own pace. And finally, instead of wishing they had lived according to our expectations, how blessed we'd be to be grateful even when they weren't able to love us perfectly, and how loving it would be to allow them to die in peace. Jesus gives us good advice: "Leave your father, leave your mother, leave your sister, and leave your brother." He knows that letting our parents and siblings go free is creating space in us not only to welcome God's unconditional love but also to gradually become a compassionate parent figure for others.

More and more I sense that the opposite of love is not hate

but fear. Even though I don't feel that I hate anyone, I do know that I am afraid that people will not love me if I act freely in my relationship. I see more and more clearly how this fear moves me toward isolation and violence. Let me explain.

> *The practice of the trapeze has acquainted me with many unholy ghosts that hide in the dark regions of the psyche. . . . I am afraid of failure. I am afraid of what others will think of me. I am afraid I will embarrass myself. I am afraid I will lose control. I am afraid I can't trust you. I am afraid I will be abandoned if I do not measure up to your expectations.*
>
> —From *Learning to Fly: Reflections on Fear, Trust, and the Joy of Letting Go* by Sam Keen, 1999, Broadway Books, New York, pp. 36–37.

Not having fully claimed myself as a beloved child of God I carry real and imagined suffering around being unloved, abused, rejected, and unacceptable. This false sense of being not very good awakens feelings of loneliness, fear, and anguish. From there I move out, sometimes frantically, to find acceptance in others. I divide my world between those on my side and those who are against me. In self-protection I cling to the few who respond to me, and I fearfully begin to challenge those who befriend my friends in case they steal affection away from me. I do this not because I am hateful, but because I am afraid and I view people with suspicion and see them as dangerous. When I sense danger, I become preoccupied with survival and I begin to build real or imagined walls to protect my space. Then, of course, I begin to hoard things for emergencies and I withhold emotions, money, knowledge, material things, and love in case another will become stronger or more successful than me.

I hear the cry of suffering sisters and brothers: "Look. You have all these friends, all this knowledge, and silos full of grain. You have more than you need and I have not enough. I want some of what you have. Why don't you share with me and let me have part of your wealth?" But now fear is the master and I reply, "It's true that there's more than enough now, but you never know about tomorrow, so I cannot share with you."

Everything we have is on loan. Our homes, businesses, rivers, closest relationship, bodies, and experiences, everything we have is ours in trust, and must be returned at the end of our use of it. As trustees we have the highest and strictest requirements of fiduciary duty: to use nothing for our sole benefit; to manage prudently; and to return that which has been in our care in as good or better condition than it was when given into our custody.

—From *Always We Begin Again: The Benedictine Way of Living* by John McQuiston II, 1996, Morehouse Publishing, Harrisburg, PA, p. 52.

When panic dominates my horizons I always anticipate the worst. Behind my walls I'm fearful people out there are plotting to tear them down, so I top them off with shards of broken glass and explosives. I've become violent toward unseen enemies. And I have also to worry that my explosives could topple my way instead of toward the enemy. Fear consumes me and prevents me following my inner aspirations to love and be loved.

I hope you can see that hatred is really secondary to the fear that consumes our inner space and compels us to build prisons around ourselves. I hope you can reflect how fear

Breeds feelings of being unsafe, unloved, and alone.
Makes us believe we won't be loved if we act freely.

Prompts us to divide the world between friends and
    enemies.
Inspires us to hoard.
Robs us of our capacity to love and be loved in return.
Obliges us to cling to people and things.
Limits our ability to relate with the Spirit of Love within.

When we freely allow fear to dominate and change us, we live
in misery far from our home of unconditional love.

Some old men came to see Abba Poemen, and said to him:
    "Tell us, when we see brothers dozing during the sacred office,
should we pinch them so they will stay awake?"
    The old man said to them:
    "Actually, if I saw a brother sleeping, I would put his head on
my knees and let him rest."

—From *Desert Wisdom* by Yushi Nomura, ed., 1982, Doubleday, New
York, p. 17.

Meanwhile Jesus, our example, says to the disciples and to
us, "Don't be afraid. Perfect love casts out fear." He walked
freely, lived freely, and carried on an intimate relationship with
the One who sent him into the world. Throughout the nights
or early in the mornings Jesus spent time communing with the
One who loved him. Among his last words he tells us, "As the
Father has loved me, so I also love you. . . . If you keep my word,
the Father and I will come to you and we will make our home
in you. . . . I will send you my Spirit, who will dwell with you forever, and will remind you of all I have said to you." Jesus came
to convince us that

Our Maker's love is pure gift, unearned and free.
We are free to relate with the Source of all life or not.
A greater love embraces all the love that you and I have
    ever known, from father, mother, spouses, brothers,
    sisters, children, teachers, friends, partners, or
    counsellors.
Welcoming unconditional love automatically makes us
    more like the Unconditional Lover. Divine love lasts
    forever.

The prodigal son story is an amazing image of how God pa-
tiently waits to be in communion with us. Even if we leave home
for a while, Love waits for our return. We may condemn ourselves, but we are not objectively being judged for our misguided
decisions, nor is the One who loves us saying, "Away from me, I
do not love you anymore. You are a bad person. You're going to
hell." No! That response is against the very nature of the eternal
Lover that Jesus invites us to know. The God of Jesus is, in the
words of Thomas Merton, "mercy, within mercy, within mercy."
As we receive mercy we become merciful, we become like the
Father figure.

Even in all its beauty this story cannot fully articulate the
great truth about how the One who created us loves you and me
with passionate joy. Certain images of God from Scripture say
more about the limitations of human expression and a given
worldview than about the heart of the One who fashioned the
universe. Since the writing of these texts our knowledge of the
vastness of our universe and of our interconnectedness has
evolved, so we no longer need to rely on older concepts about
a God who does not offer second chances and whose compassion does not include those children who sometimes make poor

choices. We do need to try to imagine the universal heart of the God that Jesus reveals to us. This is a Creator who says, "For I have come to call not the righteous but sinners" (Matthew 9:13). And through the parable of the prodigal son, the Lord of the Universe is saying to each one of us, "Don't make up speeches to give but trust my compassionate heart. Servants, bring out the best robe and put it on my child. Put a ring on her finger and sandals on his feet. Kill the fatted calf and prepare a feast. For this beloved of mine was lost and is found, was dead and has come back to life."

Yes, I left for the foreign country because I needed to get out and discover life for myself, but I ended up with the swine. I suffered and I also discovered a lot. And yes, I worked in my father's vineyards with angry feelings, but that is not because God wanted it that way. The One whose love is unconditional is saying, "I love you so much that I freely give you liberty to live and choose. But remember, all that is mine is yours. You've been always with me. My love for you is real and unchanged despite your unwise choices, so return to it and be shaped by it into my image."

Let us try to grow in our knowledge of the true Source of our lives. Let us allow this Spirit of all Truth into our hearts to dispel our fear, resentment, and hatred, and to shape our lives in the image of the Divine Lover. And let us not be scandalized because we have to return again and again. Leonard Bernstein wrote *The Mass,* an incredible opera about a priest saying Mass in a very contemporary setting. What you see is how the priest allows himself to be dressed by the people and then lifted up, central, important, and like a very highly respected and adorned royal person. Suddenly he falls and as he tumbles downward the chalice and the plate are broken and shattered. Next you see that same priest, now dressed in blue jeans and walking amidst all the shards of broken glass. He makes an incredible statement. He says very slowly, "I never knew how bright the light was until I saw it here in the broken glass." It wasn't being lifted up that enlightened him. It was in the broken glass and in the shattered image of himself that he recognized the light of his true identity.

You prepare a table before me
in the presence of all my fears;
you bless me with oil
my cup overflows.
Surely goodness and mercy
will follow me
all the days of my life;
and I shall dwell in the heart
of the Beloved
forever.

—From *Psalms for Praying* by Nan C. Merrill, 1996, The Continuum International Publishing Group, New York, Psalm 23, p. 40.

So homecoming for us is turning away from pervasive fears that cripple relationships, imprison us in misery, and steal our freedom. Our return means that we also recognize the light of truth in the broken shards of our individual lives. We are but fearful children, unable to relate faithfully, intimately, and permanently with Divine Love. But, constantly forgiven, we have power to love others more.

Jesus' whole mission in coming to live among us was to call us home to the truth of our lives. He lives and teaches belonging in the womb of Unchanging Love, in the intimacy of Companioning Presence, in the house of the giver of Life and Breath, in the name of the Compassionate Creator. God's name is our home, our dwelling place. When asked, "Where are you?" you answer, "I'm home. I'm in the name and that is where I live and find safety." From this home with the Guiding Spirit we walk out into the world without ever leaving this source of belonging. The name, the home, the family, the womb, and the communion are where we dwell, rooted and held. "You do not belong to the world," Jesus said to the disciples. "I do not belong to the world. I belong to the Father." Jesus is saying that he is totally and completely living in an intimate relationship with the Divine and that there is nothing in him that isn't held in this embrace. He knows that he is sent into the world to offer us the same gift. We, too, live in the intimate embrace of the Holy One. Like Jesus, we do not belong to the world but to the Divine Comforter. And we are sent into the world just as Jesus was sent into the world to freely offer our love to others and to personify that love is possible.

How do we welcome home our lost brothers and sisters? By running out to them, embracing them, kissing them. By clothing them with the best clothes we have and making them our honoured guests. By offering them the best food and inviting friends and family for a party. And, most important of all, by not asking for excuses or explanations, only showing our immense joy that they are with us again. . . . The past is wiped out. What counts is the here and now, where all that fills our hearts is gratitude for the homecoming of our brothers and sisters.

—From *Bread for the Journey: A Daybook of Wisdom and Faith* by Henri J. M. Nouwen, 1997, Doubleday, New York, entry for July 3.

Jesus draws us all into the heart of Love. "I go to my God and to your God." When we are in the heart of the Divine we are also in the heart of the world, because the world dwells in the heart of its Creator. It is from the heart of Love that we finally step into the shoes of the God figure and become compassionate lovers of others in the human family. From our dwelling place in the heart of Love we are free, we can be generous and welcoming while always remaining at home.

LISTENING

Listen to Love speaking to you through the ages.

> "Do not be afraid for I have redeemed you. I have called you by your name. You are mine . . . since you are precious in my eyes and honoured and I love you. Do not be afraid, for I am with you." (Isaiah 43:1)
>
> "I call you friends because I have made known to you everything I have learned from the Father." (John 15:15)
>
> "Anyone who loves me will keep my word, and my Father will love him, and we shall come to him and make a home in him." (John 14:23)
>
> "It is to the glory of my Father that you should bear much fruit and be my disciples. I have loved you just as the Father has loved me." (John 15:9)
>
> "Love your enemies, do good to those who hate you, bless those who curse you, pray for those who treat you badly." (Luke 6:27–28)

Listen with all your heart.

Holy Spirit, Lord of life,
From your clear, celestial height,
Thy pure beaming radiance give.

Come Father of the poor,
Come with treasures which endure,
Come Thou Light of all that live.

Thou of all Consolers best,
Visiting the troubled breast,
Dost refreshing gifts bestow.

Thou in toil art Comfort sweet,
Pleasant coolness in the heat,
Solace in the midst of woe.

Light immortal Light divine,
Visit Thou these hearts of thine,
And our inmost being fill.

If you take your grace away,
Nothing pure in us will stay,
All our good is turned to ill.

Heal our wounds our strength renew,
On our dryness pour thy dew,
Wash the stains of guilt away.

Bend the stubborn heart and will,
Melt the frozen, warm the chill,
Guide the steps that go astray.

Thou on those who evermore,
Thee confess and Thee adore,
In thy sevenfold gifts descend.

Give us comfort when we die,
Give us life with Thee on high,
Give us joys that never end.
Amen

—Paraphrased by Henri Nouwen in original manuscript tapes;
attributed to Pope Innocent III, published in 1570 in *Catholic Encyclopedia*.

JOURNALING

Write your willingness to forgo living from your wounded past, and step courageously into the shoes of the One whose heart is filled with love for each person. Write of your desire and willingness to gently open yourself to compassion for those whom you fear. Write of the people in your life and of ways that you will try to embrace them more as brothers and sisters on the journey of life with you. Write of your readiness to allow your maternal and paternal gifts to flower in the service of others.

COMMUNING

Speak now to the God who has spoken into your life. Ask the Great Awakener to open the sealed reservoir of compassion, forgiveness, and welcome to all those in your life today. Speak and listen for gentle reassurance. "Fear not. Abide. Come home. Dwell in your deepest soul."

Heart speaks to heart.

Practice #9—ASK FOR SUPPORT

Far from home and isolated, the young prodigal was hungry and thirsty for food, but also for a helping hand to reclaim some of what he had lost by leaving home. He was able to overcome his load of guilt and shame, and to turn back toward home and family where he would ask for the necessary support to stand again and repossess himself in truth. His elder brother had not yet come to terms with his need to accept support in the places of his vulnerability. Both, however, were invited to grow into the parental role.

Because of being unconvinced that I am loved, I cling to my strong negative emotions as safety measures. My pattern is to fall back from good resolutions, make a faltering return, and then quickly leave again. After my breakdown and during my time in Winnipeg I knew that, despite my sense of shame, I needed support. Two people accompanied me through those long and lonely months, listening and offering consolation and questions. I cannot imagine where I would be had they not been there. Today other friends know me when I am well and when I am not so well and I meet regularly to share about my leavings, my returnings, and my increasing desire to be home to welcome others like myself.

The spiritual life is a treacherous undertaking that we best not attempt alone. In some traditions this discipline is called spiritual direction. Good mentors are themselves on this road, so they are not shocked to hear us say how often we return and then leave again. Directors listen, help us clarify motivations, and recognize destructive patterns. We want to find mentors who don't judge us or tell us what to do. We need people who encourage us to reach within for our own directions for the future, and who challenge us to stand up and reclaim love as our heritage. Good mentors point us toward truth as well as toward our many brothers and sisters in the human family who are waiting to be welcomed home by our compassionate love.

EPILOGUE

HOME TONIGHT

🎇

We do not have to be saviours of the world! We are simply human beings, enfolded in weakness and in hope, called together to change our world one heart at a time.

—From *Becoming Human* by Jean Vanier, 1998, House of Anansi Press, Toronto, p. 163.

T hank you, Henri, for telling us what God spoke deeply into the painful and impenetrable places in your life. Thank you for revealing the door to *our* most intimate story, and for giving us the freedom to walk our own walk into the parable. Thank you for teaching us to "stand in" our pain and with integrity live it in solidarity with others in the world who suffer, and for pointing us to the small ways of claiming home while "on the way home." Thanks, too, for the gift of the spiritual practices and workouts that move us slowly into the same intimate relationship that Jesus enjoyed with the One who sent him into the world.

Did you ever realize that by so honestly sharing your identification with the two young people in the parable you unwittingly *became* for us the loving father figure, passionately awaiting *our* return to the truth?

Maybe you only ever superficially heard John's question, "Henri, are you home tonight?" But perhaps his persistent repetition supported you to courageously stumble through your second loneliness so you could return home to Daybreak. There is nothing superficial about the way you confidently invite us to do likewise. Thank you.

And now, we editors grant you, Henri, the final summary of your response to John's question, "Are you home tonight?" It is an edited quote of you speaking in the PBS documentary *Journey of the Heart: The Life of Henri Nouwen*:

"When I saw the poster of the Rembrandt painting with the returning son being embraced by his father, I was totally overwhelmed and I said, 'That's where I want to be.' I began to think of myself as the runaway son wanting to return home. But then . . . the older son suddenly started to speak to me. I'm the oldest son myself and I recognized a lot of resentment in me, a lot of not fully enjoying where I was in my life. I woke up to the truth that both those young people lived in me.

"More than a year later something incredibly important happened for me. I suffered from depression and was on a long sick leave from L'Arche Daybreak. One member of my community came to visit me and in the course of the conversation she said, 'Henri, you're always talking about yourself being the prodigal son, and you're often talking about yourself being the elder son, but now it's time for you to become the father! That's who you're called to be.'

"*Look at the father figure in the painting. This person has the hand of a mother and the hand of a father, the male hand and the female hand touching a beloved child. Look at the figure of a father who is like a mother bird with a big cloak to safely enwrap her young close to her body. Look at the one who wants to welcome the child home without asking any questions. The father doesn't even want to hear the story of the younger son. The father doesn't even want to hear the story of his elder child. He simply wants them 'home,' around the same table with him, growing up to become like him.*

"*In a moment I suddenly realized that my final vocation is not only to return home but also to welcome people home by saying, 'I'm so glad you are here! I'm so glad you're here! Come now. Bring out the beautiful cloak, bring the precious ring, find the best sandals. Let's celebrate because you've finally come home!'*"

I stand with awe at the place where Rembrandt brought me. He led me from the kneeling dishevelled young son to the standing, bent-over old father, from the place of being blessed to the place of blessing. As I look at my own aging hands, I know that they have been given to me to stretch out toward all who suffer, to rest upon the shoulders of all who come, and to offer the blessing that emerges from the immensity of God's love.

—From *The Return of the Prodigal Son* by Henri J. M. Nouwen, 1992, Doubleday, New York, p. 129.

Excerpts from the original talks by Henri Nouwen are available for listening at HenriNouwen.org.

Post your thoughts on *Home Tonight* at www.henrinouwen .org/nouwen_blog.

ALSO AVAILABLE FROM HENRI NOUWEN

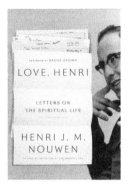

Read *Love, Henri* and discover over two hundred previously
unpublished letters that stretch from the earliest years of
Henri's career up through his last ten years at L'Arche Daybreak.

ALSO AVAILABLE FROM HENRI NOUWEN

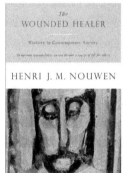

The Inner Voice of Love, Reaching Out, and *The Wounded Healer*